MW00655776

IMAGES
of Aviation

LOS ANGELES INTERNATIONAL AIRPORT

On the Cover: The official dedication of Mines Field took place on June 7, 1930. The field had been used by aircraft for several years, but this event marked its inauguration as an airport. Aviation aficionados and others crowded onto the field and runways for the occasion. (Courtesy of LAX Photo Archives.)

IMAGES
of Aviation

LOS ANGELES INTERNATIONAL AIRPORT

William A. Schoneberger, Ethel Pattison,
Lee Nichols, and Flight Path
Learning Center of Southern California

ARCADIA
PUBLISHING

ISBN 978-0-7385-5582-9

Published by Arcadia Publishing
Charleston SC, Chicago IL, Portsmouth NH, San Francisco CA

Printed in the United States of America

Library of Congress Catalog Card Number: 2007931269

For all general information contact Arcadia Publishing at:
Telephone 843-853-2070
Fax 843-853-0044
E-mail sales@arcadiapublishing.com
For customer service and orders:
Toll-Free 1-888-313-2665

Visit us on the Internet at www.arcadiapublishing.com

Contents

Acknowledgments

Particular thanks go to the former public relations directors of Los Angeles International Airport, including Peggy G. Hereford, Jack Francois, Virginia Y. Black, and Lee Nichols. We thank current LAX public and community relations directors Nancy Niles, Tom Winfrey, and Nancy Castles. We would also like to thank staff photographer Jay Berkowitz. David Mellen tracked down portions of the text that had been archived. All of the photographs in the book were supplied by the LAX Photo Archives of Los Angeles World Airports (LAWA). Among the photographers whose work was collected by the LAX Photo Archives were Ken Brown, Brent Cook, Abe Creekmore, Bill Eccles, Johnny Johnson, and Wen Roberts.

FOREWORD

Los Angeles International Airport is unique in many ways, as this history so clearly indicates. Location has made this airport a primary contributor to the singular growth and prosperity of Southern California. In turn, LAX shares in the region's prominence, serving millions of travelers, handling impressive tonnages of high-value cargo, and providing a popular filming location for scores of movies and television shows.

LAX also shares a common heritage with many other airports, including its origins in aviation's age of barnstorming and air shows, importance as the site of World War II aircraft manufacturing and testing, and continual adaptation to the needs of air travel from the era of the biplane to today's wide-body jets.

My career as a commercial airline pilot for 40 years and, since 1968, as owner of an aircraft leasing and maintenance company has brought me to LAX countless times. I never cease to be impressed with the ever-changing face of the airport. New terminals and hangars, airfield and air traffic control upgrades, and many other improvements over the years are all chronicled in this beautifully illustrated volume.

After my last visit to LAX, one of my clients asked me, "Is the construction work at the airport almost completed?" I didn't need to check with anyone for an answer. I replied simply, "No, and it never will be." That is the nature of LAX: ever changing to meet the travel needs of this unique place we call Southern California. The process started when the airport began in 1928 and will continue in the years ahead.

This book traces the remarkable growth of what began as a landing strip in a bean field to become today's LAX, one of the world's busiest passenger and cargo airports. Although many of the pictures are from the past, they trace a pattern of impressive improvement that points the way to even greater progress in the years ahead.

—Clay Lacy
Chief Executive Officer
Clay Lacy Aviation, Inc.

INTRODUCTION

The year was 1928. The burgeoning community of Los Angeles was struggling to meet the rising demands of the post–World War I aviation boom. Small, privately operated airports dotted the Southland map. Aviation was an exciting adventure in this land of Hollywood glamour.

A group of enlightened businessmen, with support from the Los Angeles City Council, recognized that the growing city desperately needed a single airport that would meet the exploding demands for passenger flight while airmail and cargo service were also expanding.

In a prescient editorial on March 17, 1928, the *Daily Californian* expressed, in part:

> The great metropolitan airport of a thousand acres, an area comparing with the largest similar airports of the world, is to be on the site . . . in Los Angeles. . . . The reader can no doubt vision the importance to this community that the choice of the site entails. . . . in a comparatively few years (giant liners of the air) will make port here, with hundreds of passengers where one to a dozen now travel by air.

A wind-blown bean and barley field "out in the country" at the crossroads of the Inglewood-Redondo Road and Imperial Highway was selected by the Los Angeles City Council. Considerable influence on site selection was brought by its choice for the 1928 National Air Races in September. They would attract 200,000 spectators and include three dirt runways, a 200,000-square-foot display building, a 40,000-car parking lot, and a 20,000-seat grandstand. Mines Field, which was named for realtor William W. Mines, who brokered the land, was created on 640 acres of land leased for 10 years. Two 100-by-100-foot "modern hangars" were constructed. Hangar No. 1, off Imperial, is the sole remaining building of the original airport.

Famed American aviator Charles "Lucky Lindy" Lindbergh helped promote the site selection. In addition to Lindbergh, who flew with the U.S. Army Air Corps's Three Musketeers Flying Trapeze aerobatic team, the 1928 National Air Races attracted aviation boosters such as Will Rogers, Amelia Earhart, Jimmy Doolittle, and Roscoe Turner. Also supportive was aviation pioneering designer Jack Northrop, who would later locate an aircraft production facility at the airport.

That same year, Mines Field, as the airport was known for many years, was officially named Los Angeles Municipal Airport. The Los Angeles Department of Airports was created that October. Cliff Henderson, known as the father of the National Air Races, was named the first airport director. Curtiss Wright established a flight school at Mines Field in 1928, then designed and constructed two original buildings. The famed Graf Zeppelin arrived in 1929 following its transpacific flight from Japan.

The airport was officially dedicated on June 7, 1930. Douglas Aircraft began operations in 1932, followed by Northrop, then North American Aviation in 1936. Los Angeles, ringed as it was by such airports as Grand Central Air Terminal in Glendale, Burbank Airport, and other airfields in Santa Monica, Torrance, and elsewhere, became known as the "Detroit of aviation."

Los Angeles Municipal Airport again hosted the National Air Races in 1933 and 1936. They eventually became the Cleveland Air Races, continuing under the aegis of Los Angeles entrepreneur Cliff Henderson. In 1937, the city purchased title to the airport for $2.24 million, saving $3 million over the life of the lease.

Those 1928 decisions laid the groundwork for continuing progress, making aviation and its elements one of the principal economic drivers in Southern California.

One

Mines Field

Although the 1928 National Air Races were not the ultimate reason for the site selection of LAX, they played a major role. Entrepreneur Cliff Henderson, who later became first airport director of Los Angeles Municipal Airport, recognized that the location was already something of a landing field—albeit scruffy and ill-prepared. Henderson and his team worked feverishly to lay out three runways; erect grandstands, temporary buildings, and fencing; build access roads; and install utilities and sanitary facilities.

The 1928 Air Races introduced more than 200,000 people—including Bill Boeing, Donald Douglas, Amelia Earhart, and Marion Davies—to the site of what would become one of the world's busiest airports. A highlight of these 1928 Air Races was the appearance of America's aviation hero, Charles Lindbergh, who flew with the U.S. Army Air Corps Three Musketeers Flying Trapeze aerobatic team.

The Air Races spotlight continued to shine on Southern California in 1933 and 1936 when this national event returned to the airport, attracting even more people than the 1928 inaugural, including well-known Hollywood celebrities.

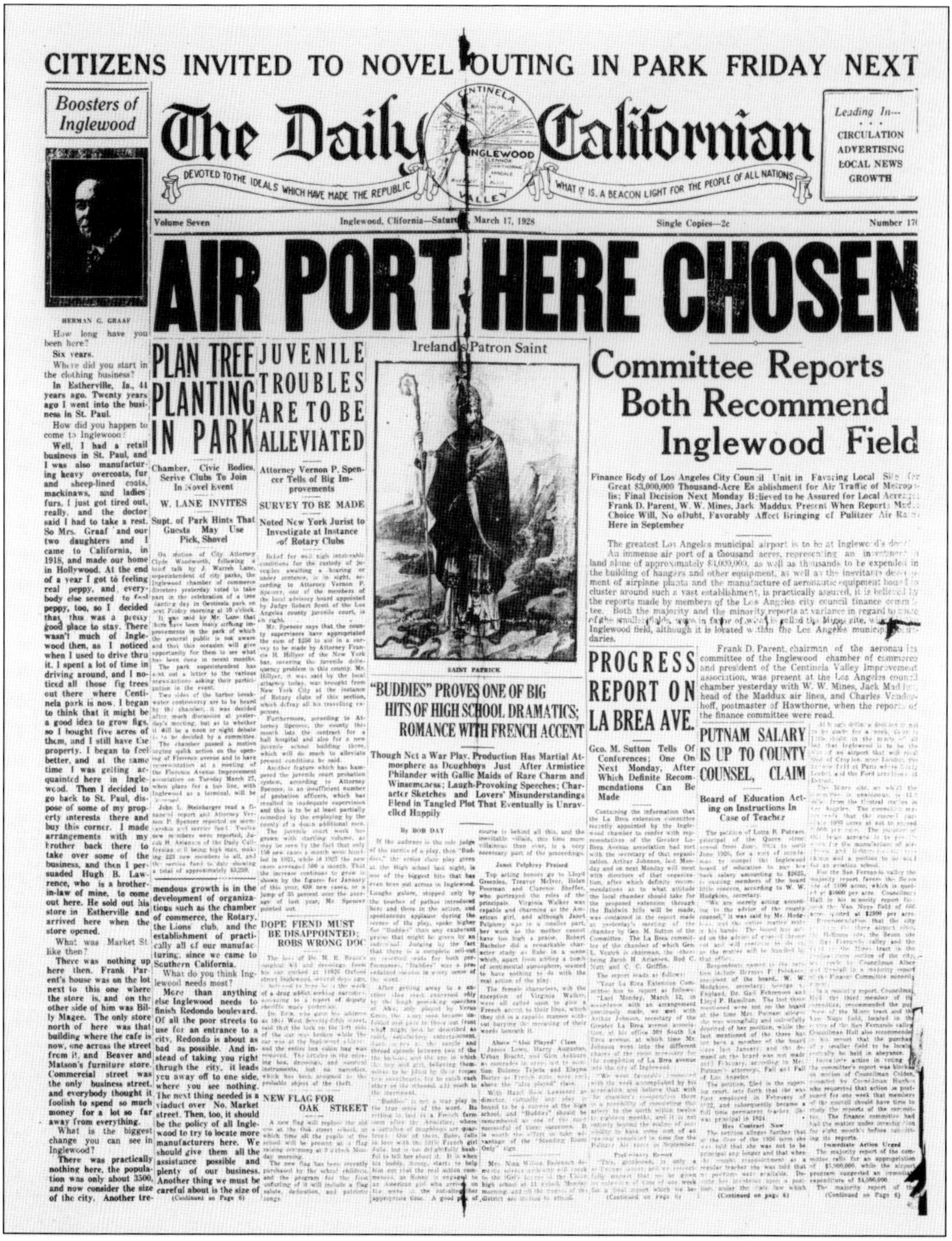

CITIZENS INVITED TO NOVEL OUTING IN PARK FRIDAY NEXT

Boosters of Inglewood

The Daily Californian

DEVOTED TO THE IDEALS WHICH HAVE MADE THE REPUBLIC — WHAT IT IS, A BEACON LIGHT FOR THE PEOPLE OF ALL NATIONS

Leading In— CIRCULATION ADVERTISING LOCAL NEWS GROWTH

Volume Seven — Inglewood, California—Saturday, March 17, 1928 — Single Copies—2c — Number 17

AIR PORT HERE CHOSEN

HERMAN G. GRAAF

How long have you been here?

Six years.

Where did you start in the clothing business?

In Estherville, Ia., 44 years ago. Twenty years ago I went into the business in St. Paul.

How did you happen to come to Inglewood?

Well, I had a retail business in St. Paul, and I was also manufacturing heavy overcoats, fur and sheep-lined coats, mackinaws, and ladies' furs. I just got tired out, really, and the doctor said I had to take a rest. So Mrs. Graaf and our two daughters and I came to California, in 1918, and made our home in Hollywood. At the end of a year I got to feeling real peppy, and everybody else seemed to feel peppy, too, so I decided that this was a pretty good place to stay. There wasn't much of Inglewood then, as I noticed when I used to drive thru it. I spent a lot of time in driving around, and I noticed all those fig trees out there where Centinela park is now. I began to think that it might be a good idea to grow figs, so I bought five acres of them, and I still have the property. I began to feel better, and at the same time I was getting acquainted here in Inglewood. Then I decided to go back to St. Paul, dispose of some of my property interests there and buy this corner. I made arrangements with my brother back there to take over some of the business, and then I persuaded Hugh B. Lawrence, who is a brother-in-law of mine, to come out here. He sold out his store in Estherville and arrived here when the store opened.

What was Market St. like then?

There was nothing up here then. Frank Parent's house was on the lot next to this one where the store is, and on the other side of him was Billy Magee. The only store north of here was that building where the cafe is now, one across the street from it, and Beaver and Matson's furniture store. Commercial street was the only business street, and everybody thought it foolish to spend so much money for a lot so far away from everything.

What is the biggest change you can see in Inglewood?

There was practically nothing here, the population was only about 3500, and now consider the size of the city. Another tremendous growth is in the development of organizations such as the chamber of commerce, the Rotary, the Lions' club, and the establishment of practically all of our manufacturing since we came to Southern California.

What do you think Inglewood needs most?

More than anything else Inglewood needs to finish Redondo boulevard. Of all the poor streets to use for an entrance to a city, Redondo is about as bad as possible. And instead of taking you right through the city, it leads you away off to one side, where you see nothing. The next thing needed is a viaduct over No. Market street. Then, too, it should be the policy of all Inglewood to try to locate more manufacturers here. We should give them all the assistance possible and plenty of our business. Another thing we must be careful about is the size of

(Continued on Page 6)

PLAN TREE PLANTING IN PARK

Chamber, Civic Bodies, Serive Clubs To Join In Novel Event

W. LANE INVITES

Supt. of Park Hints That Guests May Use Pick, Shovel

JUVENILE TROUBLES ARE TO BE ALLEVIATED

Attorney Vernon P. Spencer Tells of Big Improvements

SURVEY TO BE MADE

Noted New York Jurist to Investigate at Instance of Rotary Clubs

DOPE FIEND MUST BE DISAPPOINTED; ROBS WRONG DOC

NEW FLAG FOR OAK STREET

Ireland's Patron Saint

SAINT PATRICK

"BUDDIES" PROVES ONE OF BIG HITS OF HIGH SCHOOL DRAMATICS; ROMANCE WITH FRENCH ACCENT

Though Not a War Play, Production Has Martial Atmosphere as Doughboys Just After Armistice Philander with Gallic Maids of Rare Charm and Winsomeness; Laugh-Provoking Speeches; Character Sketches and Lovers' Misunderstandings Blend in Tangled Plot That Eventually is Unravelled Happily

By BOB DAY

Janet Pelphrey Praised

Committee Reports Both Recommend Inglewood Field

Finance Body of Los Angeles City Council Unit in Favoring Local Site for Great $3,000,000 Thousand-Acre Establishment for Air Traffic of Metropolis; Final Decision Next Monday Believed to be Assured for Local Acreage; Frank D. Parent, W. W. Mines, Jack Maddux Present When Reports Made; Choice Will, No Doubt, Favorably Affect Bringing of Pulitzer Air Races Here in September

The greatest Los Angeles municipal airport is to be at Inglewood's door. An immense air port of a thousand acres, representing an investment in land alone of approximately $3,000,000, as well as thousands to be expended in the building of hangars and other equipment, as well as the invitation to the development of airplane plants and the manufacture of aeronautic equipment bound to cluster around such a vast establishment, is practically assured, it is believed by the reports made by members of the Los Angeles city council finance committee. Both the majority and the minority reports at variance in regard to choice of the smaller fields, were in favor of what is called the Mines site, which is the Inglewood field, although it is located within the Los Angeles municipal boundaries.

Frank D. Parent, chairman of the aeronautics committee of the Inglewood chamber of commerce and president of the Centinela Valley Improvement association, was present at the Los Angeles council chamber yesterday with W. W. Mines, Jack Maddux, head of the Maddux air lines, and Charles Vonderhoff, postmaster of Hawthorne, when the reports of the finance committee were read.

PROGRESS REPORT ON LA BREA AVE.

Geo. M. Sutton Tells Of Conferences; One On Next Monday, After Which Definite Recommendations Can Be Made

PUTNAM SALARY IS UP TO COUNTY COUNSEL, CLAIM

Board of Education Acting on Instructions In Case of Teacher

This March 17, 1928, newspaper headline announced a first step in creating a municipal airport for Los Angeles. The City Council Finance Committee, prompted by local business leaders, selected a primitive landing strip known as the "Inglewood site" from among 27 competing nominations. The new airport would be called Mines Field in tribute to real estate broker William Mines, who handled details of the land transfer. The city council voted July 27, 1928, to lease 640 acres at the northwest corner of Redondo-Inglewood (now Aviation) Boulevard and Imperial Highway for 10 years.

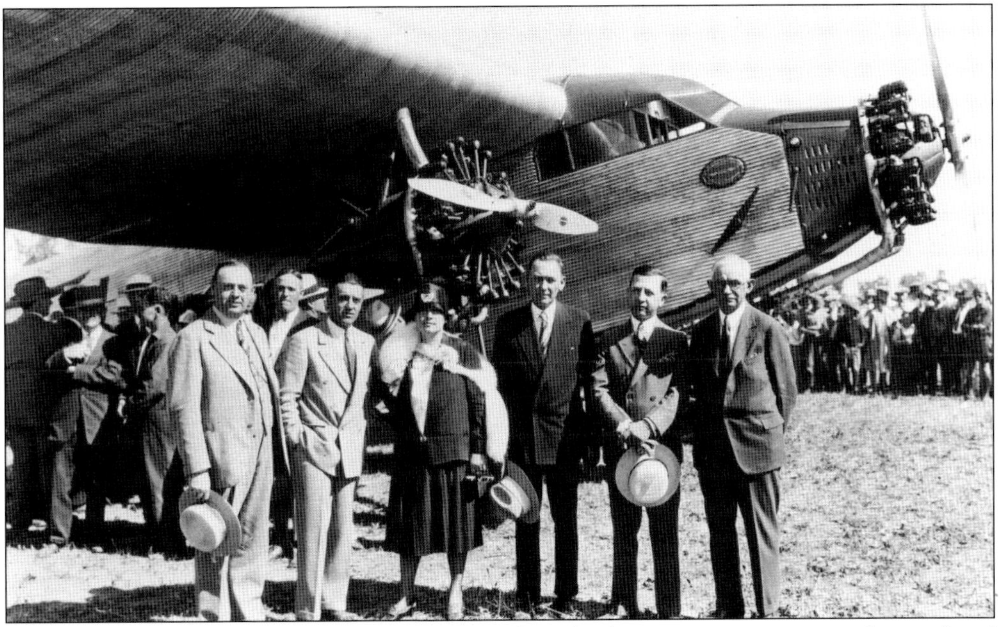

Regular airline service was nearly 20 years away when the first passenger transport plane, piloted by celebrated aviator Charles A. Lindbergh, landed at the future Mines Field and future LAX on September 27, 1927. The Maddux Airlines Ford trimotor aircraft flight from San Diego carried civic and business leaders eager to promote local air service. Pictured from left to right are George M. Sutton, Ford dealer; Judge Frank D. Parent, Inglewood Chamber of Commerce Aviation Committee chairman; Mr. and Mrs. Jack Maddux of the airline; Harry Culver, real estate broker; and W. B. Mayo, Ford Motor Company's chief engineer.

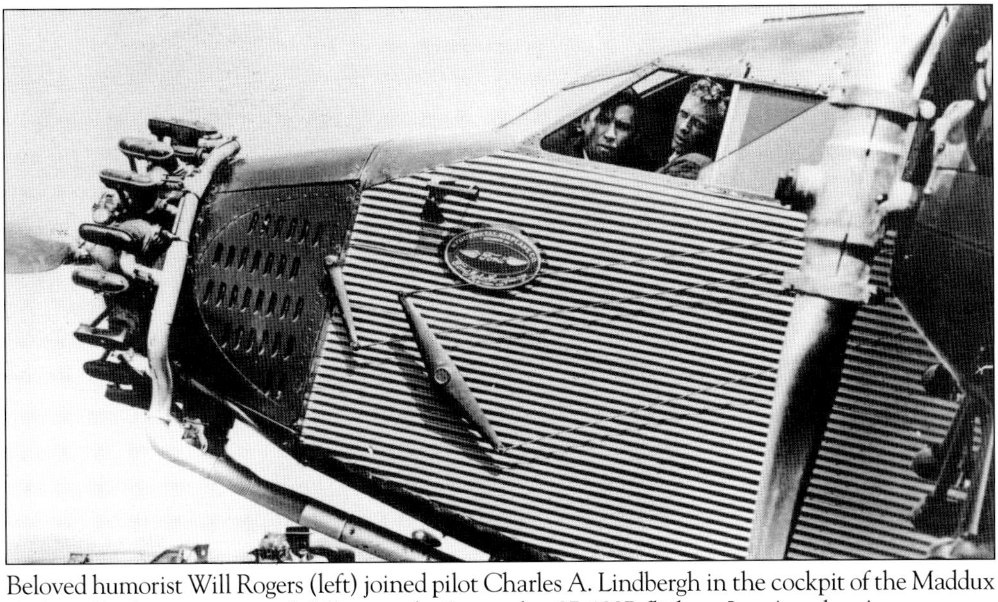

Beloved humorist Will Rogers (left) joined pilot Charles A. Lindbergh in the cockpit of the Maddux Airlines Ford trimotor aircraft following the September 27, 1927, flight to Los Angeles. A tent was set up on the field and, Prohibition still being the law of the land, lemonade and cookies served to guests. Lindbergh's promotion of the site came four months after his celebrated transatlantic solo flight and was a major boost to the selection of Mines Field as the location for a municipal airport.

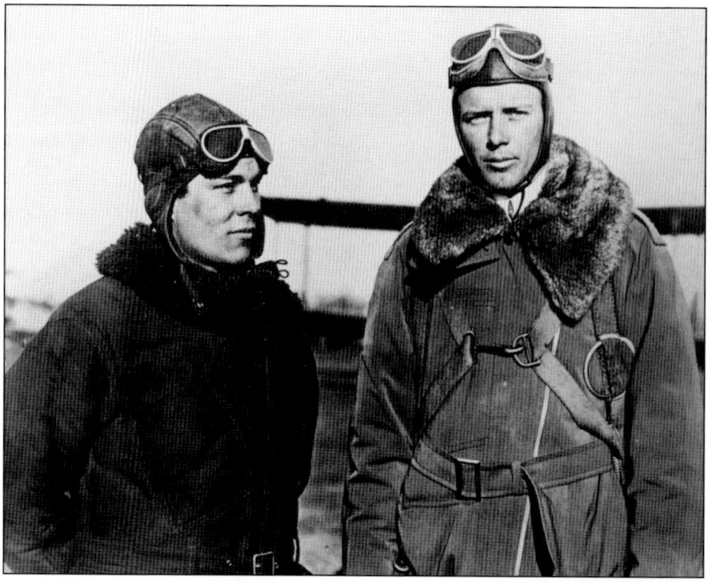

Charles A. Lindbergh, right, was idolized following his solo transatlantic flight in 1927. During his surprise visit to the future Mines Field and LAX later that year, the aviator posed for photographs, praised the airfield, and answered news media questions for about 20 minutes. At left is Harland "Bud" Gurney, barnstorming friend of Lindbergh and future United Airlines pilot.

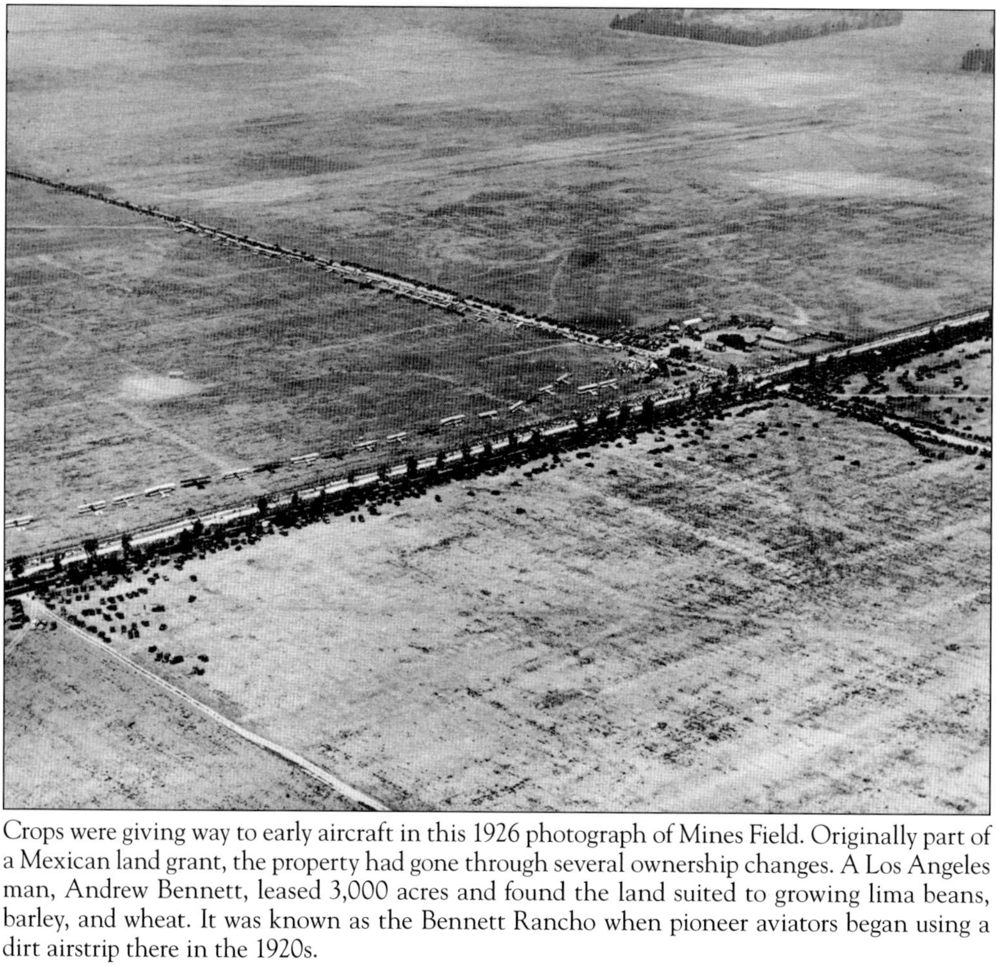

Crops were giving way to early aircraft in this 1926 photograph of Mines Field. Originally part of a Mexican land grant, the property had gone through several ownership changes. A Los Angeles man, Andrew Bennett, leased 3,000 acres and found the land suited to growing lima beans, barley, and wheat. It was known as the Bennett Rancho when pioneer aviators began using a dirt airstrip there in the 1920s.

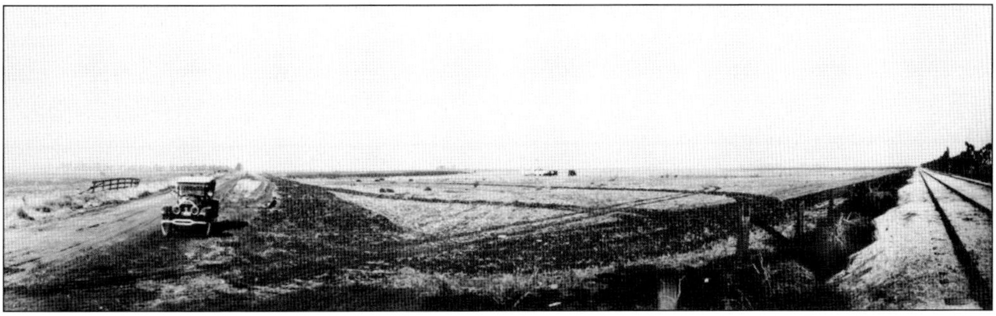

This 1928 view, looking west, shows the rudimentary beginnings of what then was known as Mines Field. Suitable terrain, favorable winds, and separation from heavily populated areas made this an ideal location for the development of the airport that would someday become LAX.

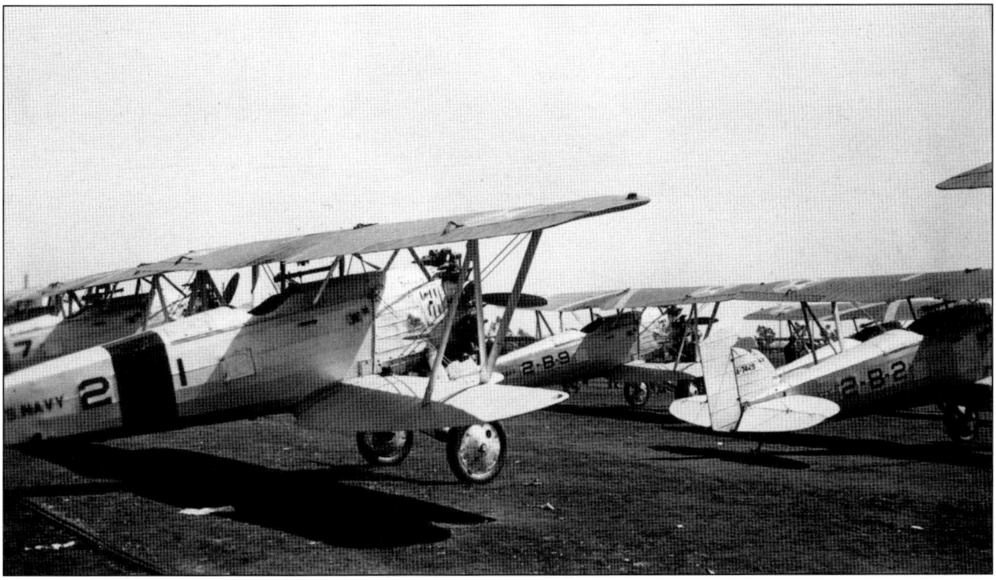

The presence of these U.S. Navy biplanes at Mines Field about 1928 provided a preview of the field's importance several years later during World War II as one of the nation's primary centers of military aircraft manufacturing and testing.

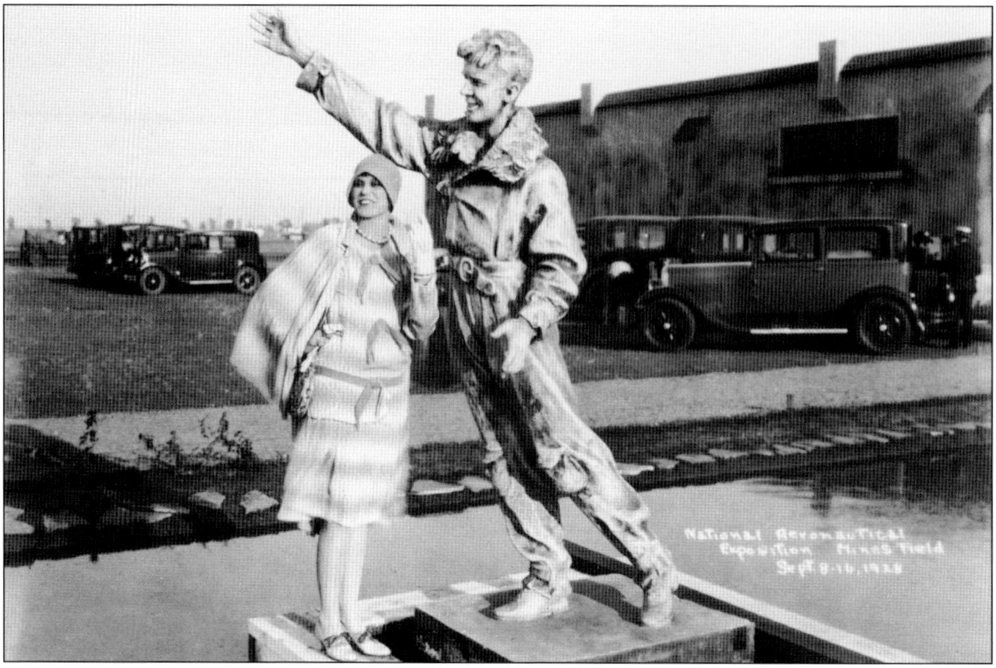

Following his pioneering transatlantic solo flight in 1927, Charles Lindbergh became the number one celebrity in the United States. For the 1928 National Air Races at Mines Field, which put Los Angeles Municipal Airport on the map, this statue of Lindbergh was placed in front of the Exhibition Hall.

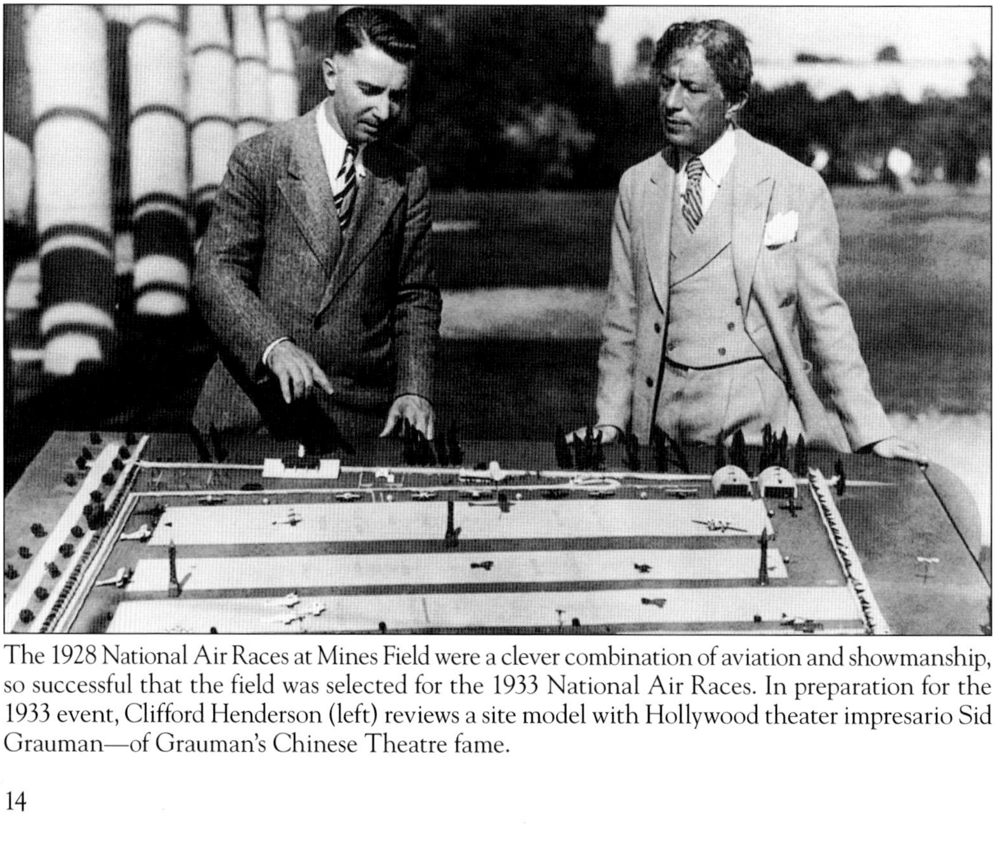

The 1928 National Air Races at Mines Field were a clever combination of aviation and showmanship, so successful that the field was selected for the 1933 National Air Races. In preparation for the 1933 event, Clifford Henderson (left) reviews a site model with Hollywood theater impresario Sid Grauman—of Grauman's Chinese Theatre fame.

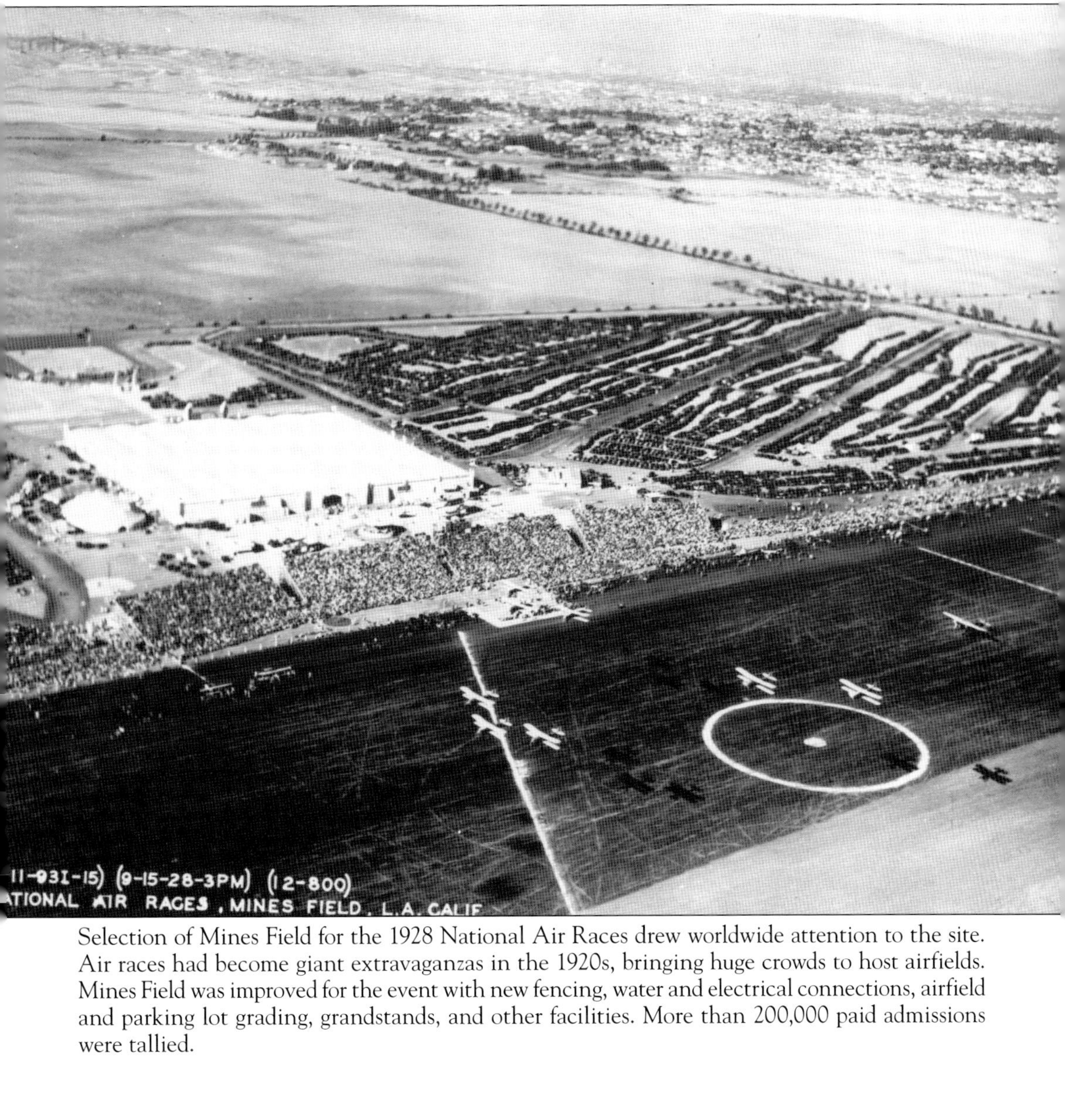

Selection of Mines Field for the 1928 National Air Races drew worldwide attention to the site. Air races had become giant extravaganzas in the 1920s, bringing huge crowds to host airfields. Mines Field was improved for the event with new fencing, water and electrical connections, airfield and parking lot grading, grandstands, and other facilities. More than 200,000 paid admissions were tallied.

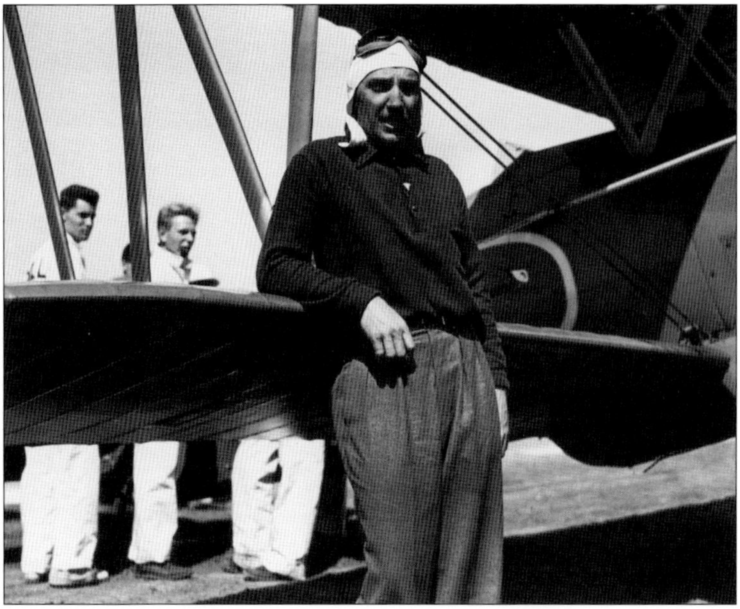

Wing-walking and other airborne stunts were featured during early air shows at Mines Field and elsewhere. Here stunt pilot Milo Brechman takes a break during the 1936 National Air Races.

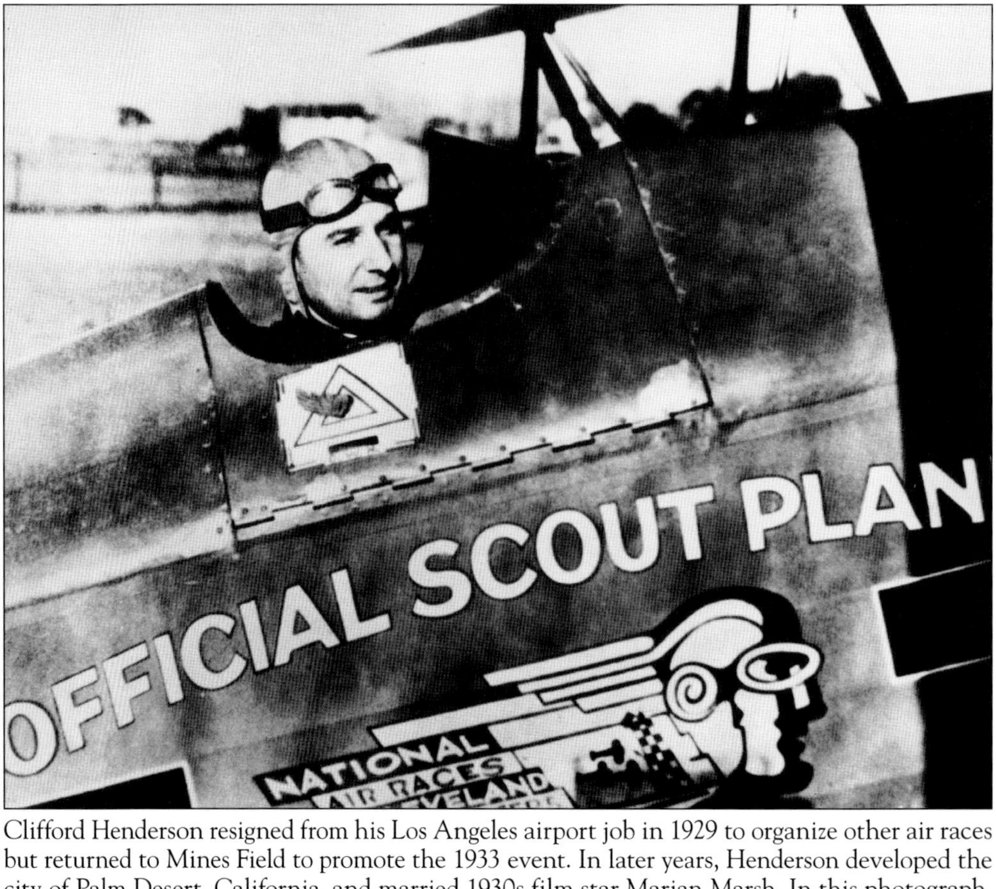

Clifford Henderson resigned from his Los Angeles airport job in 1929 to organize other air races but returned to Mines Field to promote the 1933 event. In later years, Henderson developed the city of Palm Desert, California, and married 1930s film star Marian Marsh. In this photograph, Henderson is seen promoting the 1929 National Air Race at Cleveland, Ohio.

Confusion reigned in the 1920s over site selection for a Los Angeles municipal airport. Lack of political agreement and defeat of a bond funding measure seemed to doom the project. The situation changed when the National Aeronautics Association named Los Angeles as sponsor of the 1928 National Air Races. Local leaders united to push the Mines Field site, and the city council approved Mines Field as the future municipal airport.

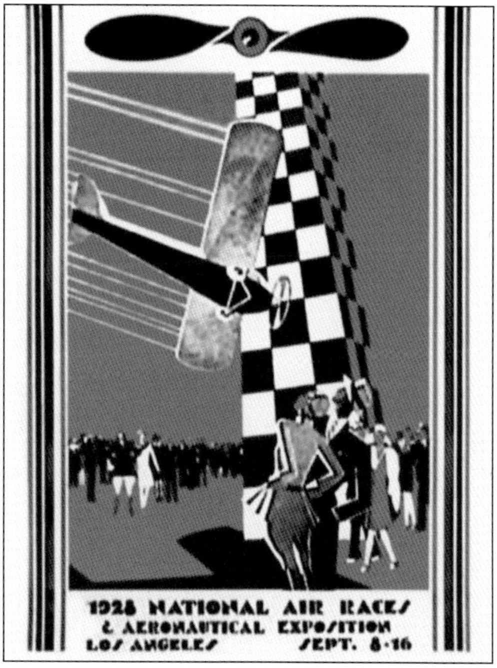

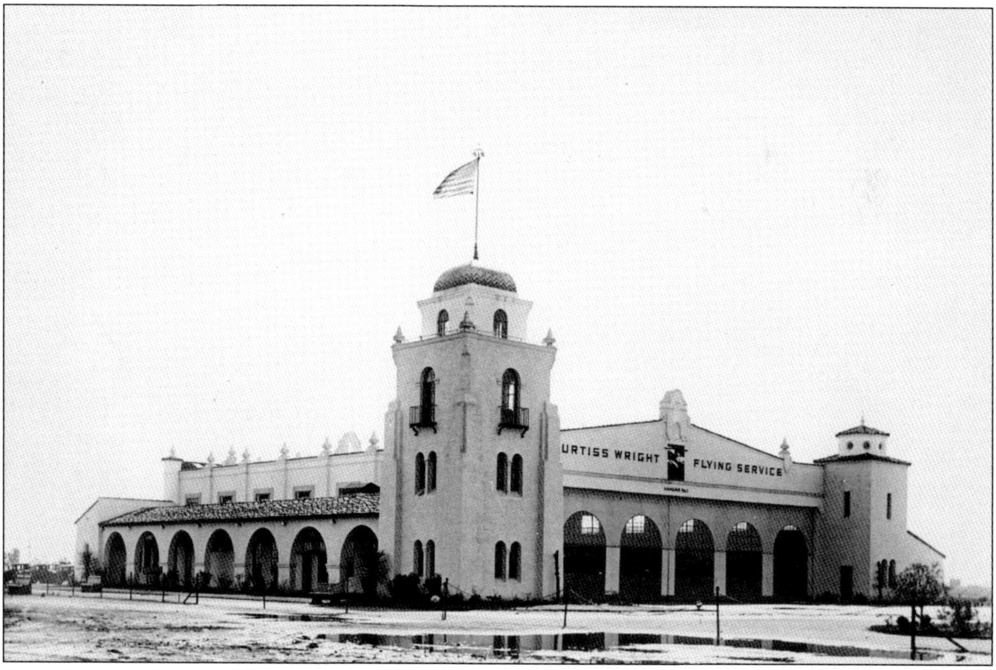

Shortly after the 1928 National Air Races, construction began on an aircraft hangar that would witness eight decades of airport history, from the general aviation era of Mines Field, through the military aircraft production of World War II, to the beginning of regular airline service in the 1940s, to the birth of the jet-age LAX in the 1960s, to a new world of aviation in the 21st century. Shown above is landmark Hangar No. 1, constructed in 1929 on the south perimeter of the airfield. It was placed on the National Register of Historic Places and is a designated Los Angeles Cultural Heritage Monument.

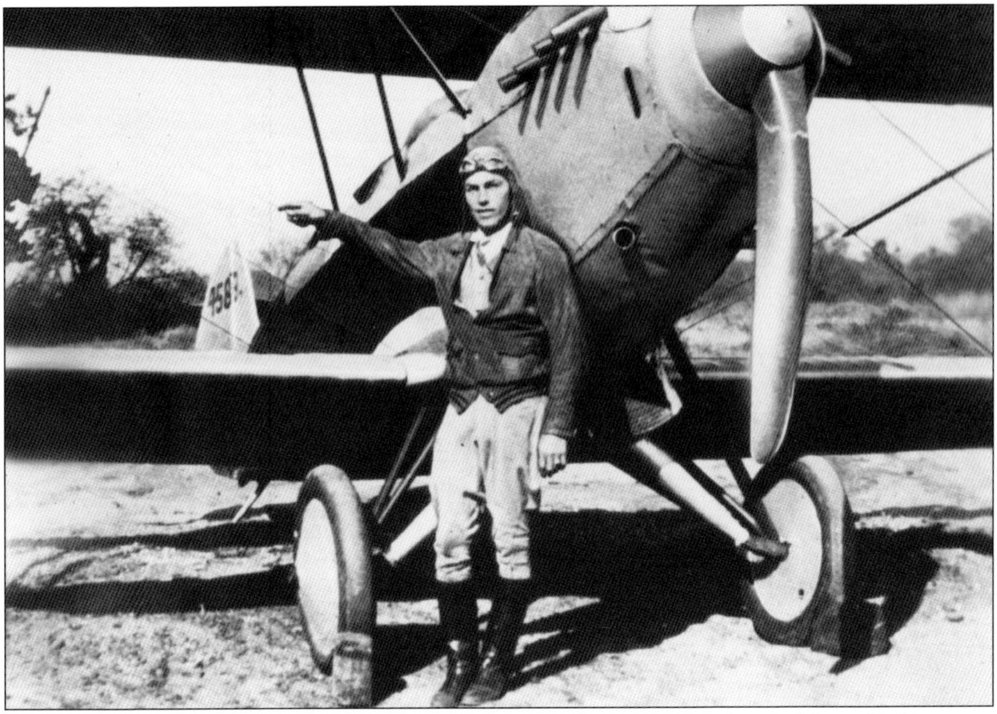

While Clifford Henderson handled administration and promotion of early Mines Field, it was superintendent of operations Henry Bakes who was responsible for the smooth functioning of the airport. Bakes, the first employee at Mines Field, is pictured here with an OX-5 Thunderbird aircraft on December 11, 1928. Bakes remained on the job for half a century, retiring after LAX had entered the jet age.

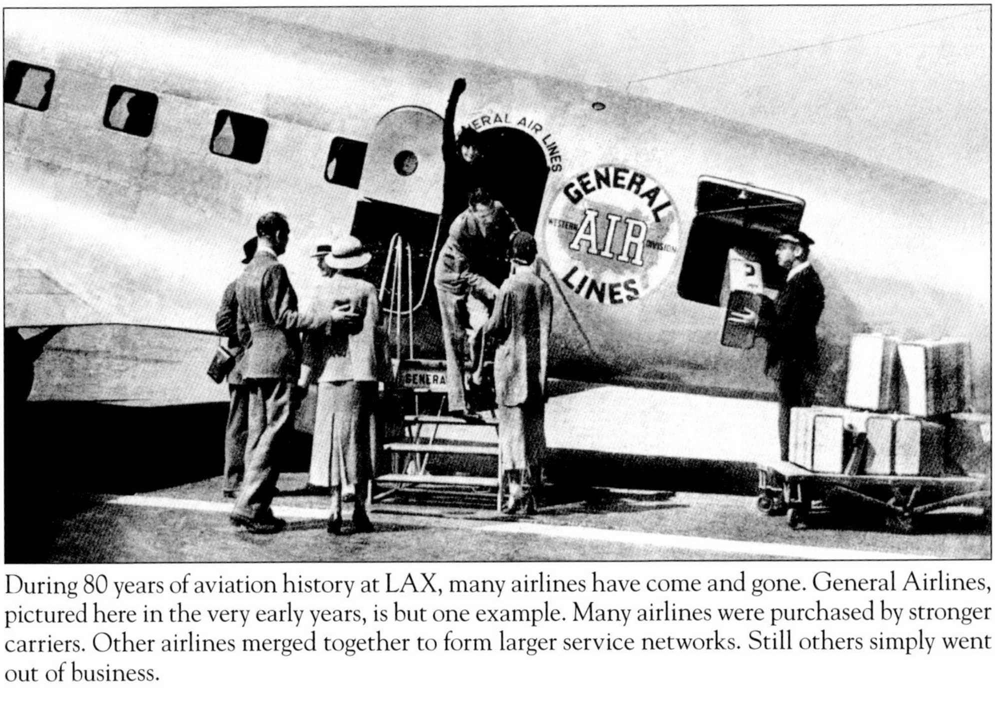

During 80 years of aviation history at LAX, many airlines have come and gone. General Airlines, pictured here in the very early years, is but one example. Many airlines were purchased by stronger carriers. Other airlines merged together to form larger service networks. Still others simply went out of business.

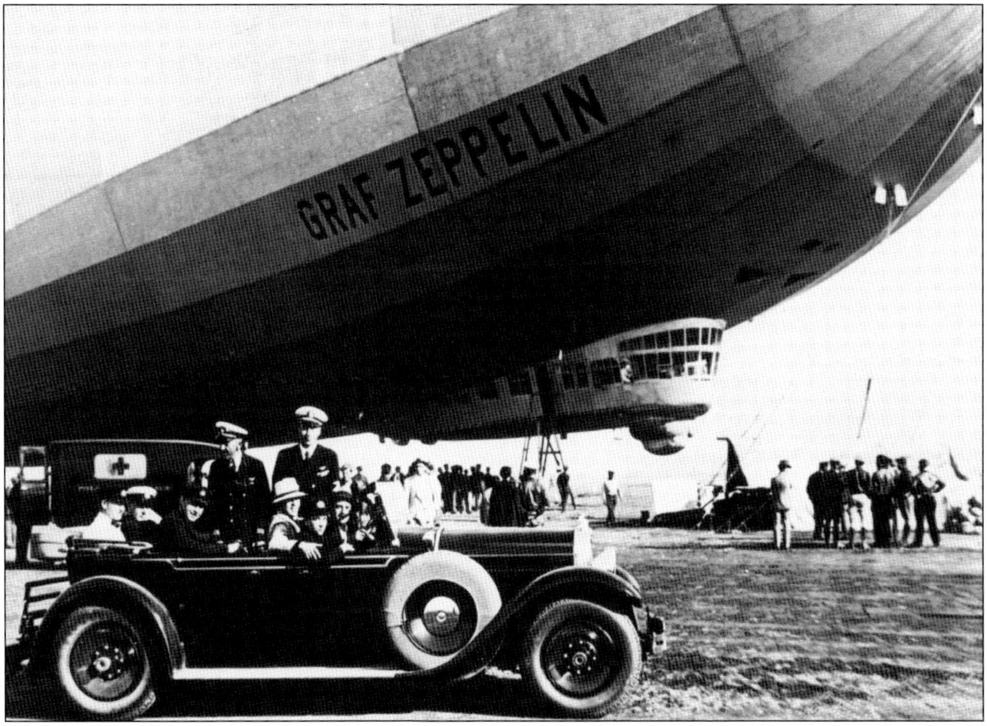

The Graf Zeppelin, a huge German airship, made a round-the-world trip in 1929, bankrolled by publisher William Randolph Hearst, aiming to demonstrate the aircraft's merit for transoceanic passenger service. Included on the itinerary was a stop at Mines Field, where the 771-foot lighter-than-air dirigible landed on August 26. Among those greeting the Zeppelin was Earle C. Anthony, a Packard automobile distributor and owner of Los Angeles radio stations KFI and KECA. He is pictured in his classic Packard Phaeton.

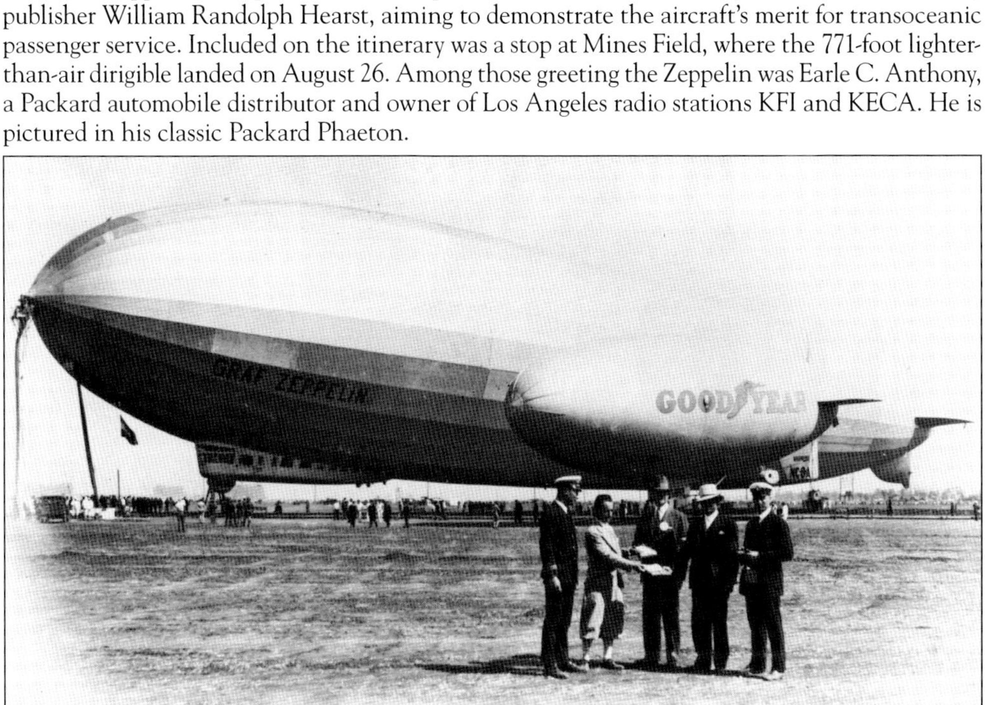

The Goodyear blimp, a familiar sight in Southern California for many years, paid a courtesy call on the Graf Zeppelin during the German airship's visit to Mines Field in August 1929.

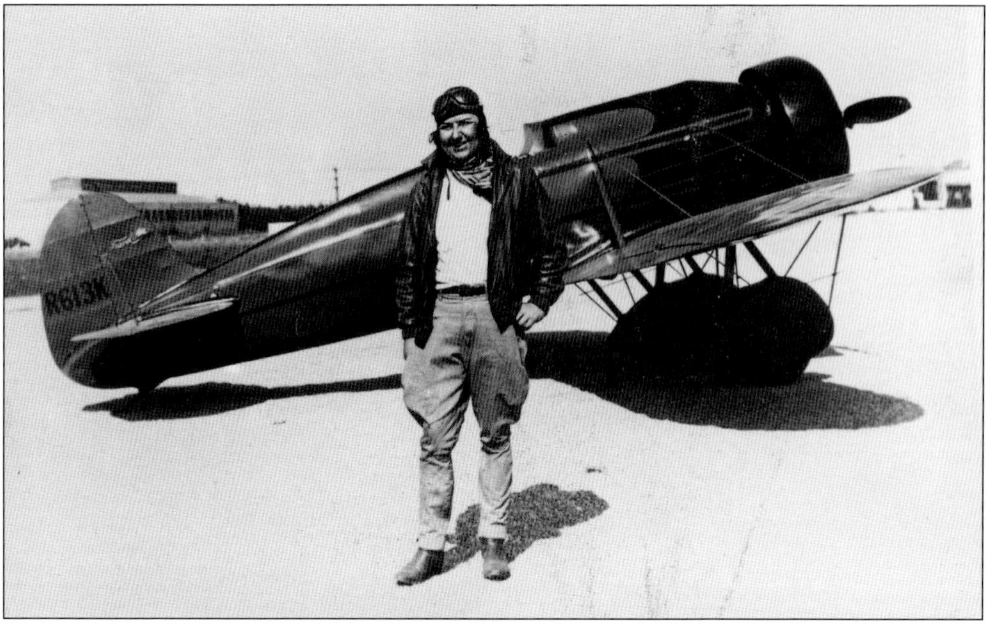

Florence "Pancho" Barnes, a record-setting early pilot who learned to fly in Southern California, was often seen at Mines Field in the early years.

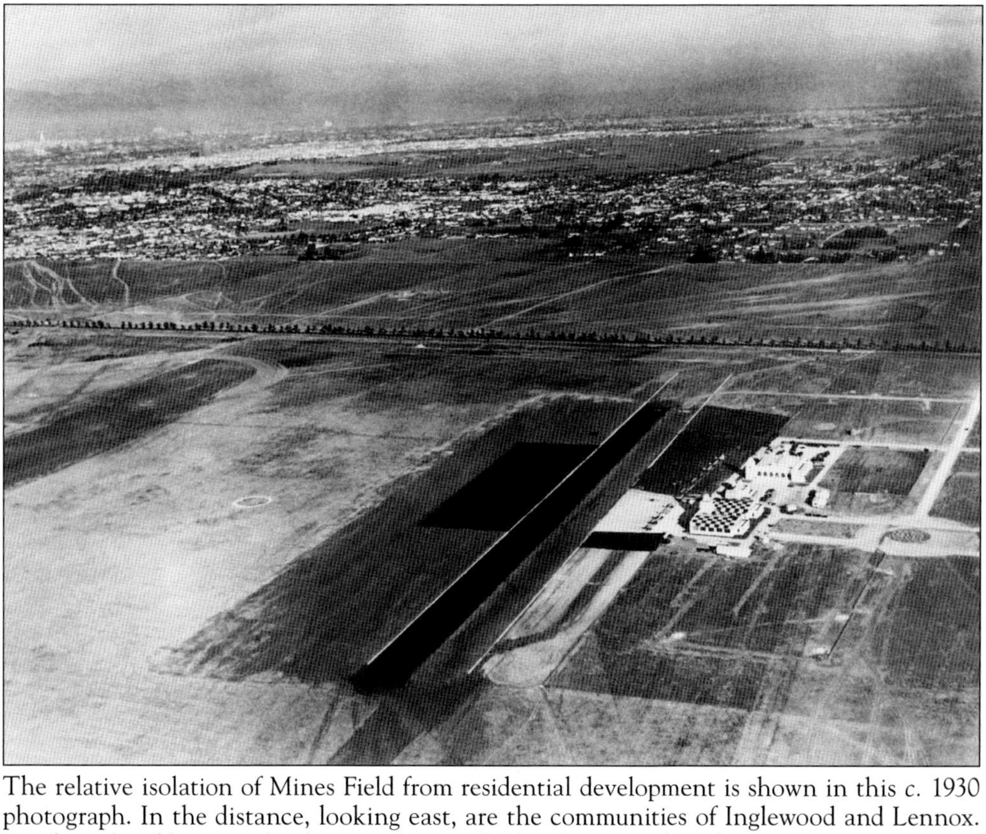

The relative isolation of Mines Field from residential development is shown in this *c.* 1930 photograph. In the distance, looking east, are the communities of Inglewood and Lennox. Residential and business development later pushed to the very edge of the airport property.

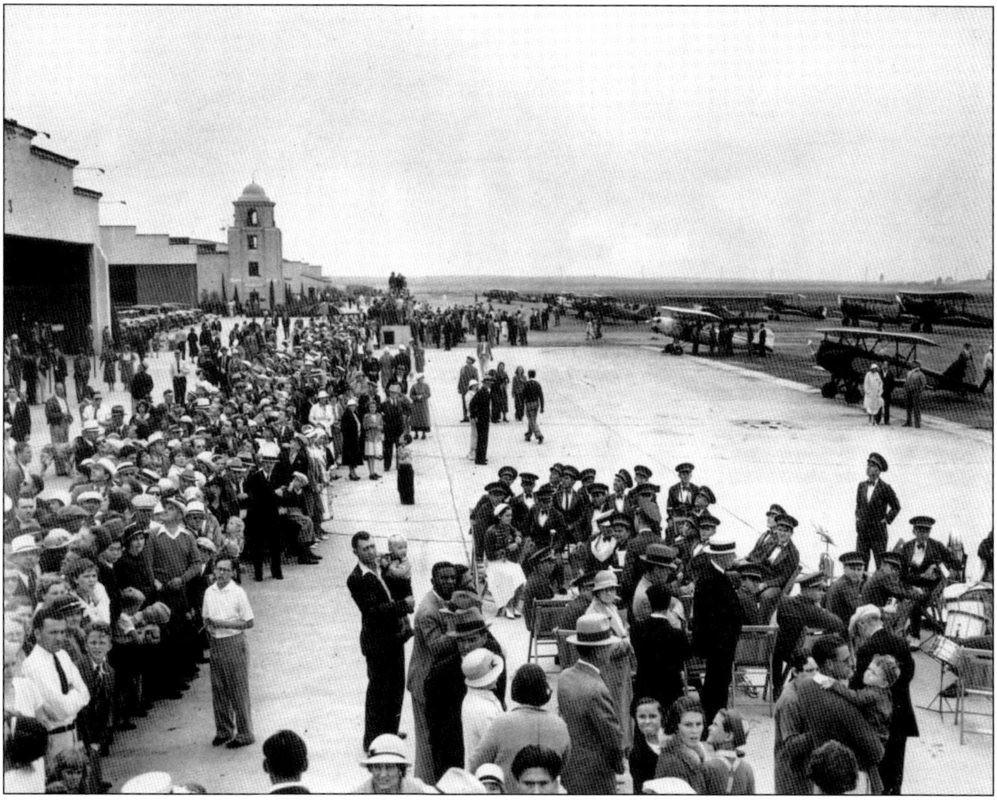

June 7, 1930, was a day of great civic pride for Los Angeles. Amid much fanfare, the city officially dedicated its own municipal airport at Mines Field. Photographs of the event, such as this one, convey a sense of celebration and anticipation. Note the band, at right, and the crowd gathered for the historic event. But it would be many years before Mines Field would grow to become the primary airport in Southern California.

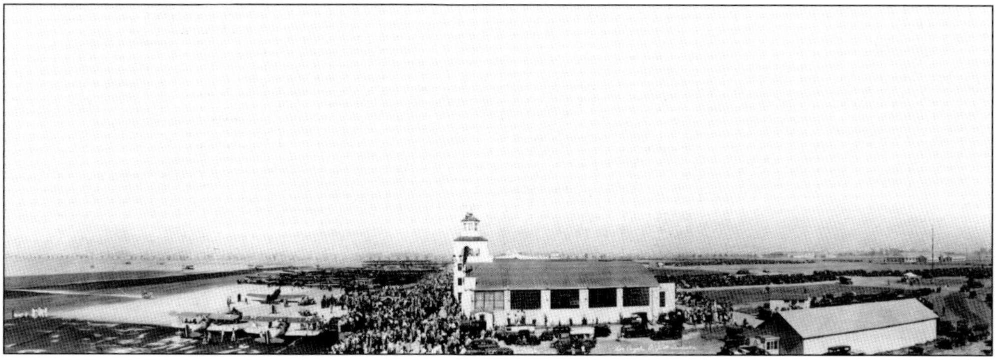

Public events connected with aviation were guaranteed to draw large crowds in the 1920s and 1930s. No exception was the official dedication of Mines Field as Los Angeles Municipal Airport on June 7, 1930. This panoramic view conveys the popular appeal and excitement of that milestone event in the history of the future Los Angeles International Airport.

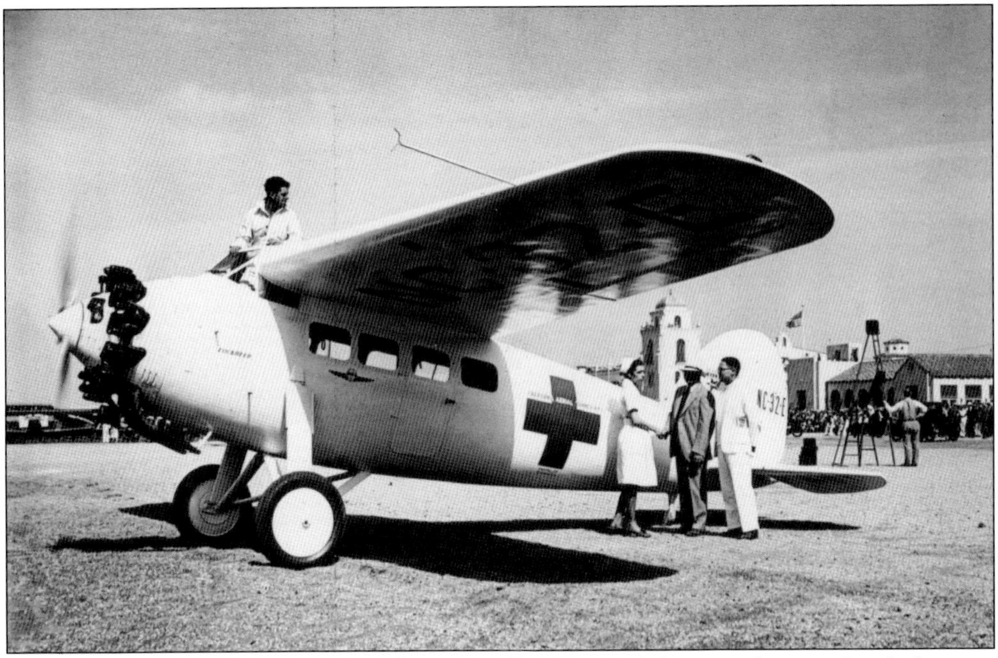

At the official dedication ceremony of Los Angeles Municipal Airport, this aerial ambulance, a Lockheed Vega-1928, was on display on the ramp. Hangar No. 1, built by Curtiss Wright Company, is partially shown on the right in the background. The structure was rededicated on December 20, 1990, after being restored by the AVIA Development Group for cargo and office use.

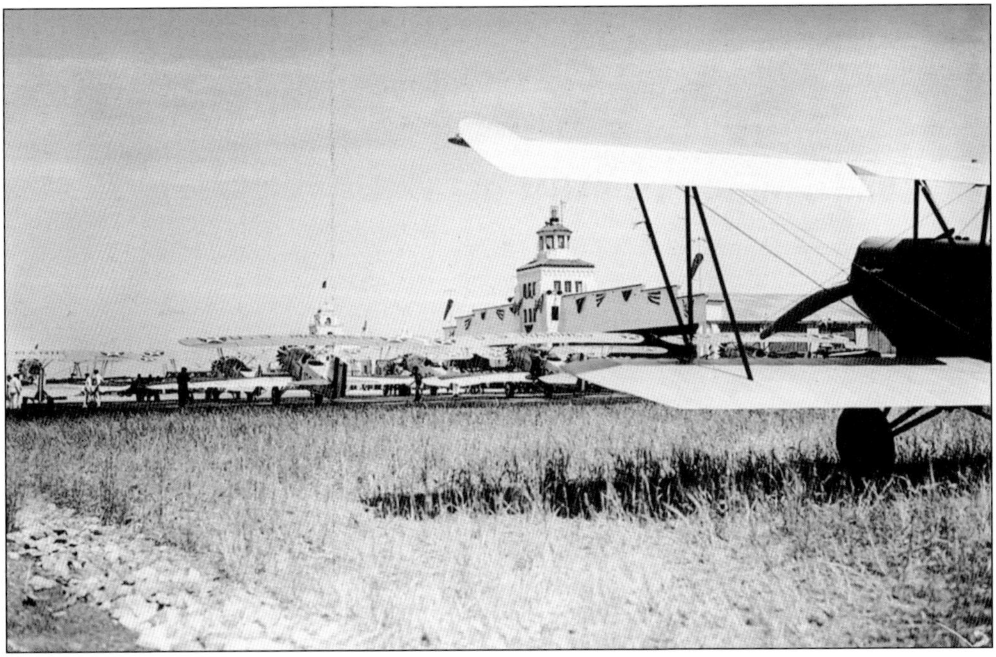

Biplanes were part of the daily scene at Mines Field in the early years, as shown in this photograph taken about 1930. Looming in the background are Hangar No. 1 at left and Hangars No. 2 and 3 flanking the early control tower. Hangar No. 1 is all that remains from this era, now designated a National Historic Landmark and a City Cultural Heritage Monument.

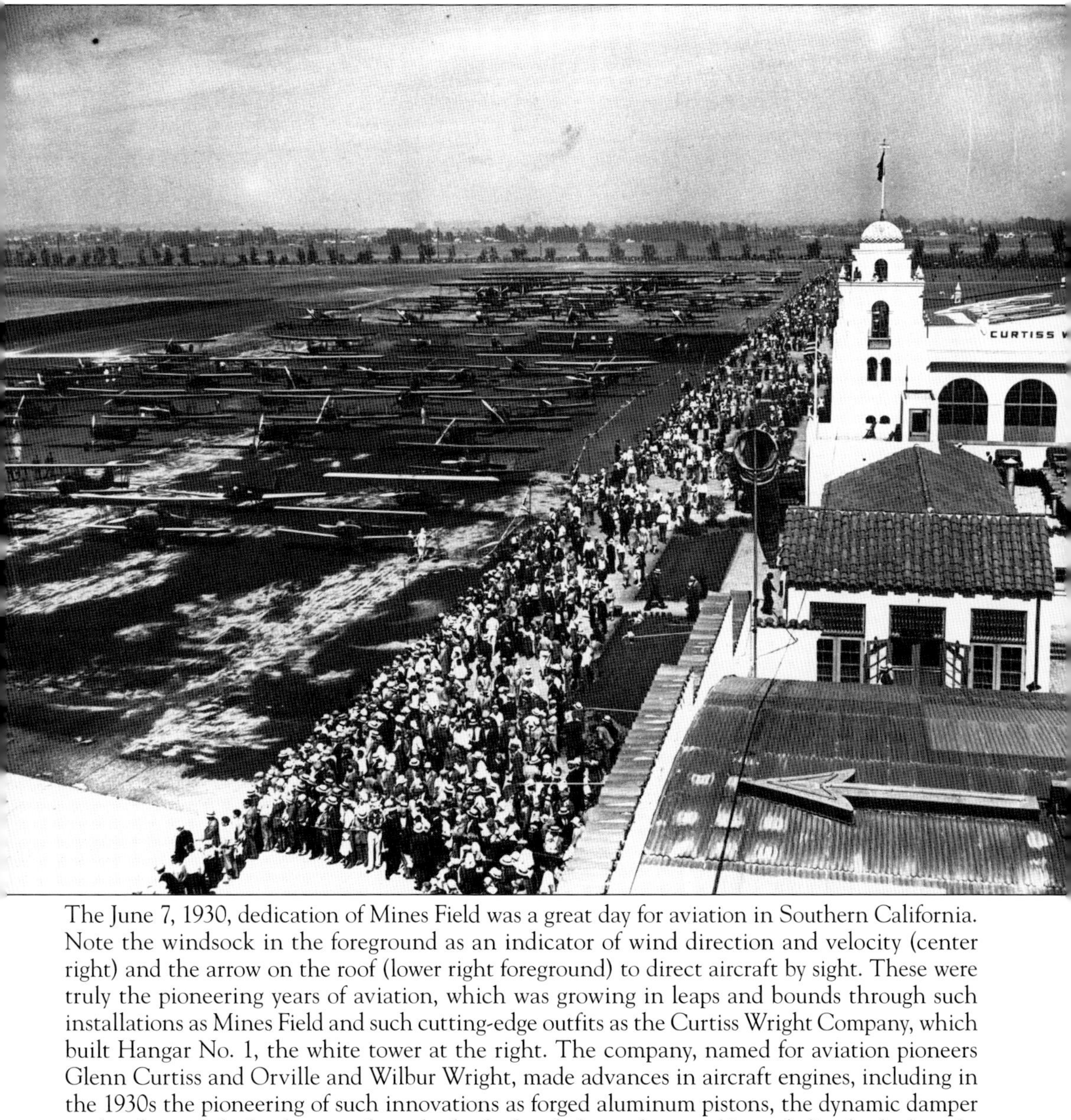

The June 7, 1930, dedication of Mines Field was a great day for aviation in Southern California. Note the windsock in the foreground as an indicator of wind direction and velocity (center right) and the arrow on the roof (lower right foreground) to direct aircraft by sight. These were truly the pioneering years of aviation, which was growing in leaps and bounds through such installations as Mines Field and such cutting-edge outfits as the Curtiss Wright Company, which built Hangar No. 1, the white tower at the right. The company, named for aviation pioneers Glenn Curtiss and Orville and Wilbur Wright, made advances in aircraft engines, including in the 1930s the pioneering of such innovations as forged aluminum pistons, the dynamic damper to absorb crankshaft vibration, finned cylinder heads for cooling, and "nitrided" cylinder barrels, a metallurgical process that vastly improved wear resistance and life. Curtiss Wright pioneered the concepts of air-cooled radial engines. By the end of the 1930s, Curtiss Wright engineers had pushed horsepower per engine above the 1,000 mark.

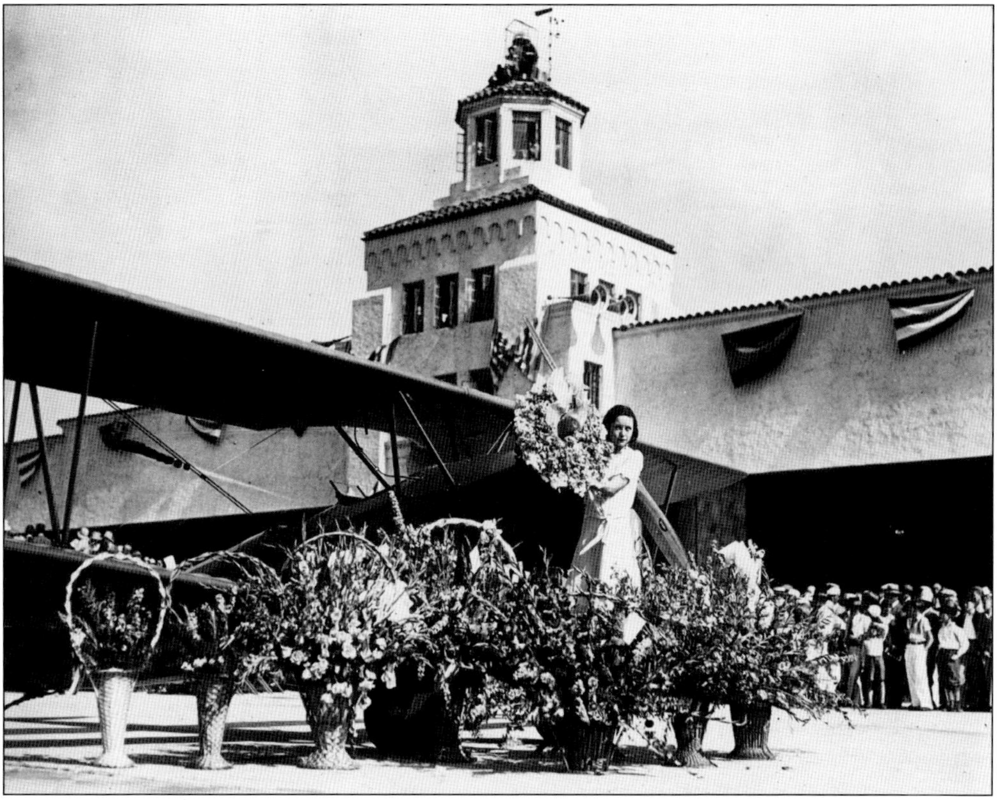

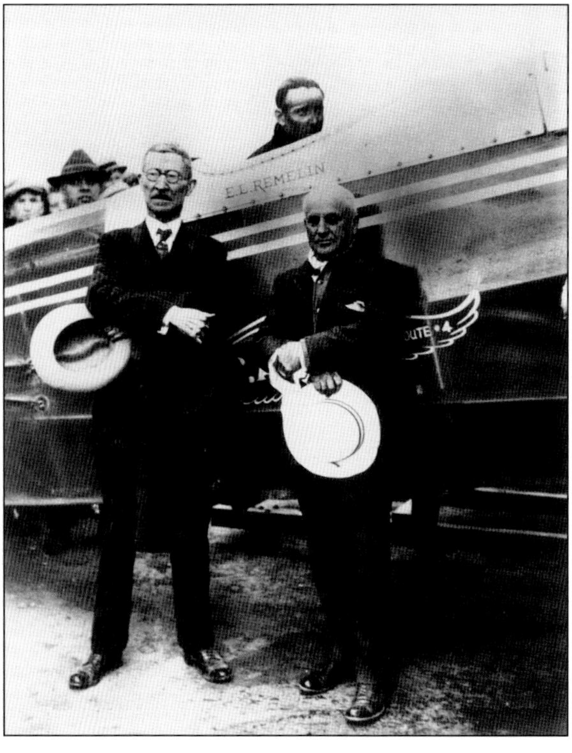

Actress Viola Peters raises a wreath amid a collection of celebratory vases of flowers at Mines Field during the dedication of the airport on June 7, 1930.

Scheduled airline service was yet to come, but charter passenger flights arrived and departed at Mines Field in the early years. The two well-dressed gentlemen, pictured here about 1930, are said to have been the first paying passengers on a local flight.

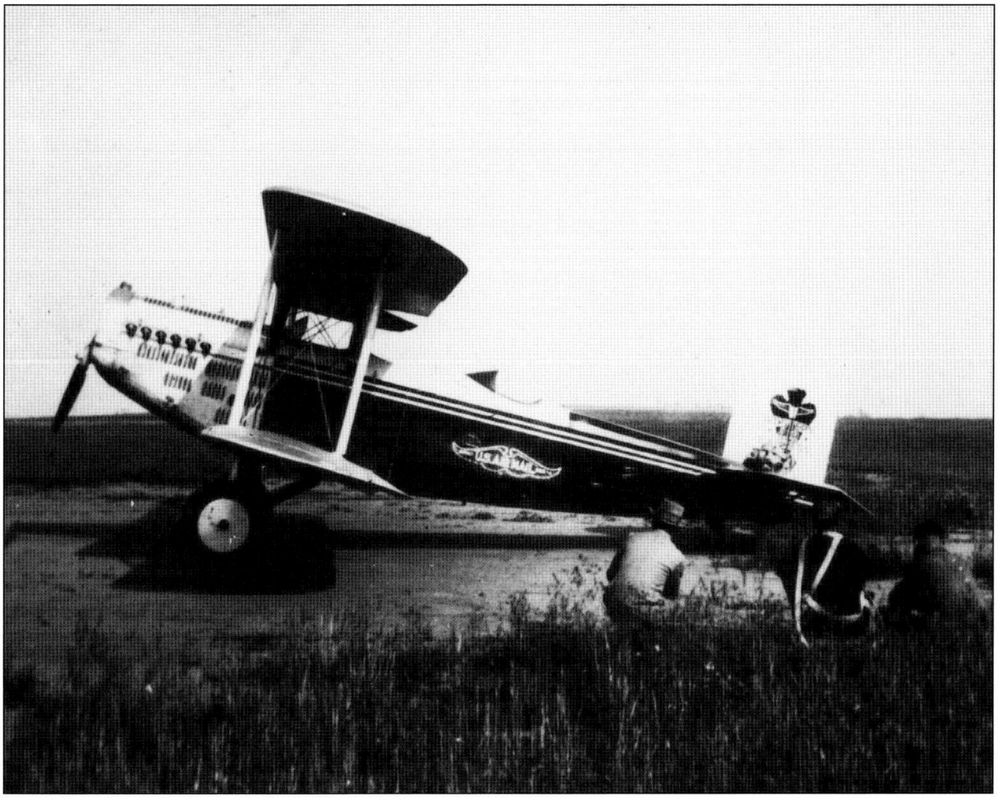

Although airline passenger service was still years away, the 1930s saw the growth of U.S. Airmail service at Mines Field. Fred Kelly was a pilot for Western Air Express, which had a contract to carry the mail. Western Air Express later became Western Airlines and ultimately part of Delta Airlines. Kelly earlier made his mark at the 1912 Olympics in Stockholm, winning the 110-meter hurdles.

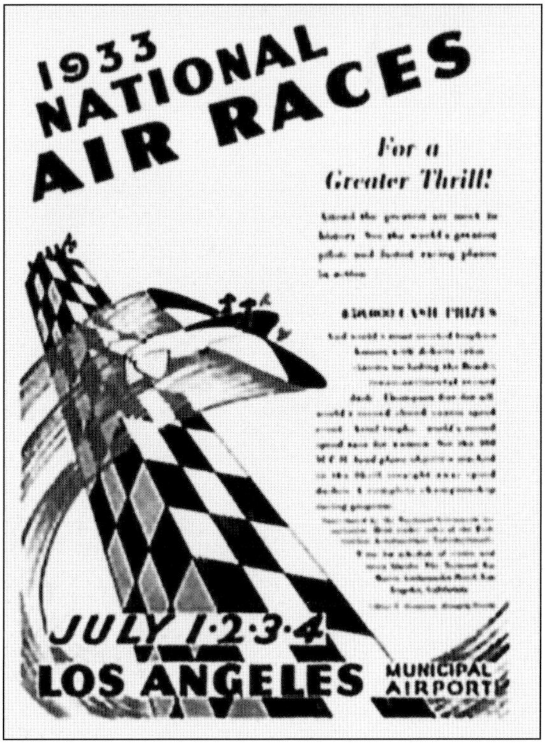

Though the focus was on aviation, the 1933 National Air Races at Mines Field also spotlighted Hollywood and the stars. One aircraft carried advertising for a 20th Century-Fox film, *The Bowery*, starring Wallace Beery and George Raft. Blonde bombshell Jean Harlow cheered flyers from the grandstands, and Mary Pickford, "America's Sweetheart," hosted a day of events. Other celebrities on hand included Hoot Gibson, Ken Maynard, and Jimmy Doolittle.

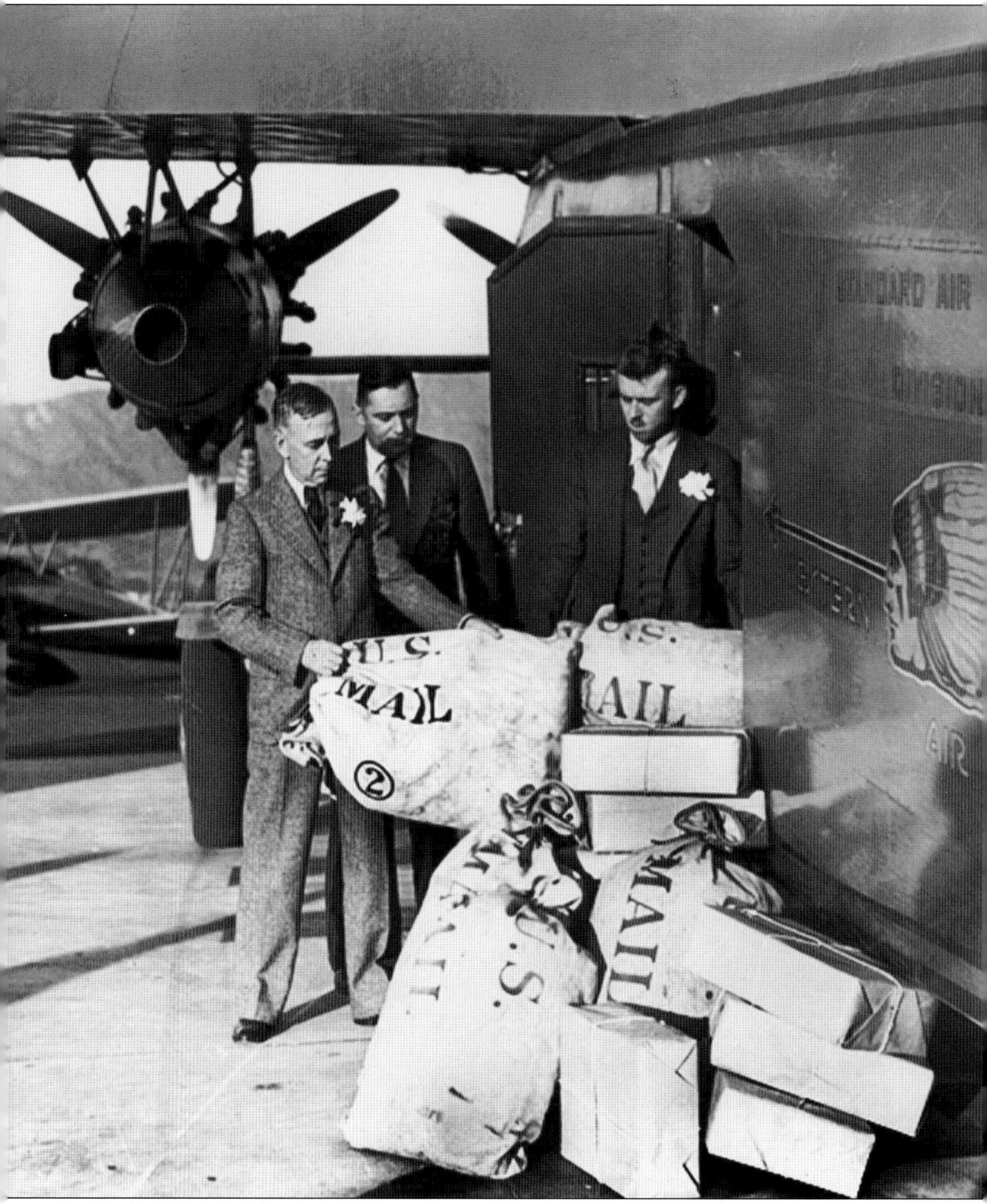

Loading airmail sacks on and off aircraft was a dirty job. These workers shed their work duds and donned their Sunday best for this photograph at Mines Field about 1930. Over the years, airmail has been carried in and out of LAX on specially designated flights, on regular passenger flights, and on all-cargo aircraft.

Sheila Brown, age nine and a half, was the mascot of the 1933 National Air Races at Mines Field. Accompanied by her father, W. Sidney Brown of Los Angeles, Sheila had already chalked up several hundred hours in the air, including two transcontinental flights, a forced landing, and other adventures. She is seated in the Shell Trophy, for which Jimmy Doolittle was the defending holder in the 3-kilometer dash.

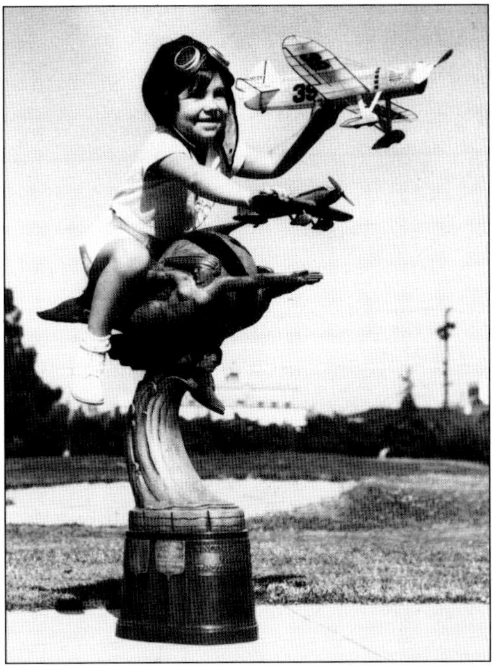

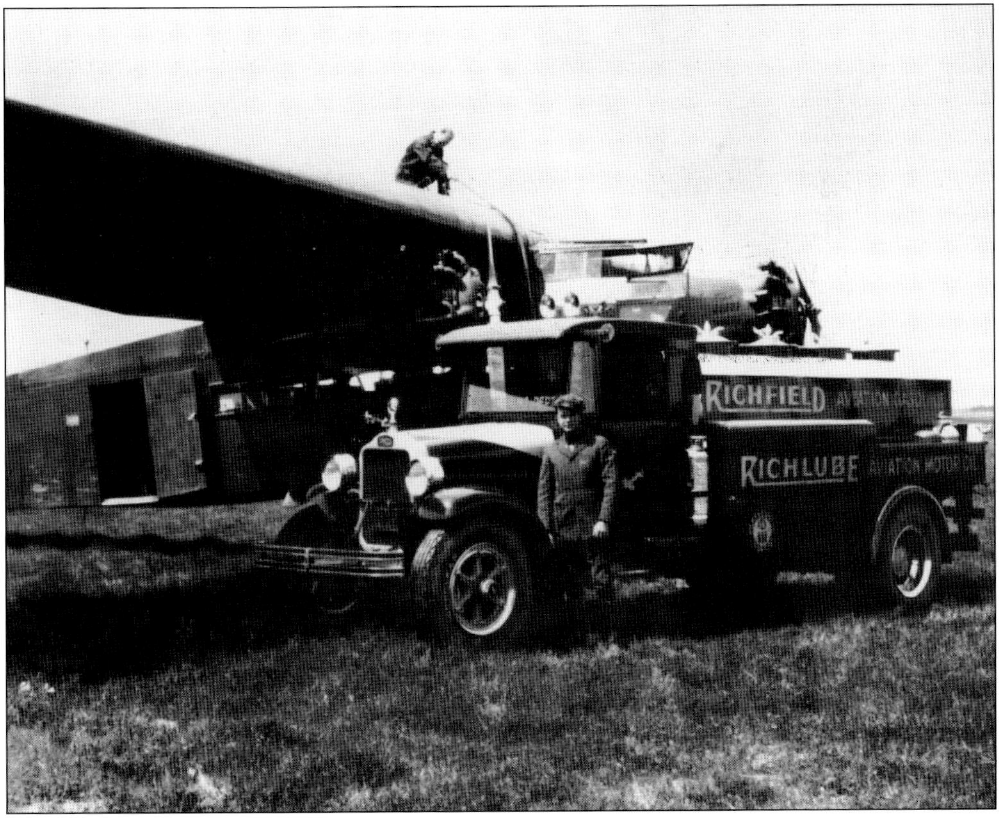

Air races were not all flash and dash. Here a Richfield Oil Company refueling truck refuels a Fokker Trimotor, the first to land at the site of the 1933 National Air Races at Mines Field.

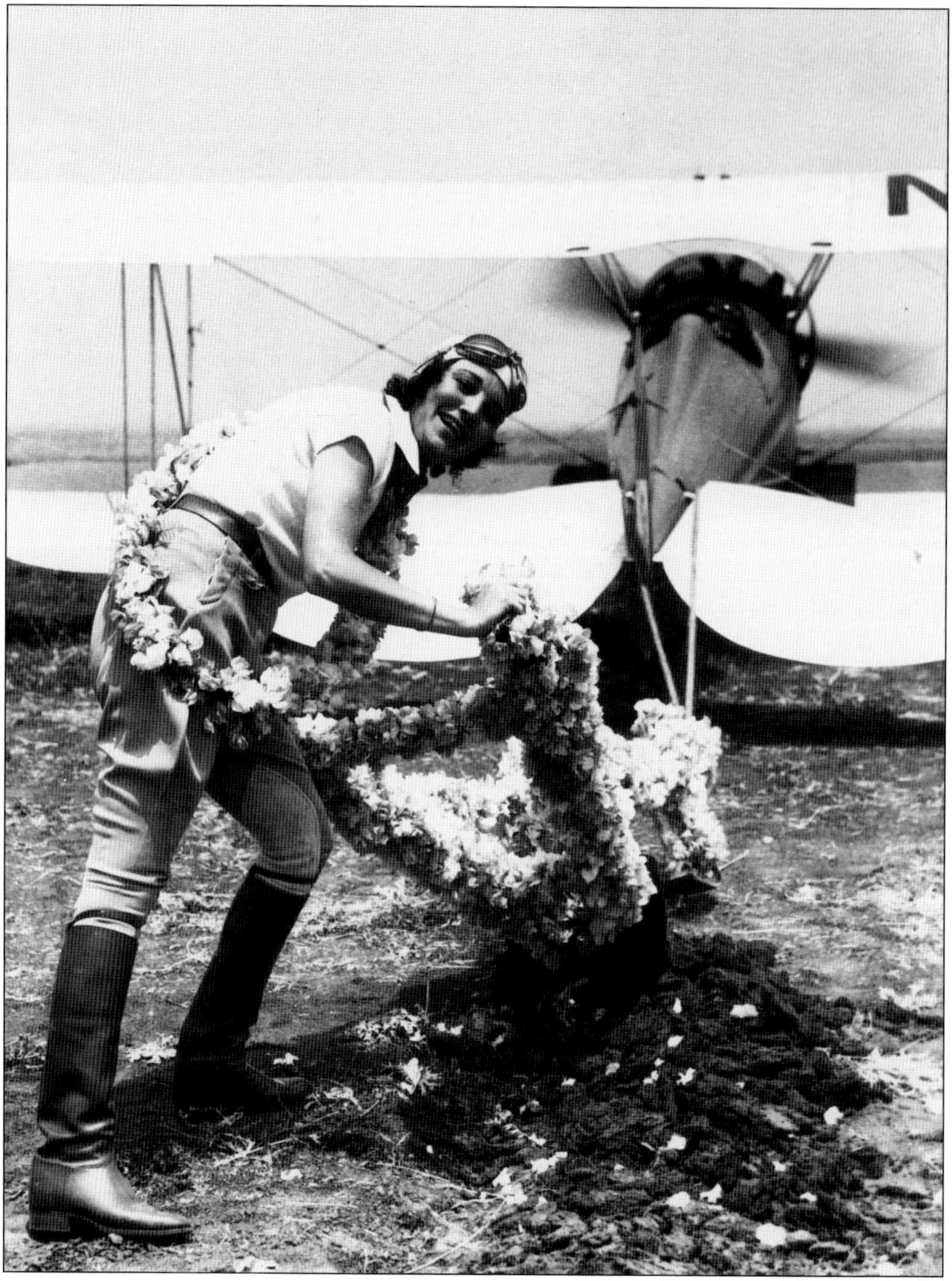

Famed aviatrix Ruth Elder Gillespie was among the celebrities on hand for the 1933 National Air Races at Mines Field. She is pictured guiding a floral plow pulled by a biplane.

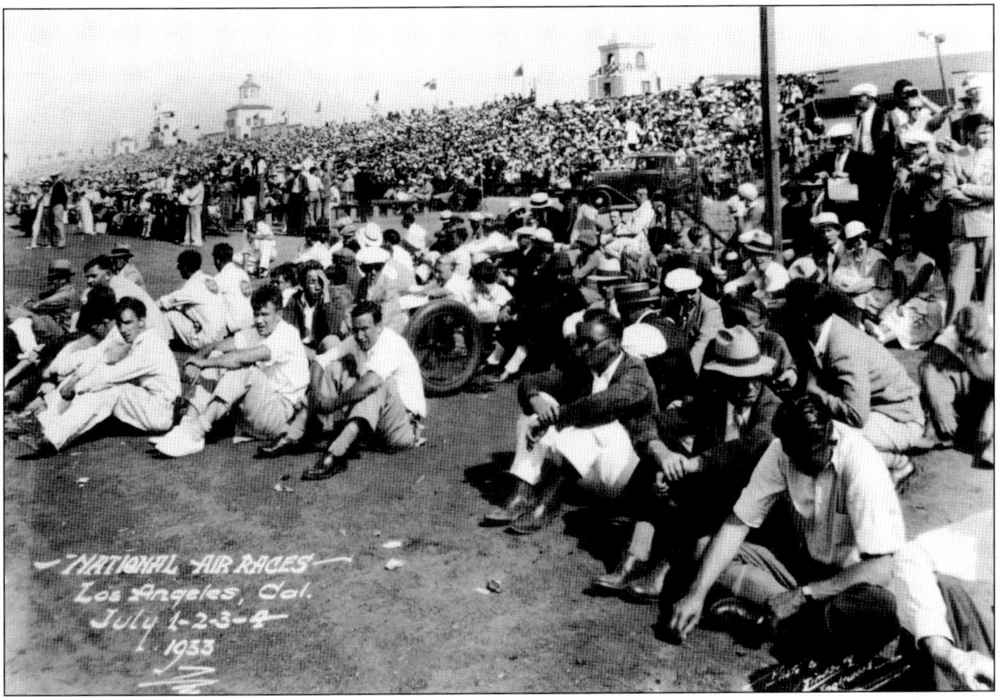

Throngs of aviation buffs attending the 1928 National Air Races were repeated for the 1933 races at Mines Field. The 1933 event was in the middle of the Great Depression, but Southern Californians still were looking to have a good time at minimum expense.

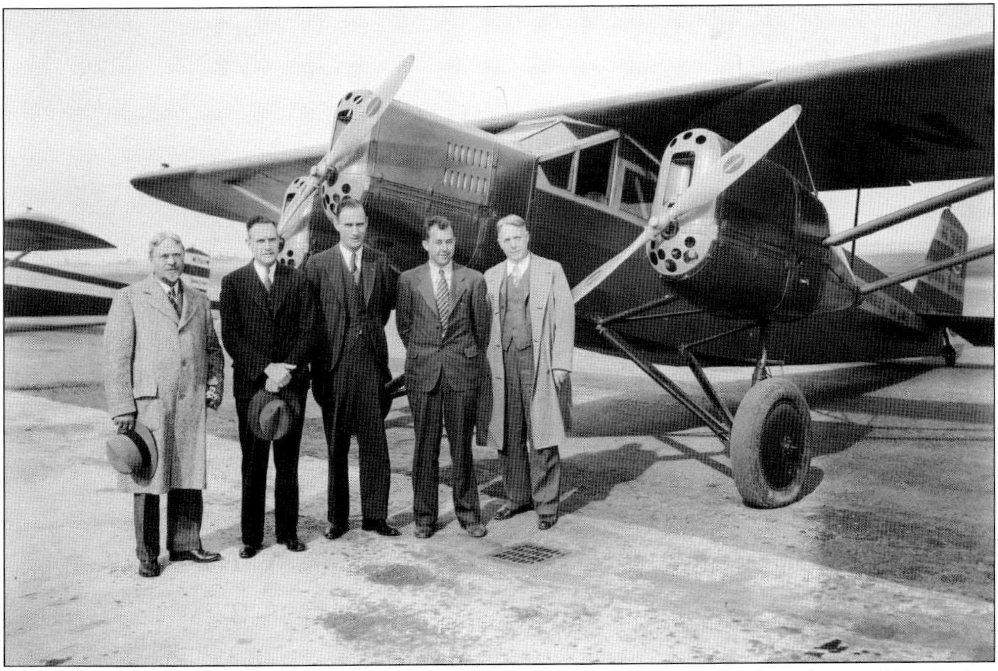

This Ogden Osprey was one of the rarer early aircraft at Mines Field. Manufactured by Ogden Aeronautics Corporation on Market Street in nearby Inglewood, the Osprey was a high-wing monoplane of limited production. This photograph was taken about 1933.

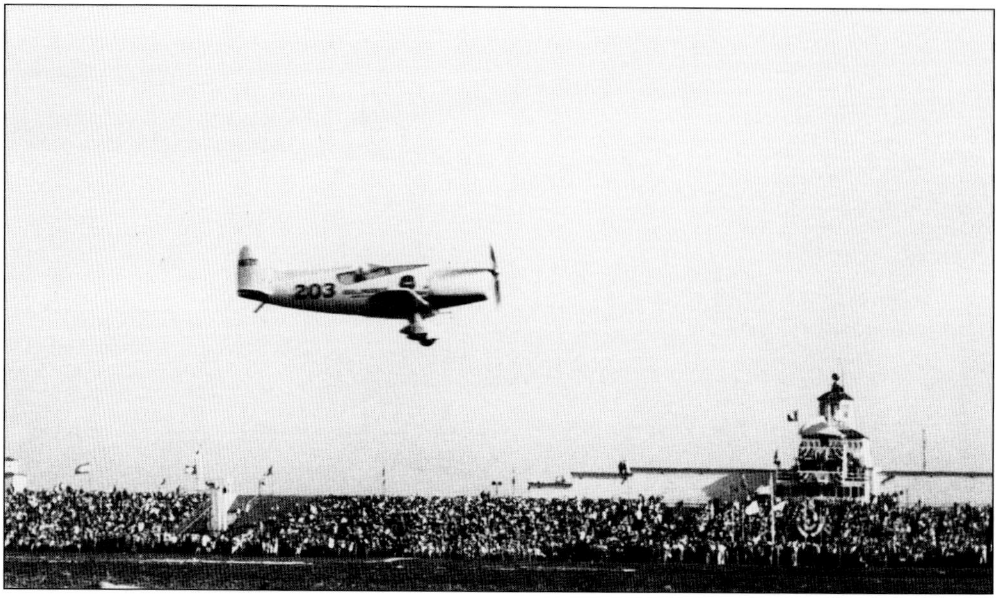

Changes in aircraft design and technology were evident in the 1933 National Air Races at Mines Field. Biplanes had dominated the 1928 races, but this monoplane pictured at the 1933 races was indicative of new trends in aviation.

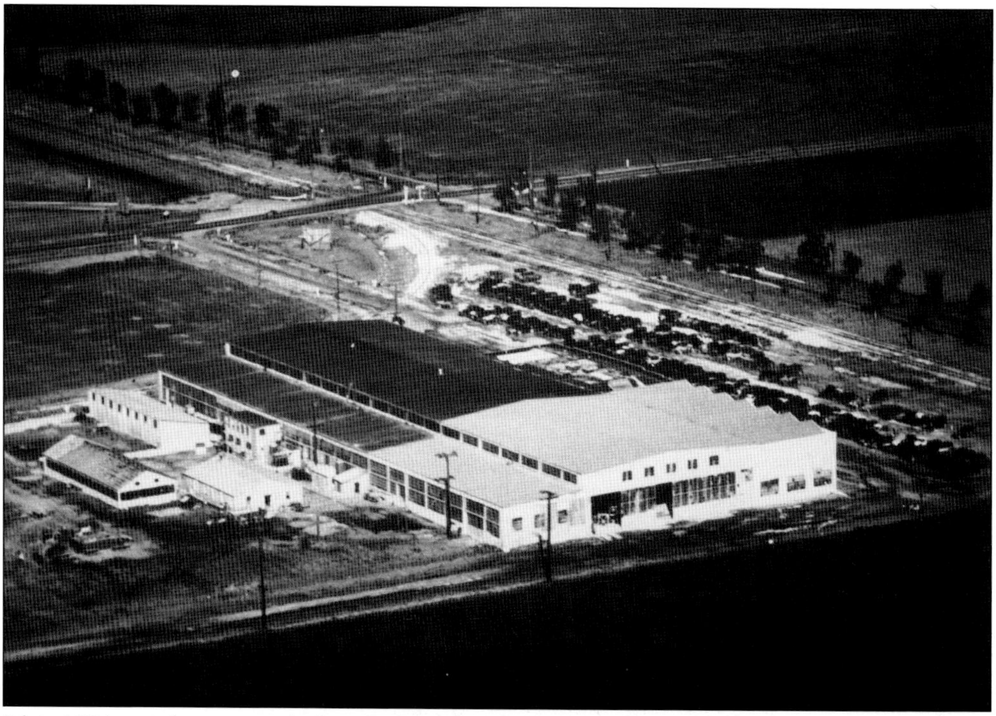

This 1934 aerial view spotlights the Northrop aviation plant at Mines Field. The building actually was owned by Pickwick Night Coach but occupied by Northrop. It later became the Douglas Aircraft El Segundo Division. Northrop remains active in Southern California aviation manufacturing in the 21st century. Pickwick Night Coaches manufactured buses for the night segments of long "flights."

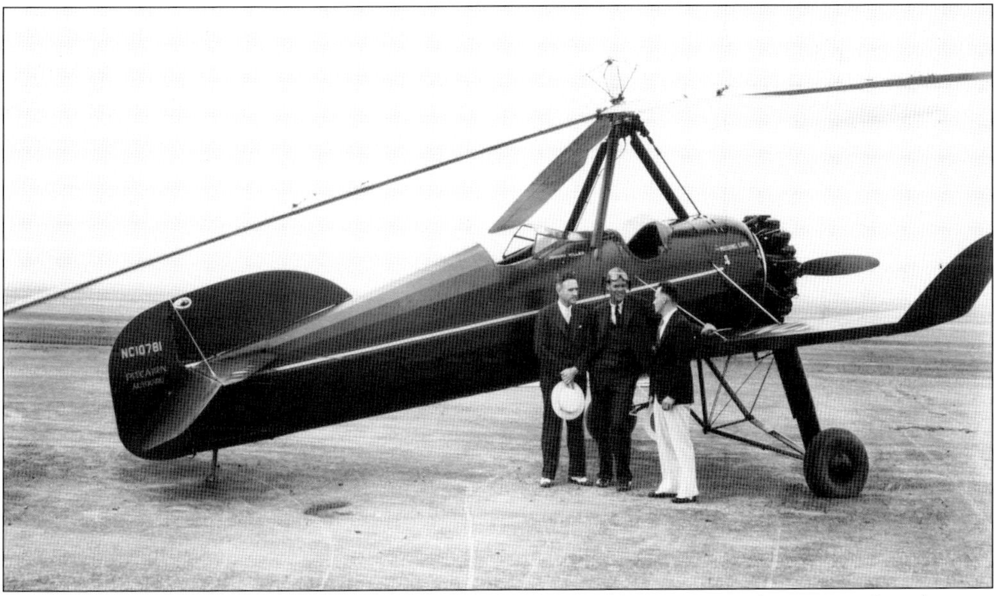

This is a *c.* 1934 view of a Pitcairn autogyro at Los Angeles Municipal Airport. Standing in front of the plane are, from left to right, Dick Barnitz, airport manager; John Miller, pilot of the autogyro; and Larry Talbot.

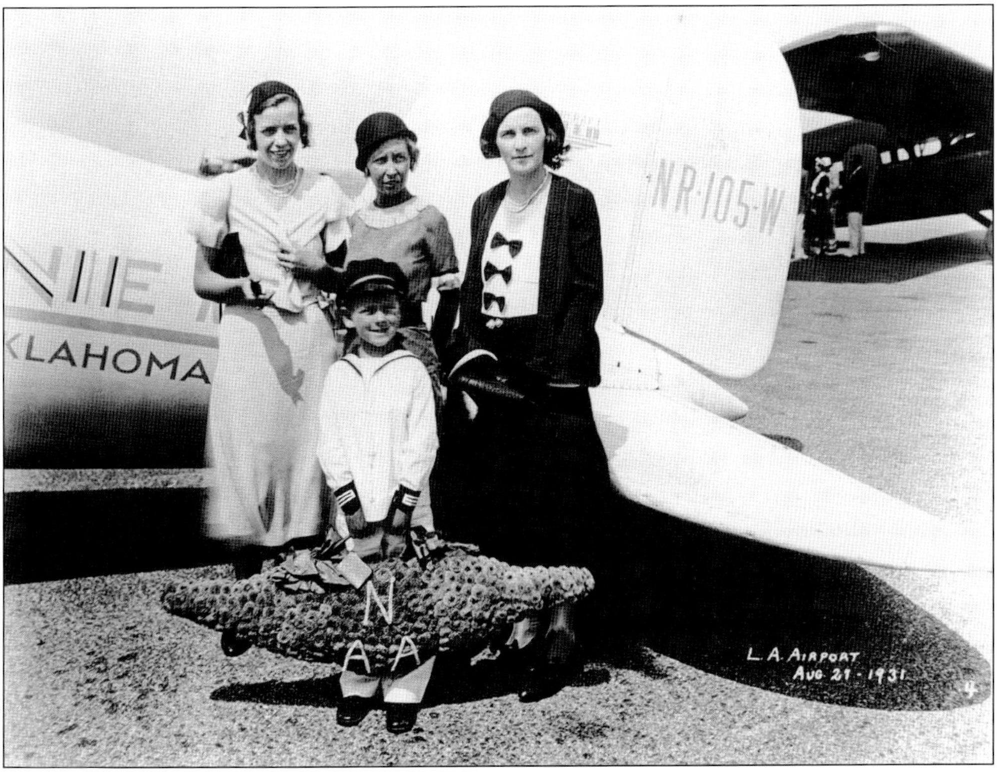

America was in the depths of the Great Depression when this well-dressed group was photographed at Los Angeles Municipal Airport on August 21, 1931. The "NAA" logo in the foreground may indicate a special event connected with the National Aeronautic Association.

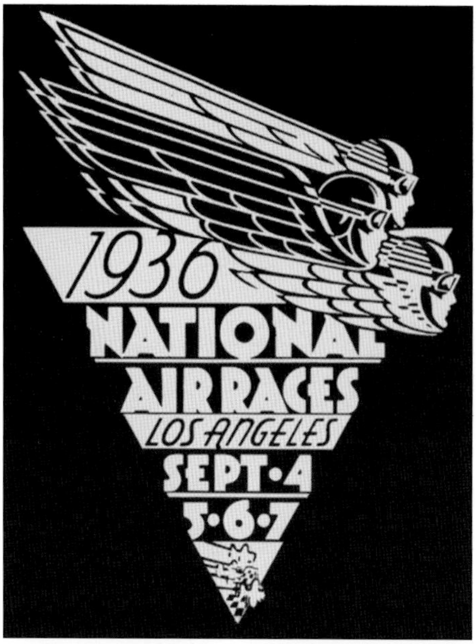

It was not surprising Los Angeles was tapped again to host the National Air Races in 1936. Radio stations KFWB and KECA beamed broadcasts of the events live from Mines Field. The airport, no longer an obscure landing strip, had acquired impressive tenants and neighbors, including North American Aviation Company, Northrop Corporation, and Interstate Aircraft and Engineering Company.

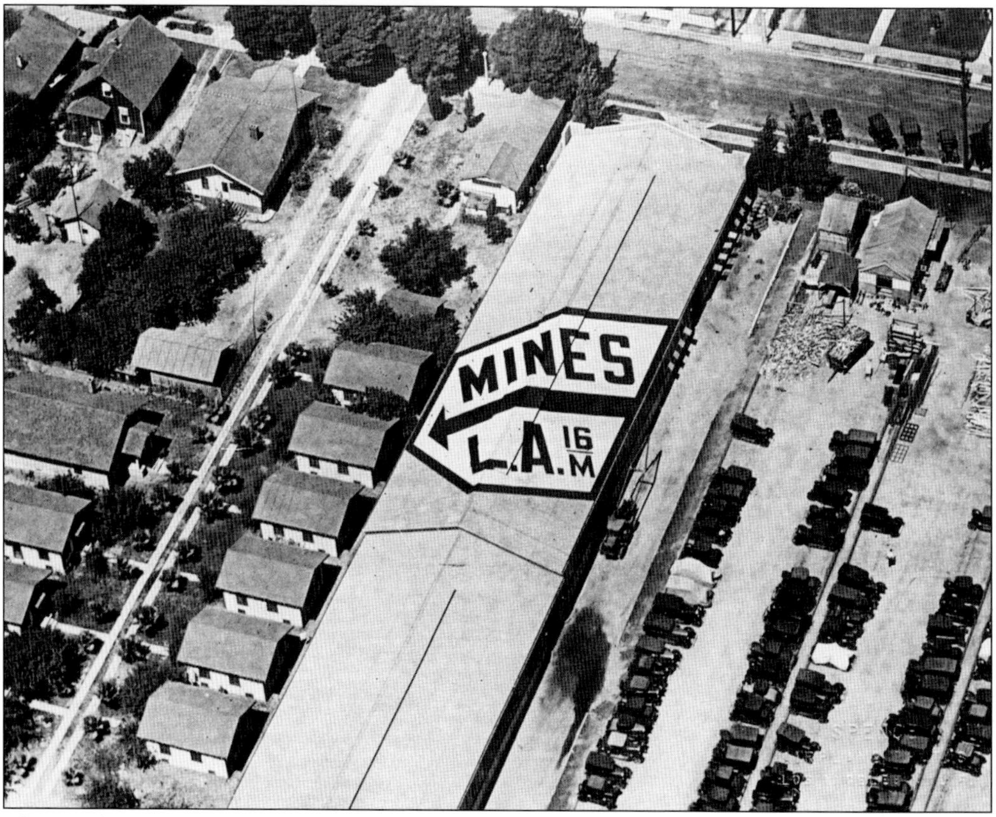

This rooftop sign helped guide pilots to Mines Field in the 1930s. Mines was one of numerous airfields in the Los Angeles metropolitan area at that time. Some, such as Compton, Van Nuys, Long Beach, and Torrance airports, have survived into the 21st century. Others, such as Alhambra, Monrovia, Glendale, and Montebello (Vail Field) airports, are long gone.

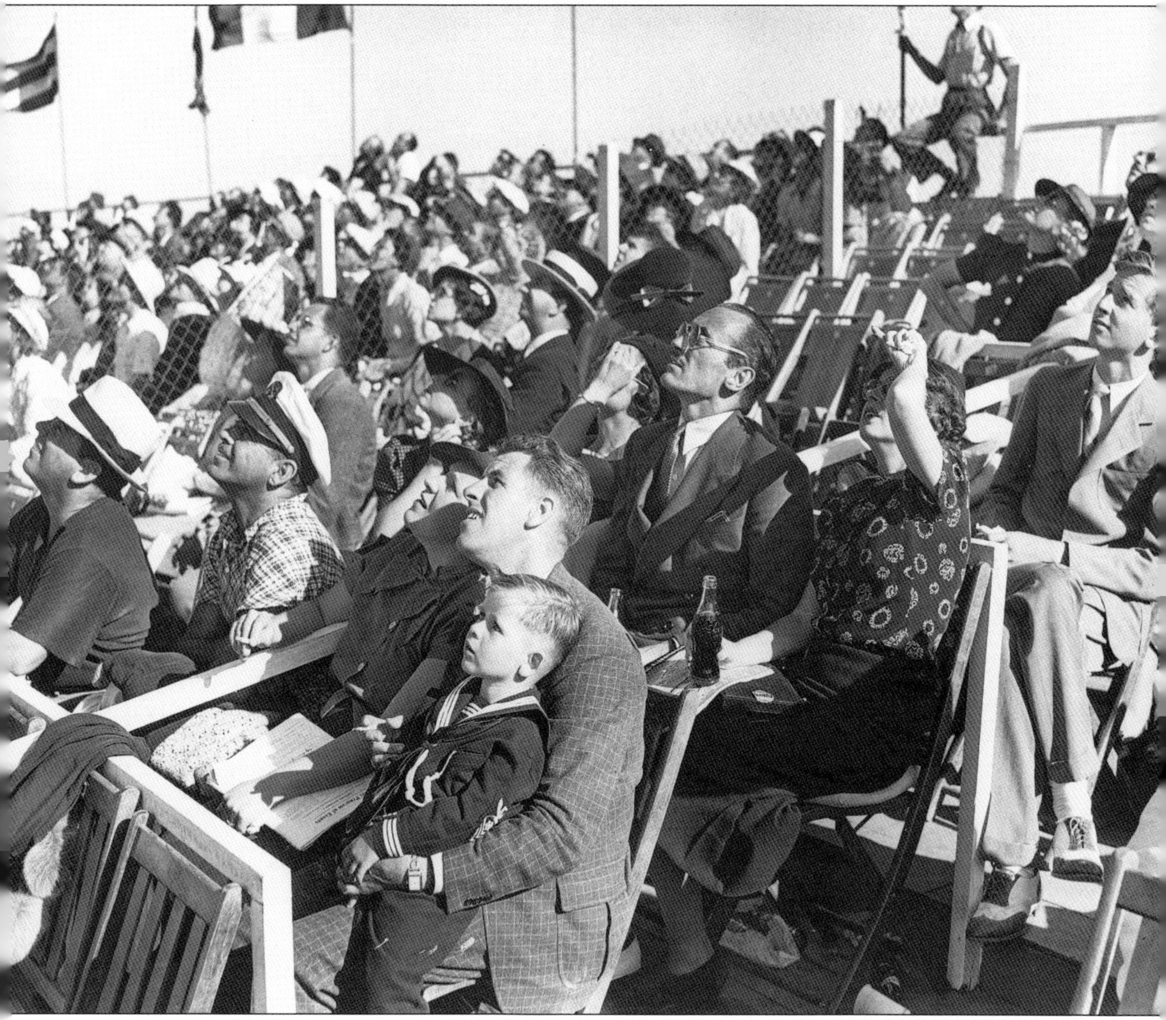

The "special event" quality of the 1936 National Air Races at Mines Field is evident in this view of the grandstands with aviation buffs dressed in their Sunday best. The races began on September 4 and continued for four days.

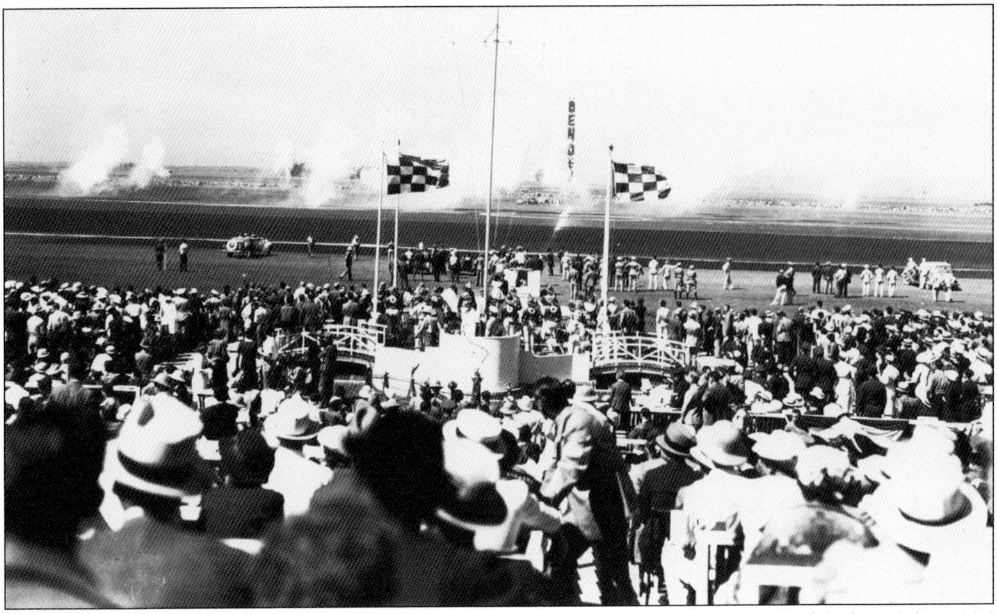

A demonstration of wartime bombing maneuvers by military aircraft was a highlight of the 1936 National Air Races at Los Angeles Municipal Airport. Radio broadcasting of the event took place from the officials' stand in the center of the photograph. In the foreground are the grandstands.

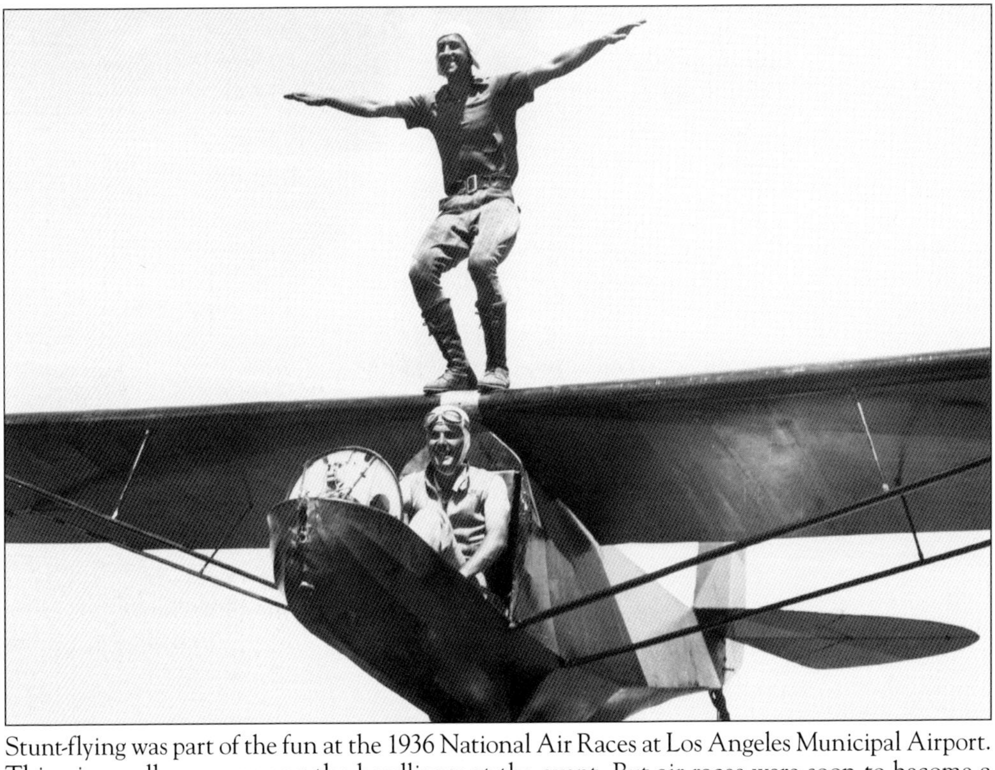

Stunt-flying was part of the fun at the 1936 National Air Races at Los Angeles Municipal Airport. This wing walker was among the headliners at the event. But air races were soon to become a thing of the past. The novelty of aviation was wearing thin as the public became more concerned with looming war clouds in Europe and Asia.

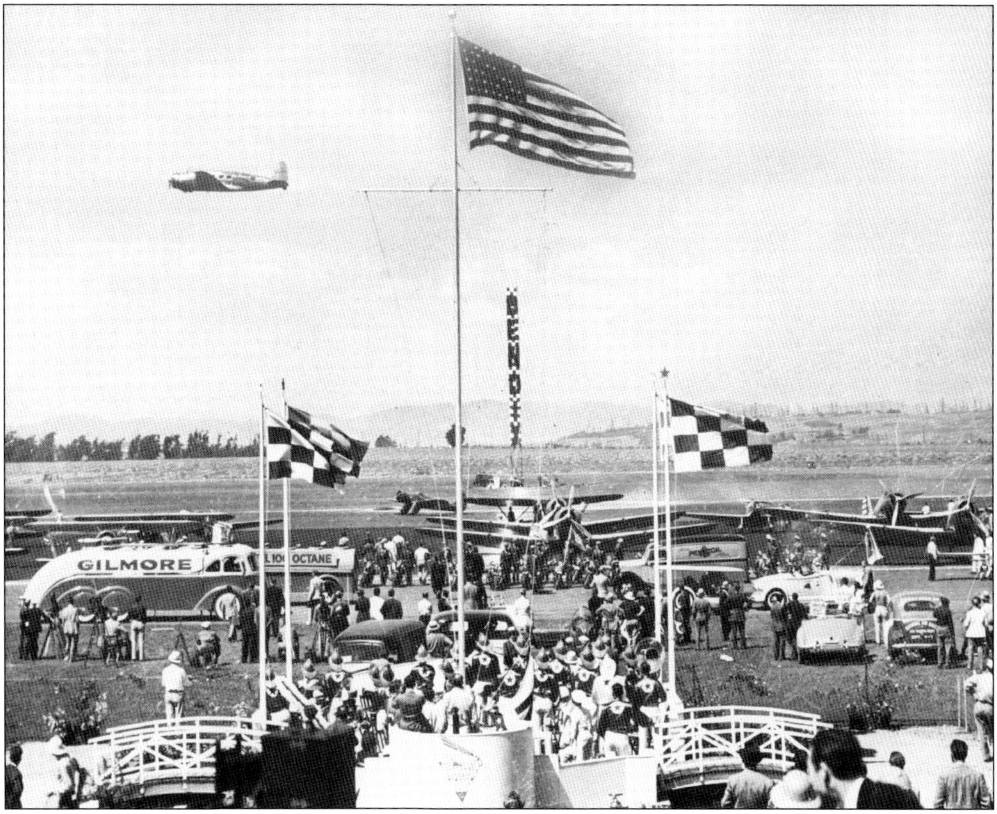

Spectators at the 1936 National Air Races at the Los Angeles Municipal Airport watch the daring flyers. Attendance was estimated at 50,000, one of the largest gatherings in the city up to that time. The mood was one of light-hearted exhilaration. The event received major coverage in the city's metropolitan newspapers and on local radio stations.

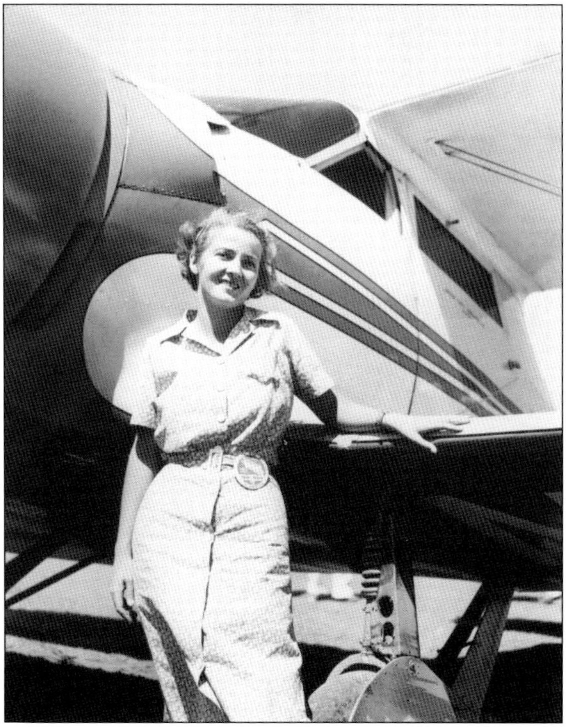

At the 1936 National Air Races at Mines Field at the Los Angeles Municipal Airport, pilot Nancy Love stands in front of her plane. The birth of aviation came at a time when women had achieved voting rights and were enjoying new influence and respect in society.

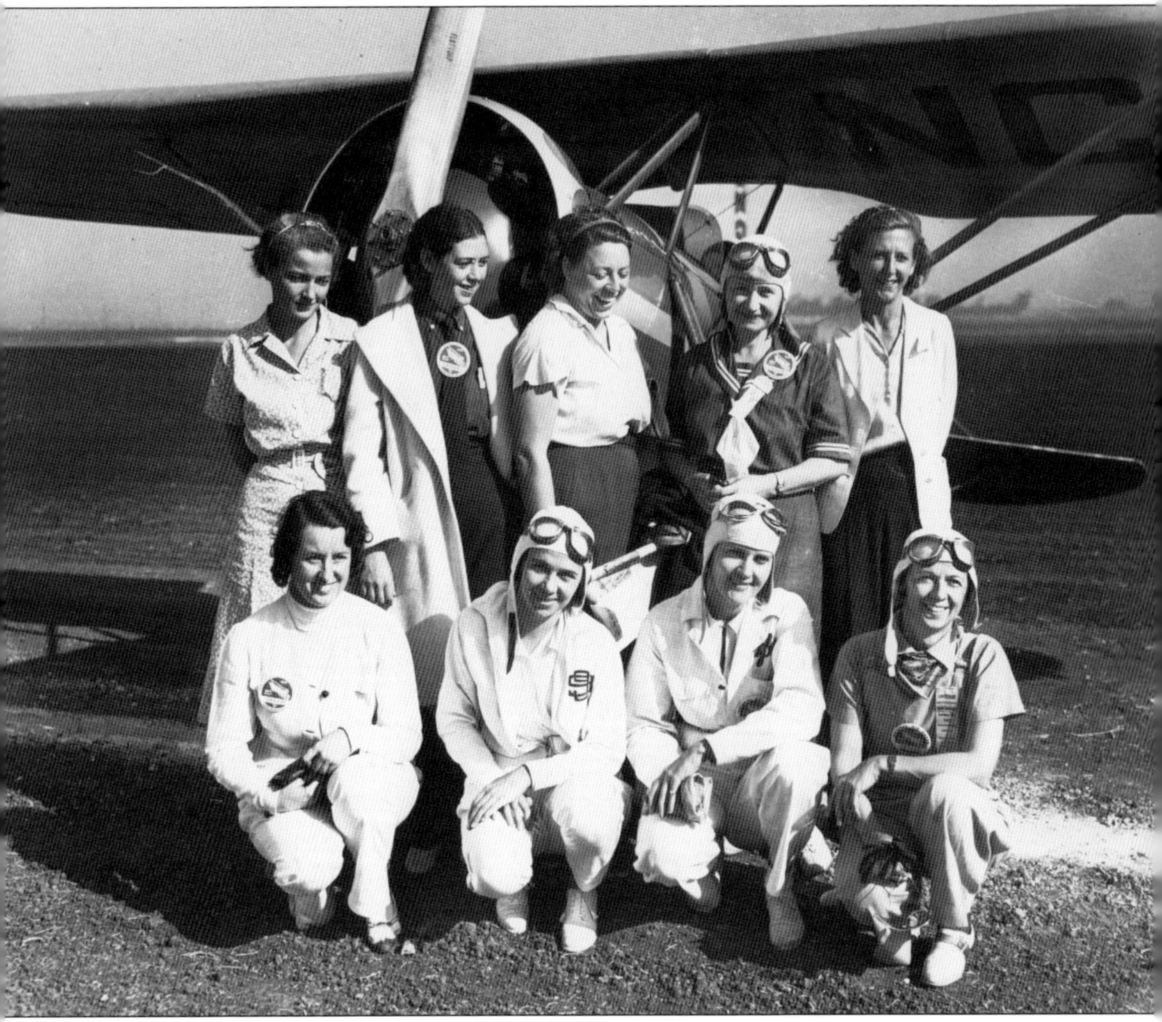

These female pilots participated in the 1936 National Air Races at Los Angeles Municipal Airport. From left to right are (first row) Lona Gardner, Melba Beard, Gladys O'Donnell, and Jeanette Lempke; (second row) Nancy Love, Betty Browning, Martie Bowman, Genevieve Salvage, and Henrietta Sumner.

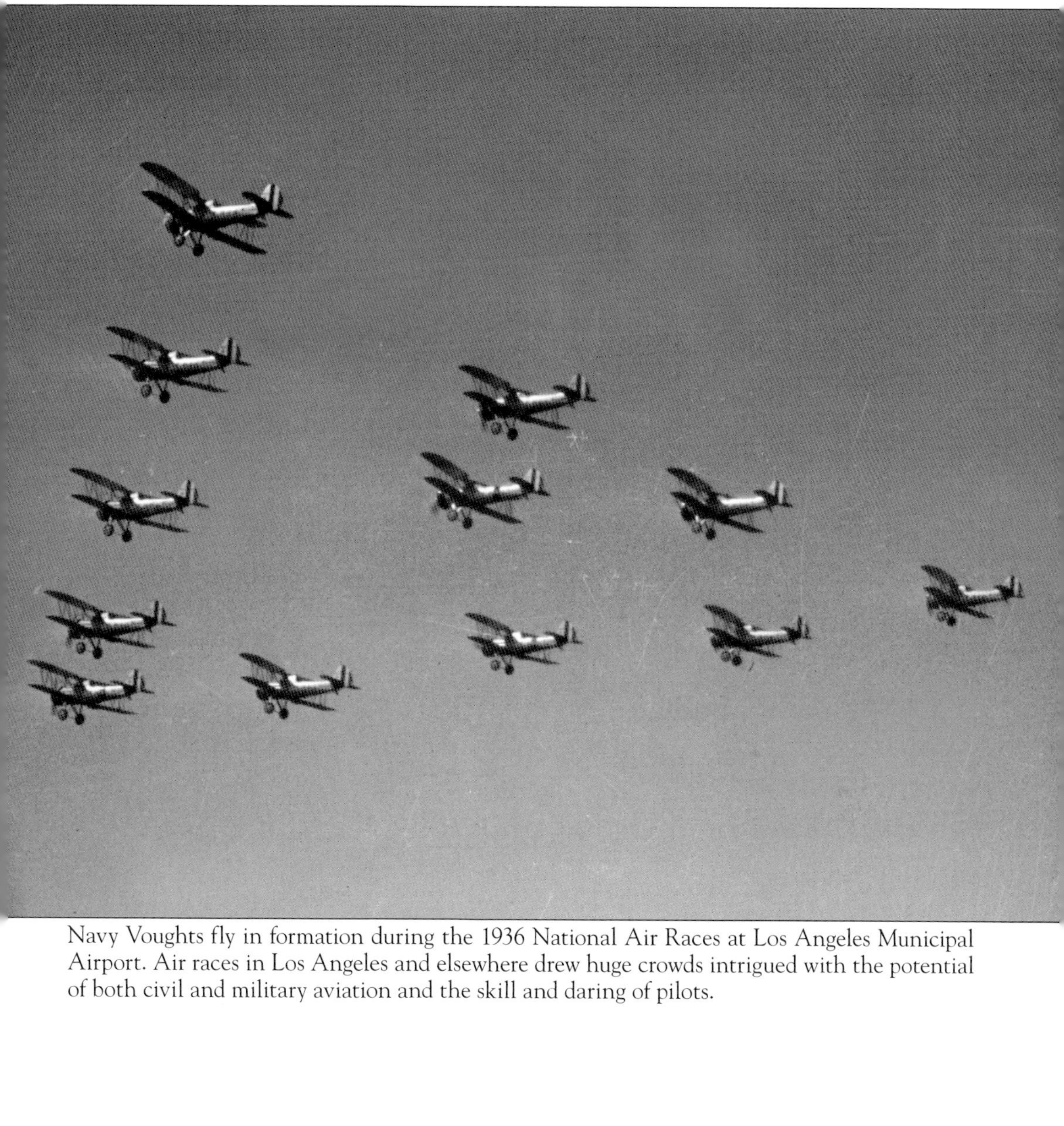

Navy Voughts fly in formation during the 1936 National Air Races at Los Angeles Municipal Airport. Air races in Los Angeles and elsewhere drew huge crowds intrigued with the potential of both civil and military aviation and the skill and daring of pilots.

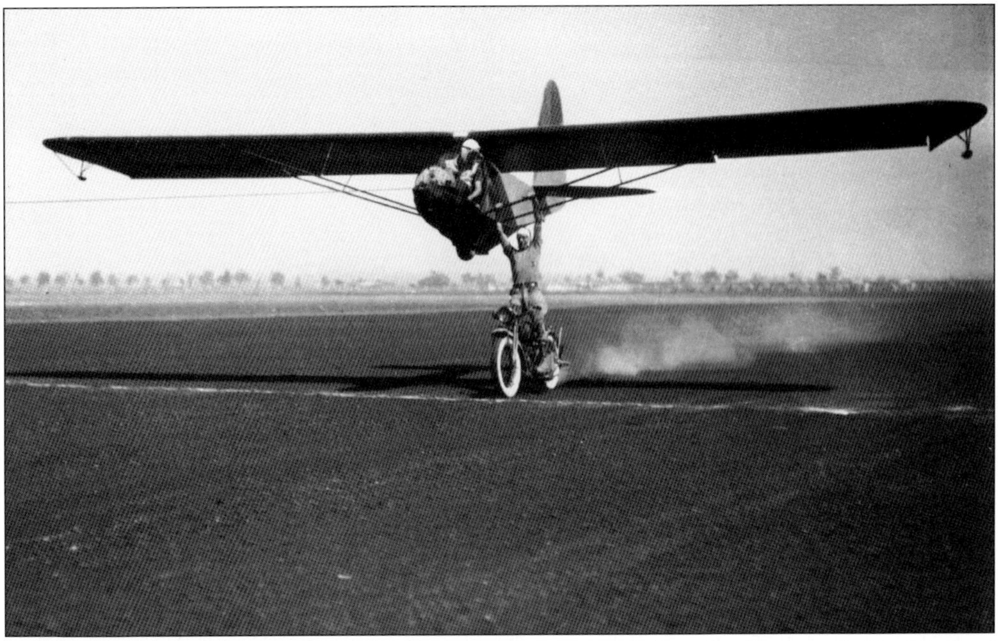

A varied program of daring stunts and other entertainment, including this "stunt cycle," highlighted the 1936 National Air Races in Los Angeles. Although the Great Depression was easing in 1936, money remained tight and the air races were a thrifty choice for family entertainment.

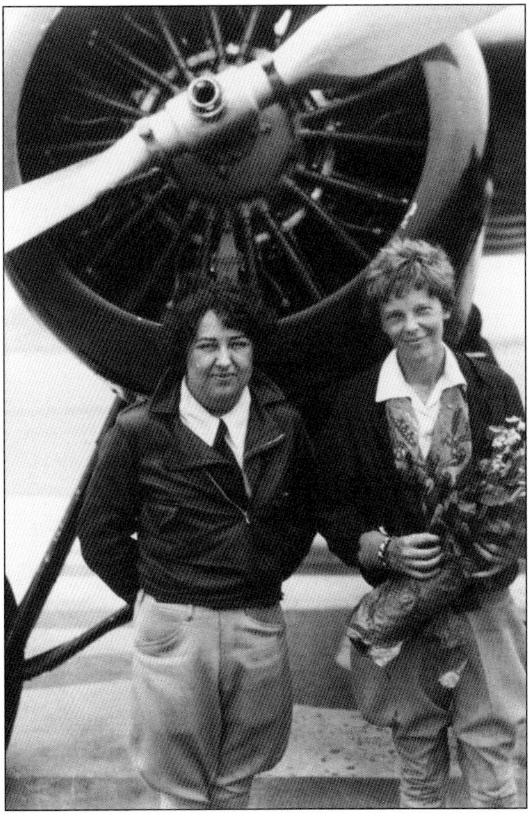

Few aviators captured the popular imagination as did Amelia Earhart. Earhart (right), with Florence "Pancho" Barnes, participated in the 1936 National Air Races at Mines Field. Vying for the Bendix Trophy, she was almost sucked out of her plane when an emergency hatch failed. The mishap caused her to finish fifth in the race. Later, for her round-the-world trip in 1937, Earhart chose the new Lockheed Electra. The plane's fuselage was almost completely filled with fuel tanks, leaving barely enough room for the pilot to crawl into the cockpit.

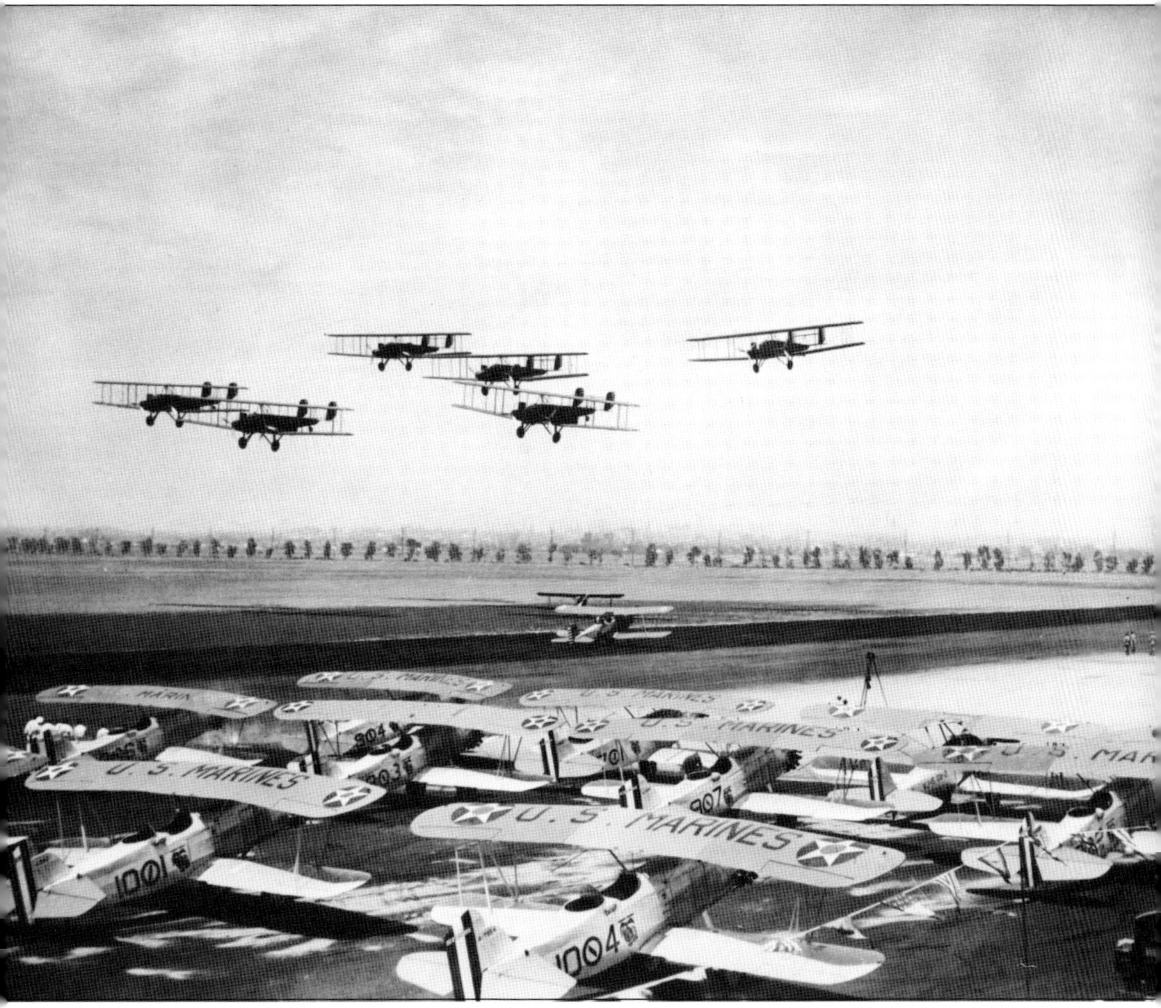

Air races of the 1920s and 1930s, including those in Los Angeles, featured an awe-inspiring variety of maneuvers, challenging pilots and delighting crowds. Daredevil exploits that would be unthinkable in today's crowded civil aviation environment were eagerly anticipated by those who flew in and viewed the early air races.

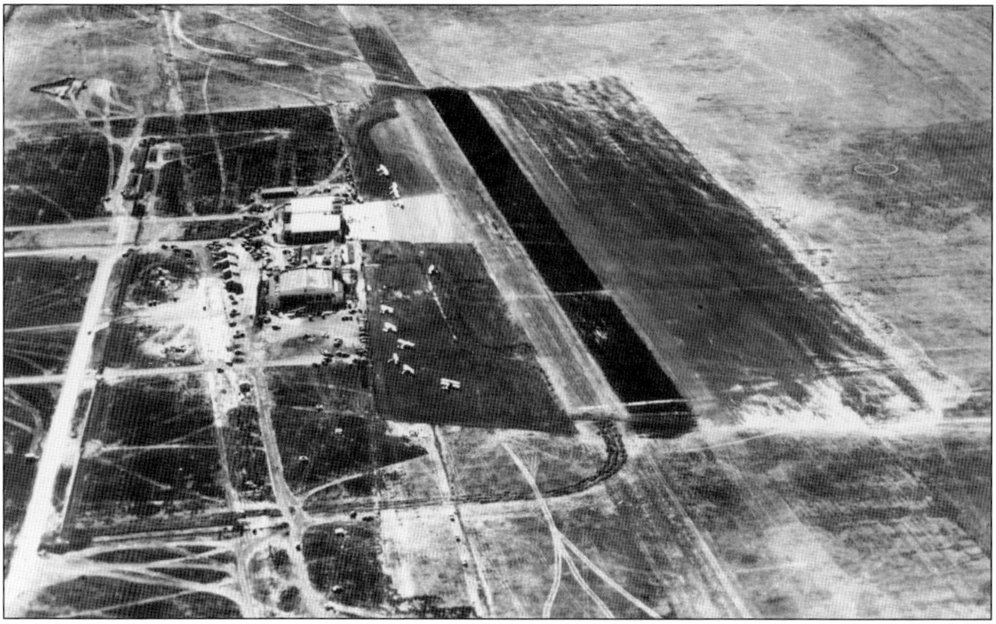

This view, looking west, shows Mines Field, officially known as Los Angeles Municipal Airport, in the 1930s. Imperial Highway is out of view to the left. The present LAX Central Terminal Area is situated off camera to the right. After years of leasing, the city finally purchased the airport land, taking title to 623 acres on October 1, 1937, at a cost of $2,692,000. The purchase was needed to comply with government regulations requiring ownership in order to receive federal funding.

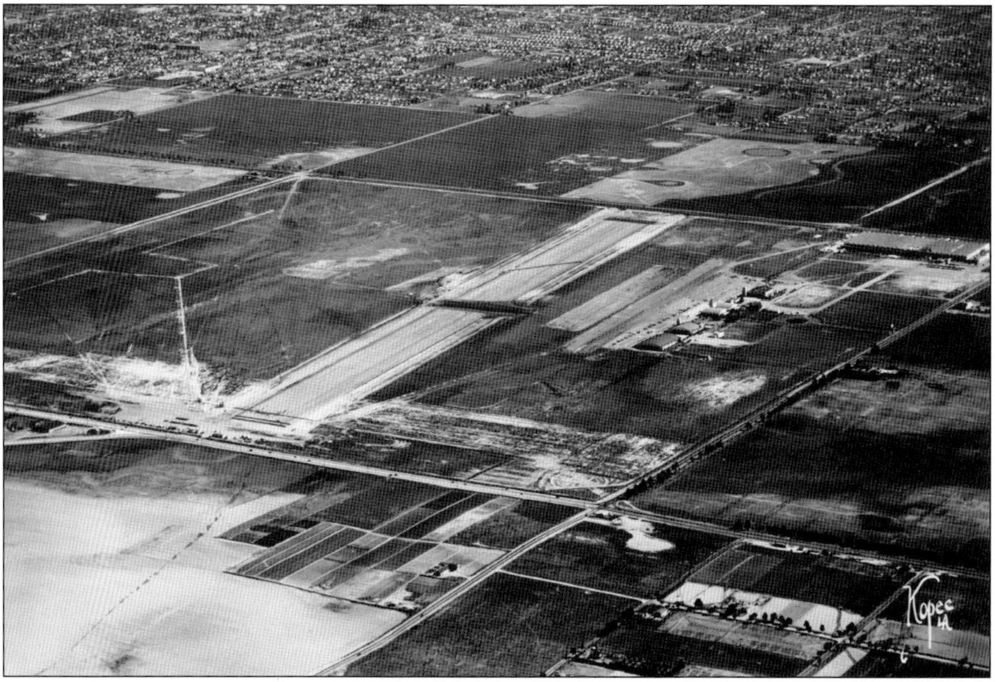

This aerial photograph of Los Angeles Municipal Airport was taken from the Goodyear Airship about 1938. After 10 years of leasing, the city had purchased 623 acres of land for the airport in 1937. More land was acquired in later years until the airport reached its present size of 3,500 acres.

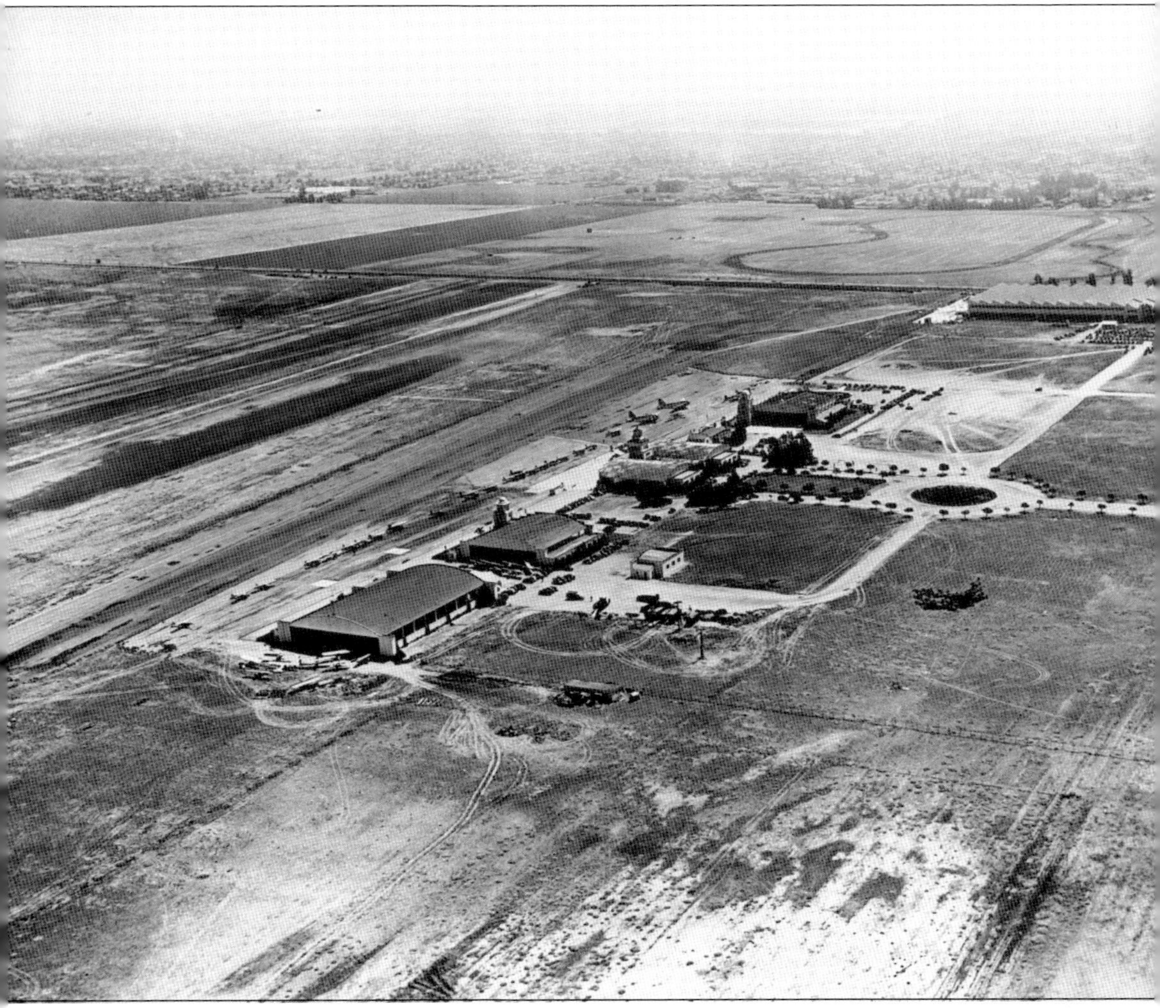

This 1938 aerial view of Los Angeles Municipal Airport, facing northeast, focuses on the municipal hangars and administration building. Imperial Highway is out of view at right. Note the automobile racetrack at the top of the photograph, east of what now is Aviation Boulevard.

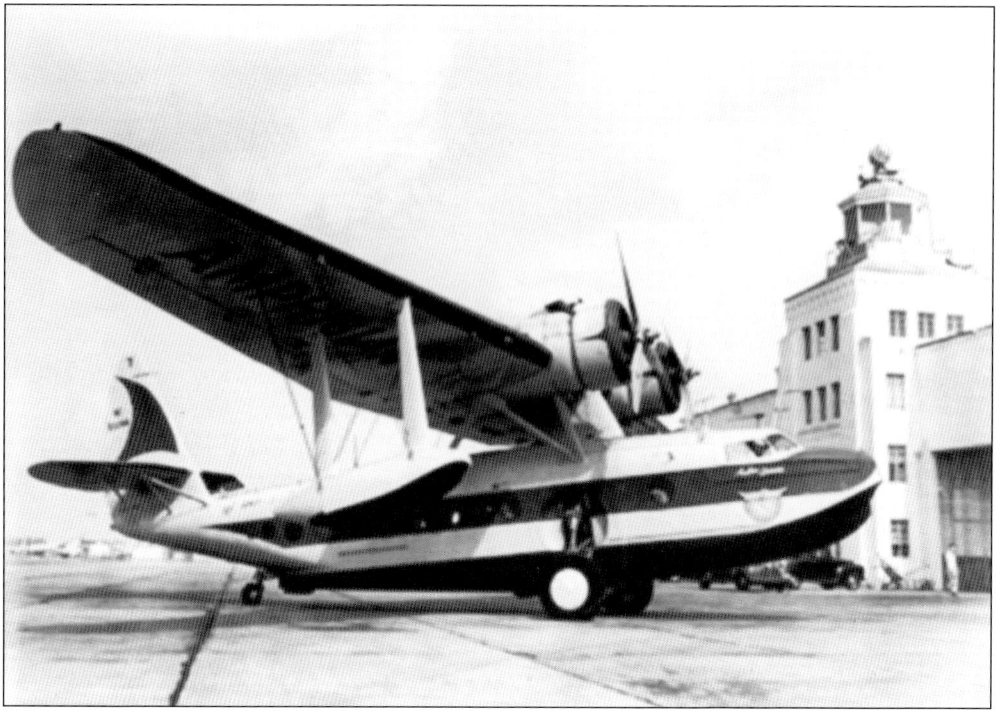

A Sikorsky S-43 aircraft is pictured near the old Mines Field Control Tower about 1938. The tower was situated midpoint between Hangars 2 and 3 just north of Imperial Highway and west of what now is Aviation Boulevard. Hangars 2 and 3 later were razed in 1970 to make way for construction of the Flying Tigers air-cargo business.

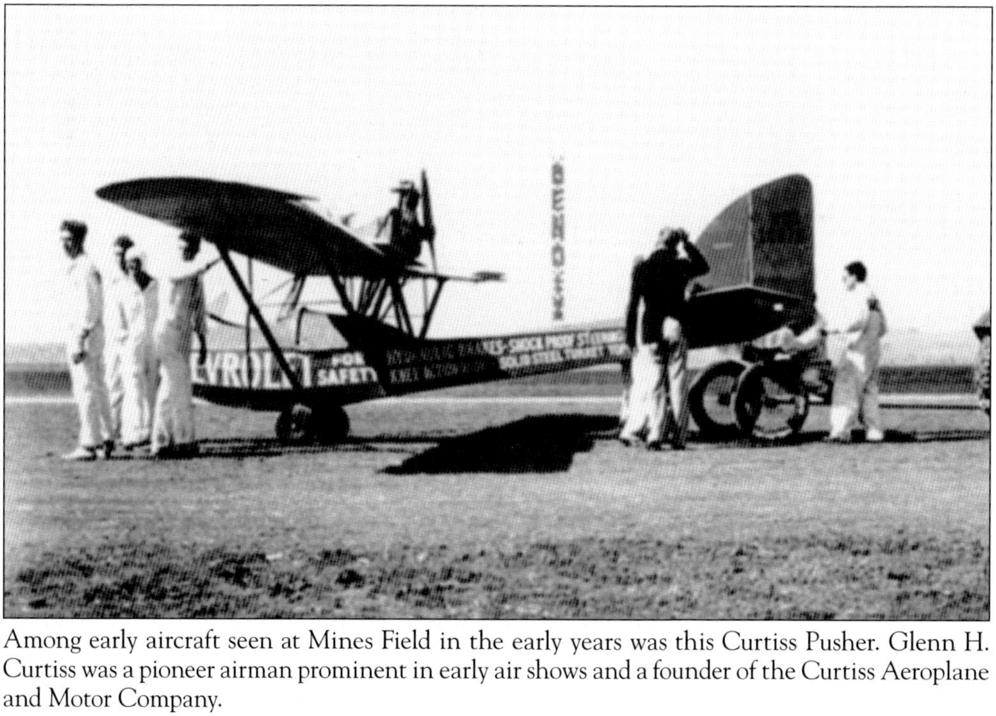

Among early aircraft seen at Mines Field in the early years was this Curtiss Pusher. Glenn H. Curtiss was a pioneer airman prominent in early air shows and a founder of the Curtiss Aeroplane and Motor Company.

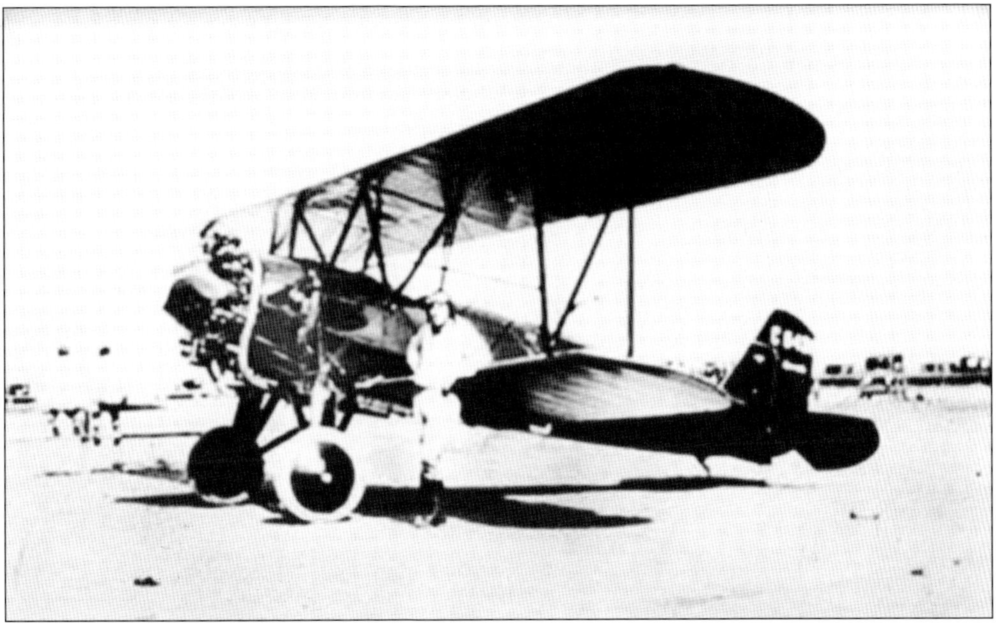

Visitors to Mines Field in the 1930s might have seen this Stearman biplane. The Stearman Aircraft Company was founded in Venice, California, by Lloyd Stearman and Fred Hoyt. It grew to become one of the most prominent light aircraft manufacturers of that era.

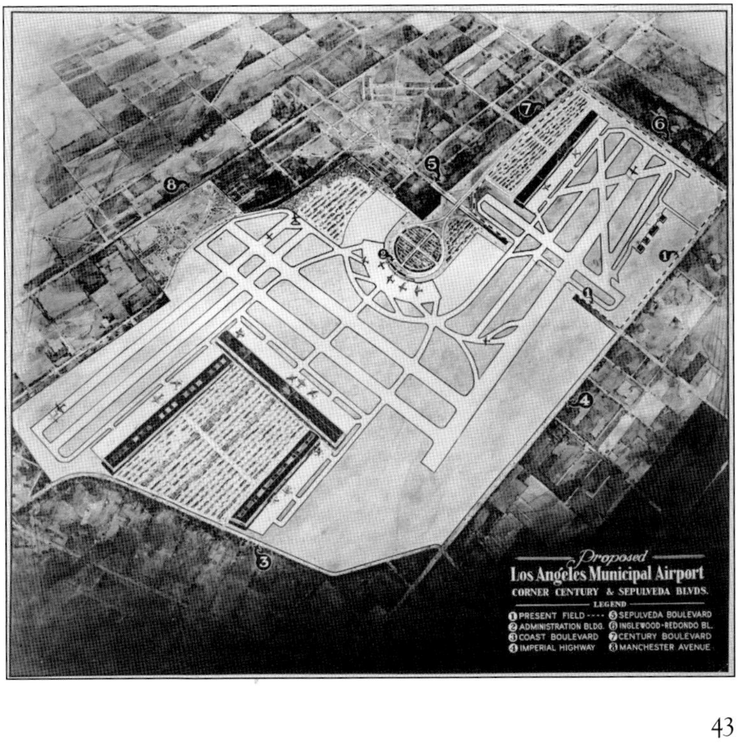

This master plan for future development of Los Angeles Municipal Airport was drawn up in the 1930s as city officials considered future aviation needs of Southern California. Note that the configuration bears a resemblance to portions of today's LAX.

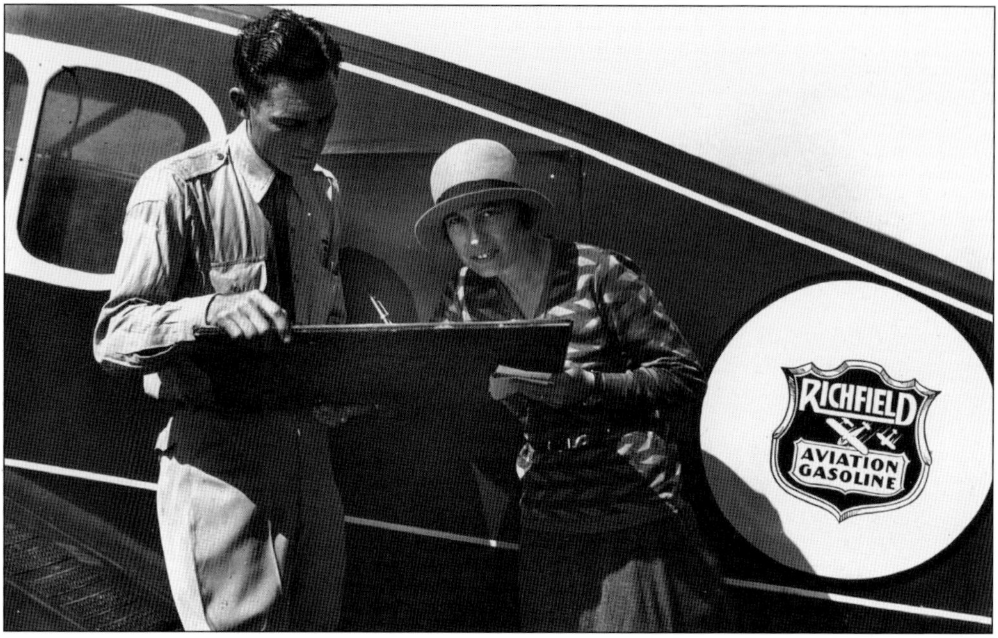

Henry Bakes, right hand to Clifford Henderson during the early years at Mines Field, checks in the first passenger for a commercial flight. Her name, unfortunately, is lost to history. Scheduled commercial service did not begin at the airport until 1946, but charter planes, like the one pictured, were an important part of air traffic at Mines in the 1930s.

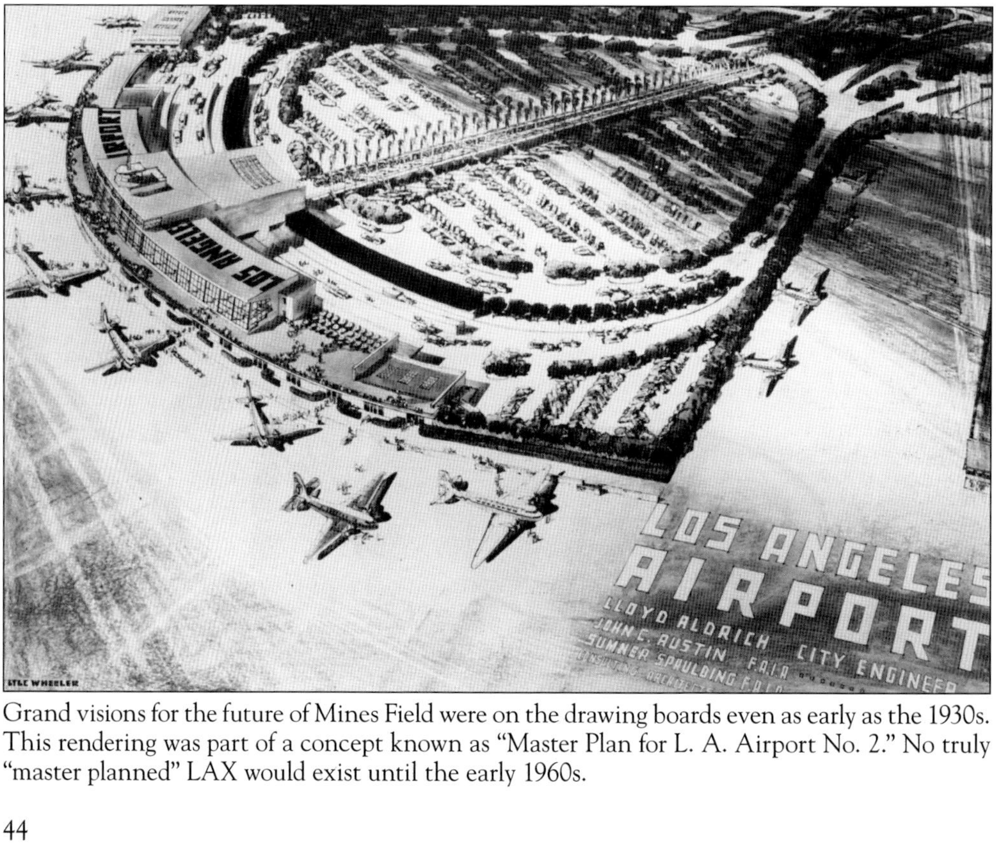

Grand visions for the future of Mines Field were on the drawing boards even as early as the 1930s. This rendering was part of a concept known as "Master Plan for L. A. Airport No. 2." No truly "master planned" LAX would exist until the early 1960s.

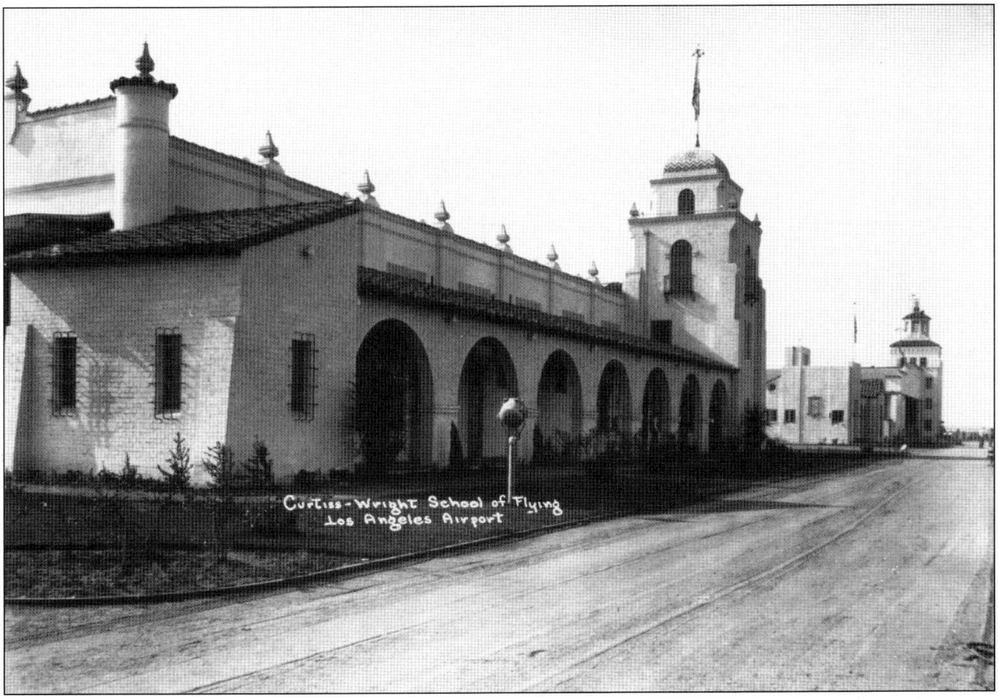

The Curtiss Wright Flying School was among the major tenants at Mines Field in the early years. Pictured is Hangar No. 1, where the flying school was based. This hangar is the only remaining structure from that era surviving at LAX into the 21st century. Below, the trainers (planes) are shown with the trainees.

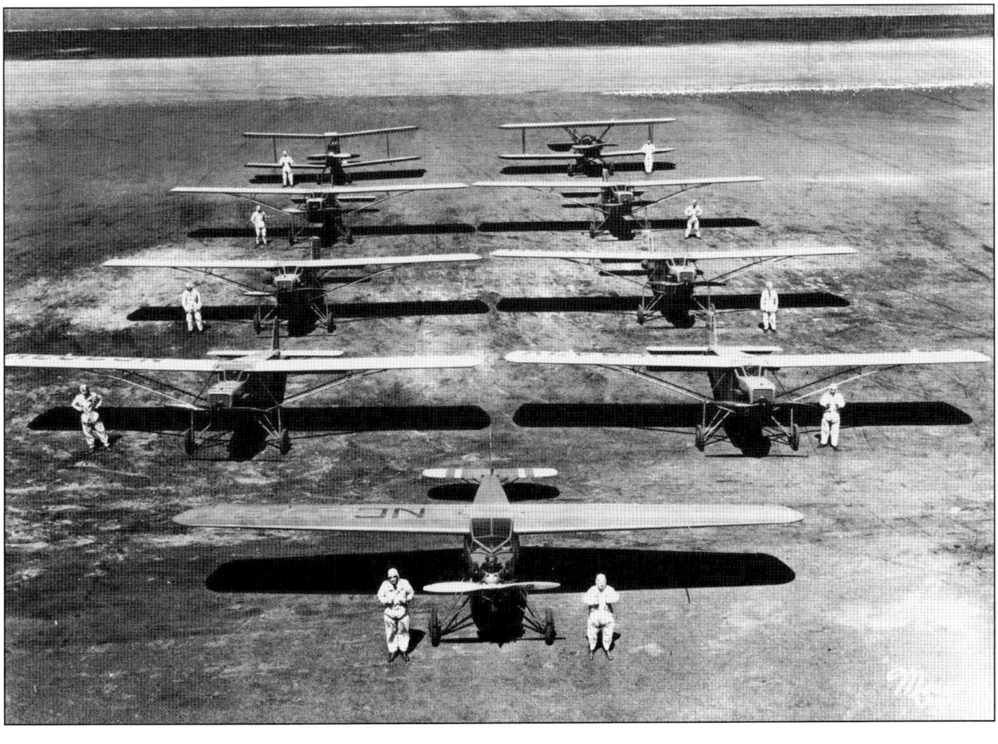

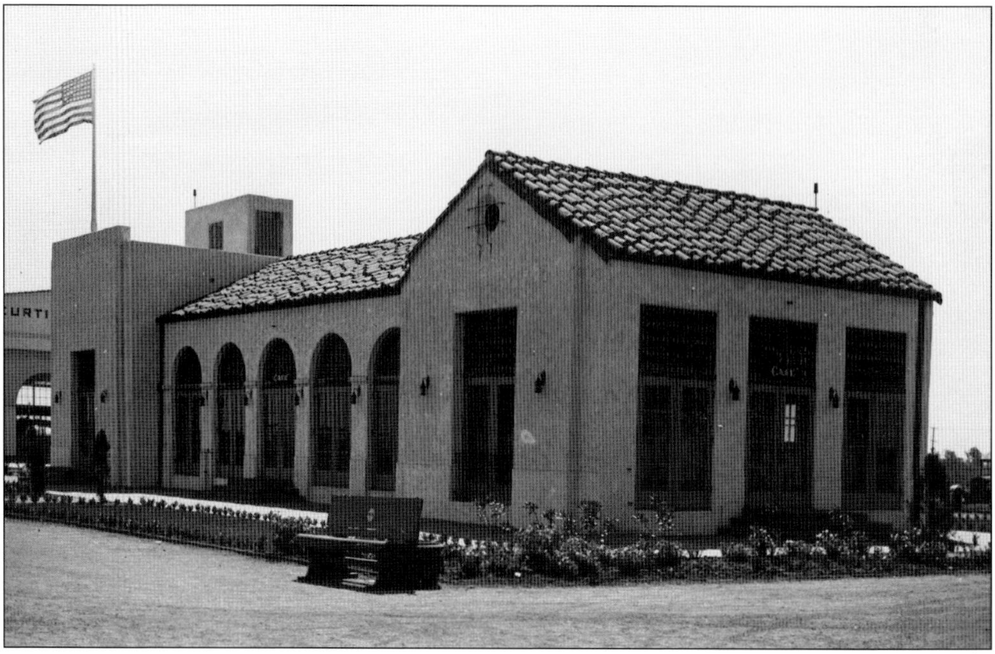

This café, operated by Interstate Host, was part of the original complex of Spanish-style buildings on the south perimeter of Los Angeles Municipal Airport. Host remained a food service provider at the airport for many years and later operated the restaurant in the famed LAX Theme Building.

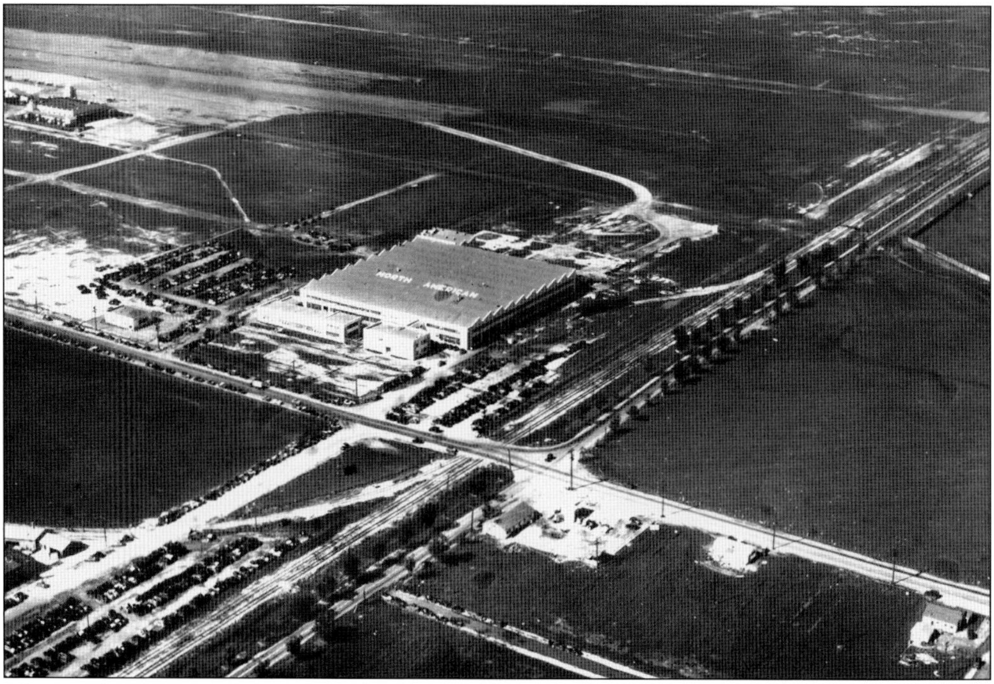

The North American Aviation aircraft assembly plant, seen here in 1936, was among the facilities that qualified Los Angeles Municipal Airport as a major strategic asset in the nation's preparation for World War II. When the United States entered the war in 1941, air races and other lighthearted pastimes were forgotten and the airport focused on the war effort.

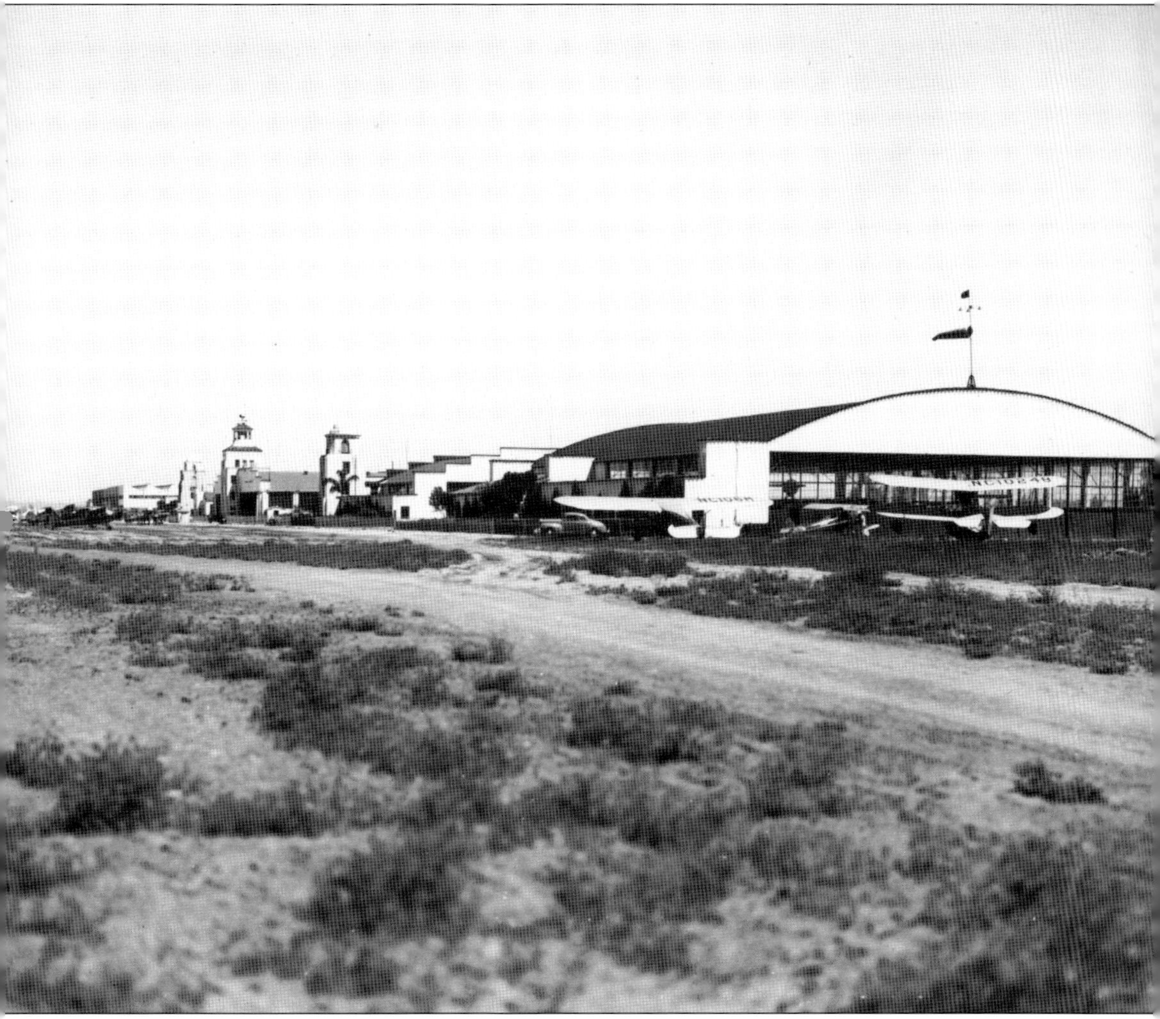

This photograph taken at Mines Field on August 20, 1940, is one of the last views of a "peaceful" airfield before the tremendous military aircraft production effort got underway. After the end of hostilities in 1945, the airport would not return to its prewar status but would become instead the main commercial air transportation hub for all of Southern California. The name Mines Field would become but a memory, replaced by the designation Los Angeles International Airport and its more popular short form: LAX.

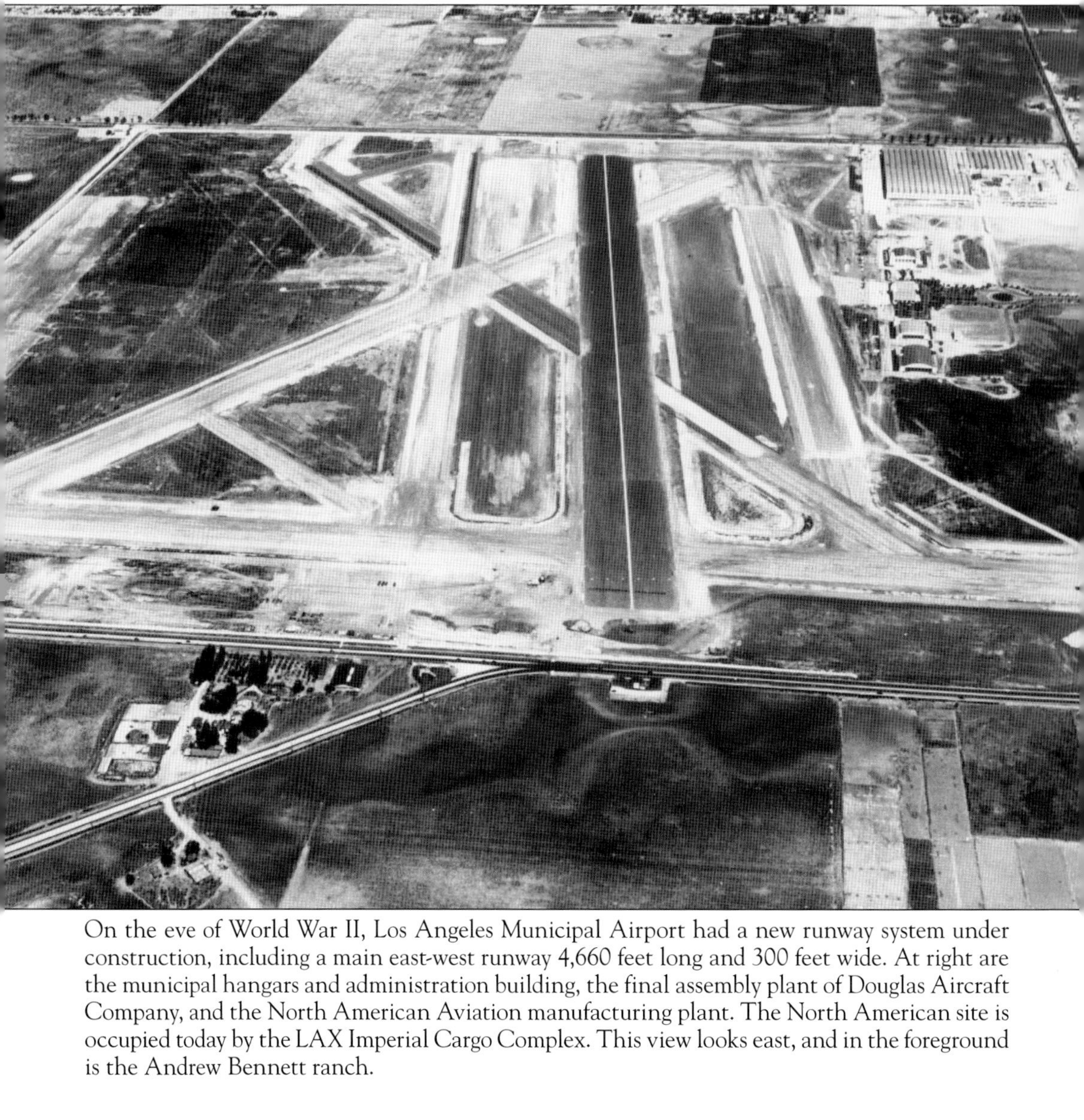

On the eve of World War II, Los Angeles Municipal Airport had a new runway system under construction, including a main east-west runway 4,660 feet long and 300 feet wide. At right are the municipal hangars and administration building, the final assembly plant of Douglas Aircraft Company, and the North American Aviation manufacturing plant. The North American site is occupied today by the LAX Imperial Cargo Complex. This view looks east, and in the foreground is the Andrew Bennett ranch.

Two

World War II Era and After

During the World War II years, Los Angeles Municipal Airport continued operations, even though from the air it looked like a farm. It was made to appear that way by some of the most massive camouflage efforts ever conceived—including wooden cows. The city turned over airport operations to the federal government "for the duration." It became the hub of a vast military complex. Southern California was the aircraft production center of America—making more than a third of the 40,000 planes produced annually in the United States.

Despite wartime conditions, a 1944 master plan called for expansion in two stages when the war ended. That plan went into effect in 1946, the year after V-J Day, with terminals and offices built and runways extended to 6,000 feet. On December 9, 1946, four major carriers—American, Trans World, United, and Western Airlines—moved overnight from Burbank and Glendale, establishing Los Angeles Airport as the region's premier air facility. A month later, Pan American Airlines moved from Burbank to Los Angeles.

When Los Angeles Department of Airports acquired Van Nuys Airport for $1 from the War Assets Administration in 1949, it was the first step toward the city department's regional airport system.

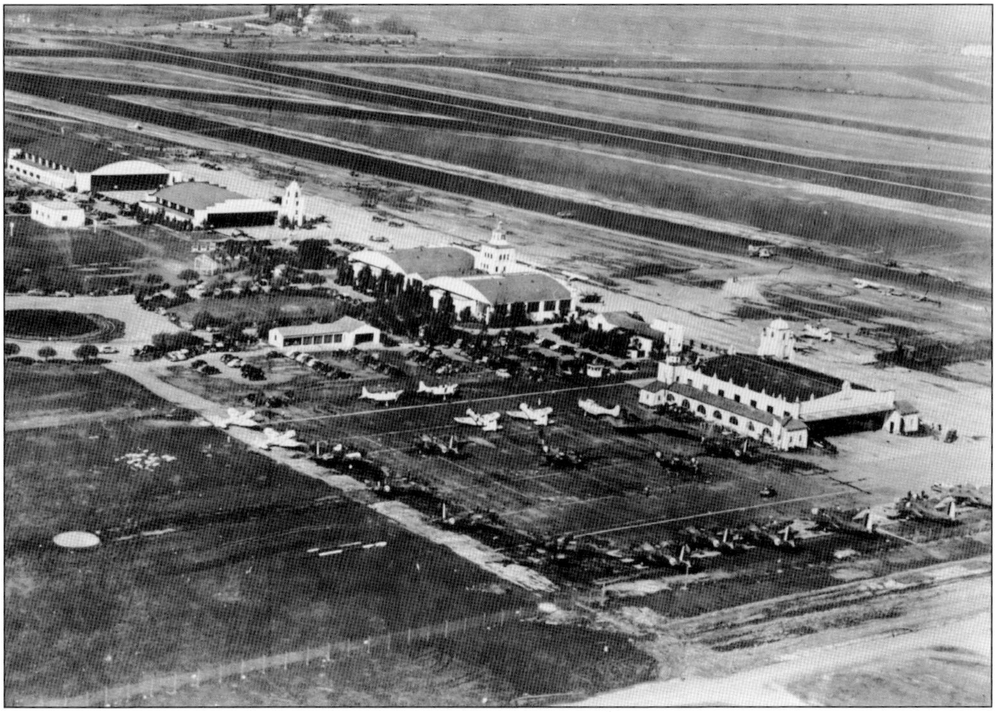

Passenger terminals and airliners were still several years in the future when this aerial view of Los Angeles Airport was taken on the eve of World War II. The Japanese attack on Pearl Harbor on December 7, 1941, would spur vastly increased manufacture of American military aircraft. The Douglas and North American plants at Los Angeles Municipal Airport were assigned a leading role in this effort.

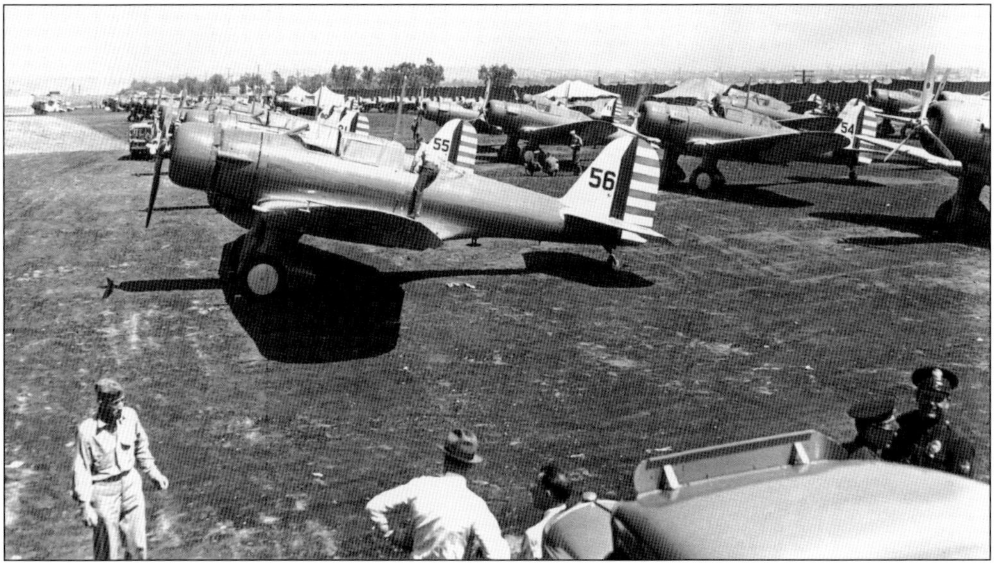

These North American Aviation AT-6 Texans were part of the scene at Los Angeles Airport during World War II. Both North American and Douglas Aircraft operated manufacturing plants at the airport during the war. This photograph was taken about 1941 as war production was ramping up. Texans were used to train fighter pilots during World War II.

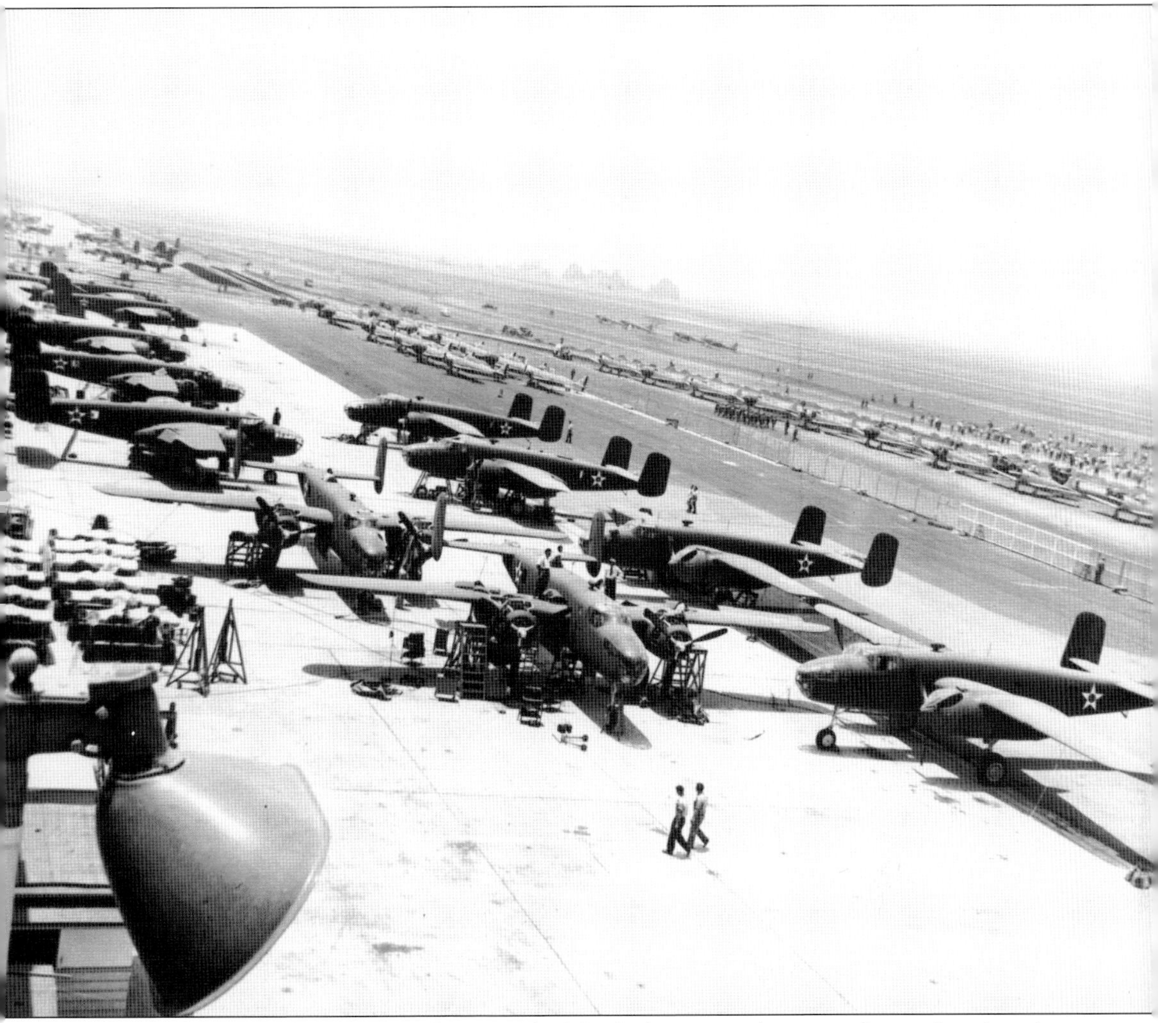

These B-25 Mitchell bombers are shown at the North American Aviation plant at Los Angeles Airport during World War II. The B-25 was used by Gen. Jimmy Doolittle of the U.S. Army Air Corps during his celebrated raid on Tokyo on April 18, 1942. After the war, Doolittle continued to take an active interest in LAX, serving as guest of honor at several airport groundbreaking and dedication ceremonies.

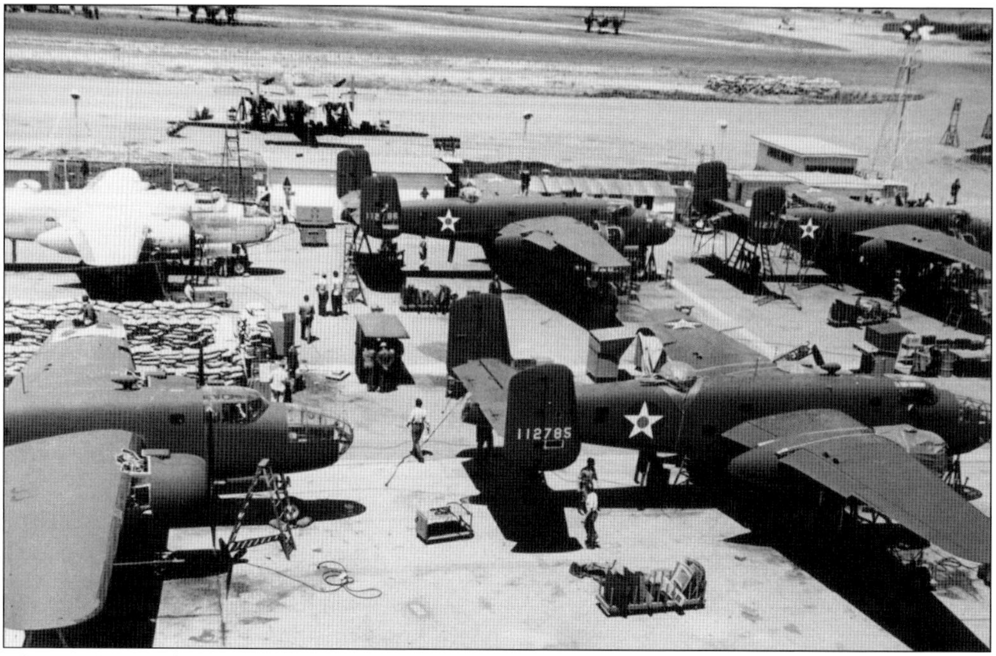

The B-25 was a key component of American air power during World War II. This aircraft was manufactured at the North American Aircraft assembly plant at Los Angeles Municipal Airport. Aircraft manufacturing provided skilled employment for many Southern California men and women during the war. The B-25, a twin-engine medium bomber, was also called the Mitchell bomber, named after U.S. military aviation pioneer Gen. Billy Mitchell.

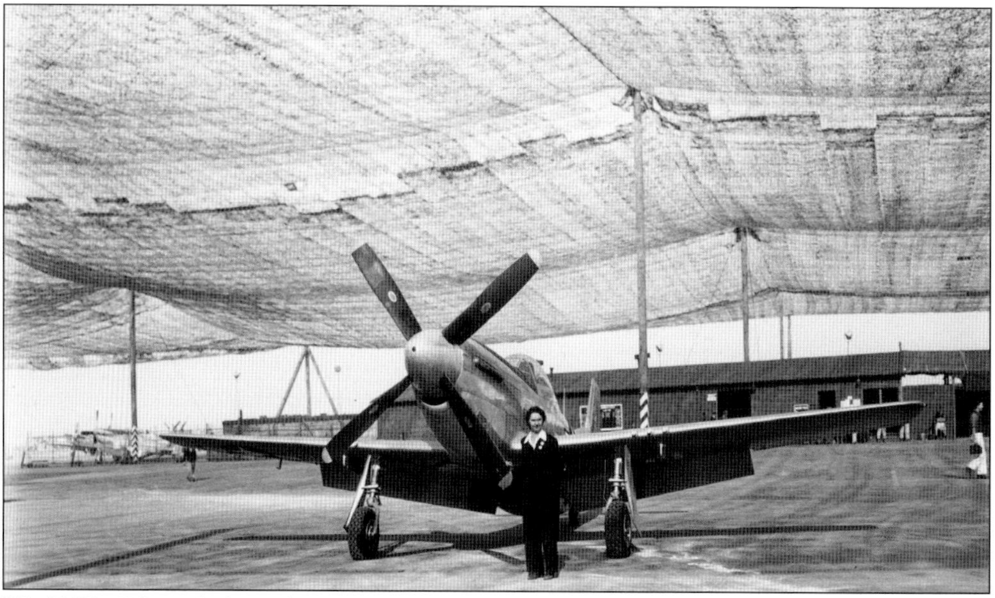

World War II brought key roles to women in aircraft manufacturing in Los Angeles and elsewhere. Here North American Aviation employee Pauline Kayes stands next to a P-51 Mustang with a modified four-blade propeller at Los Angeles Municipal Airport. The airport was under camouflage to look like a farm from the air. The P-51 was a long-range fighter and a particularly valued and familiar military plane of the war.

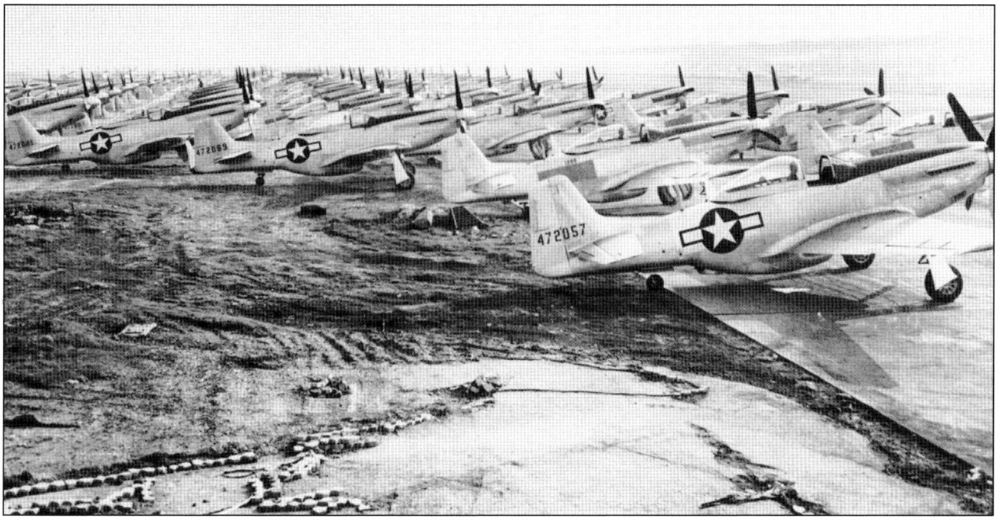

Nearly 10,000 P-51 Mustang aircraft were produced at the North American Aviation plant at Los Angeles Airport during World War II, as shown in this *c.* 1942 photograph. The growing military significance of the airport prompted the federal government to install an instrument landing system. Developed by the Gilfillan Company, it became fully operational in 1943.

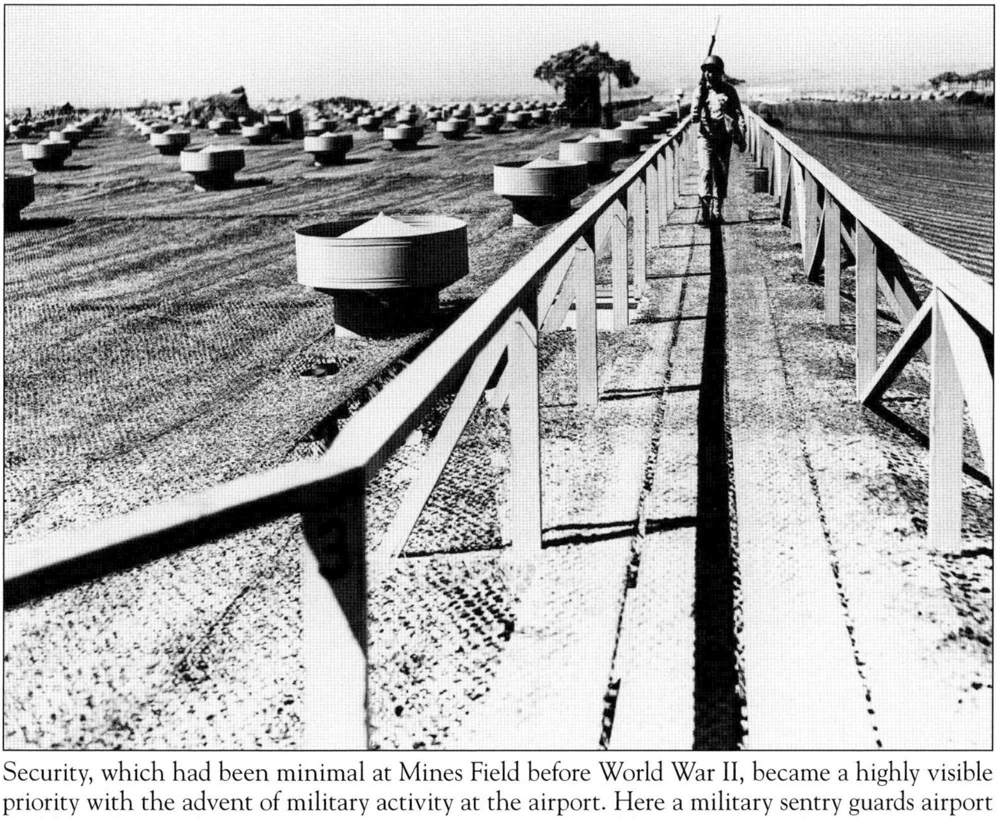

Security, which had been minimal at Mines Field before World War II, became a highly visible priority with the advent of military activity at the airport. Here a military sentry guards airport buildings during the war. Wartime jitters prompted forcible evacuation of resident Japanese nationals as well as Americans of Japanese descent. Some 2,800 were relocated from areas surrounding the airport.

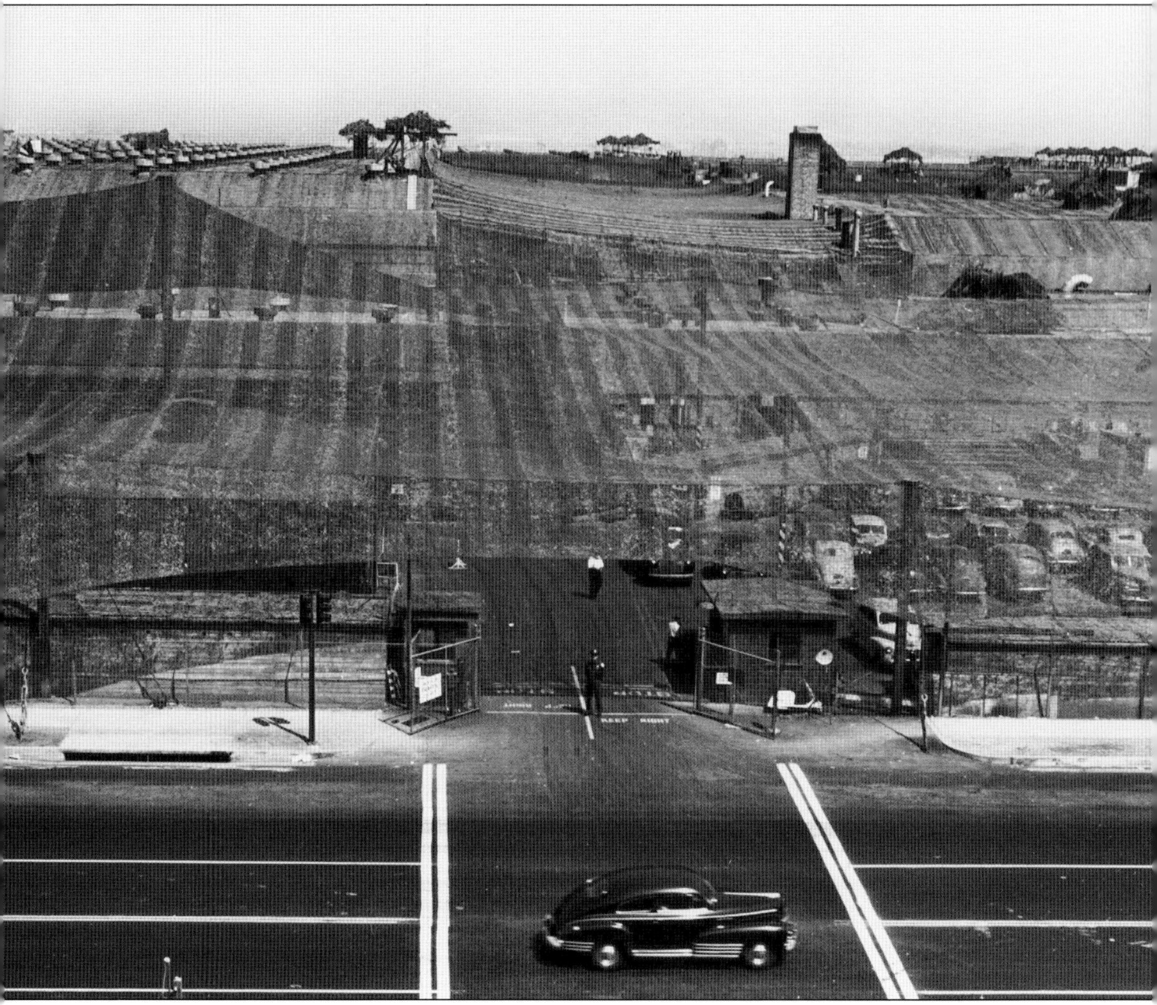

Great pains were taken to camouflage Los Angeles Airport from enemy aircraft during World War II. Netting was used to make the field appear from above to be a dairy farm. Faux trees and houses also were installed. This view along Aviation Boulevard was at the entrance of the North American Aviation plant, site of today's Imperial Cargo Complex. The 1942 Chevrolet pictured was one of the last cars manufactured before U.S. automobile factories were converted to military production.

Three

Los Angeles International Airport

The airport grew up in the 1950s. In 1949, it was officially named Los Angeles International Airport and designated LAX, with the "X" as a space filler when airport codes expanded from two letters to three to accommodate the growth in aviation.

In 1952, for the first time in its history, the airport's finances went into the black—with a net income of $185,701.

The Sepulveda Boulevard underpass was completed in 1953, allowing two runways to pass overhead. It was the first such airport underpass in the world. Anticipating the popularity of air travel and passenger growth, a new terminal complex was designed by a team of renowned architects. Ground-breaking for this new complex was in 1957. Runways were extended.

The seminal event for Los Angeles International Airport occurred on January 25, 1959, when American Airlines inaugurated the airport's first jet service with its New York–to–Los Angeles nonstop flight of a Boeing 707-123. Although there was still a plethora of piston-engine, propeller aircraft in service with most of the airlines serving LAX, more than a quarter million passengers flew in and out of LAX on jetliners that year.

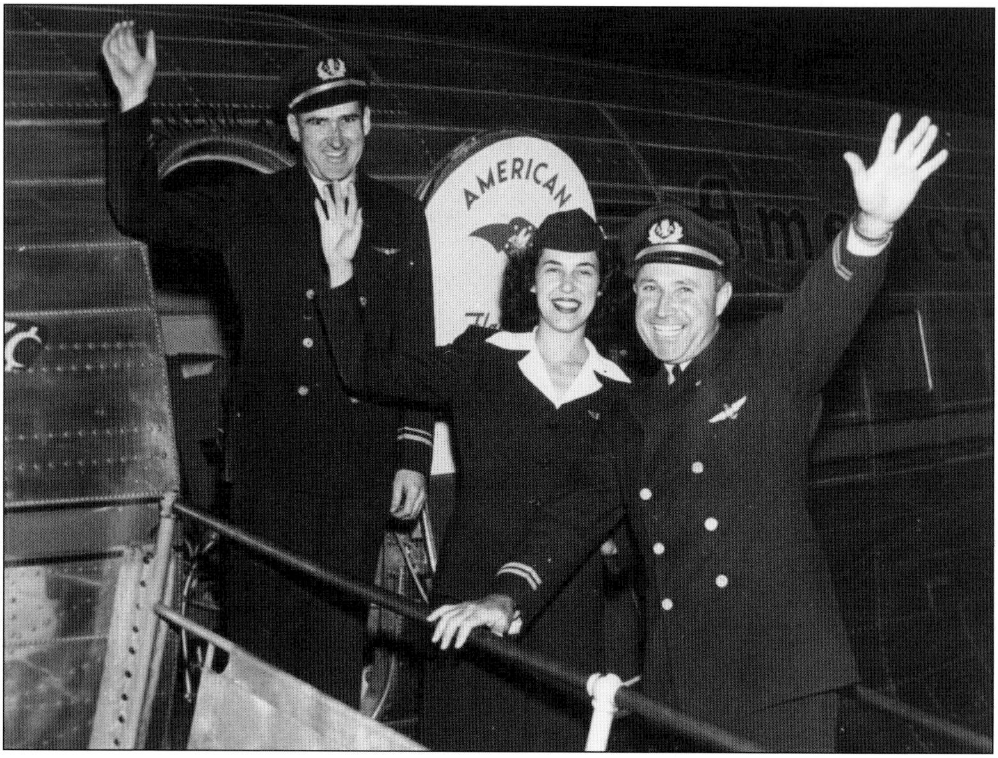

American Airlines, long one of the most popular U.S. air carriers, was one of five original airlines to begin service at Los Angeles Municipal Airport after World War II. Pictured is the first American Airlines flight at LAX in December 1946.

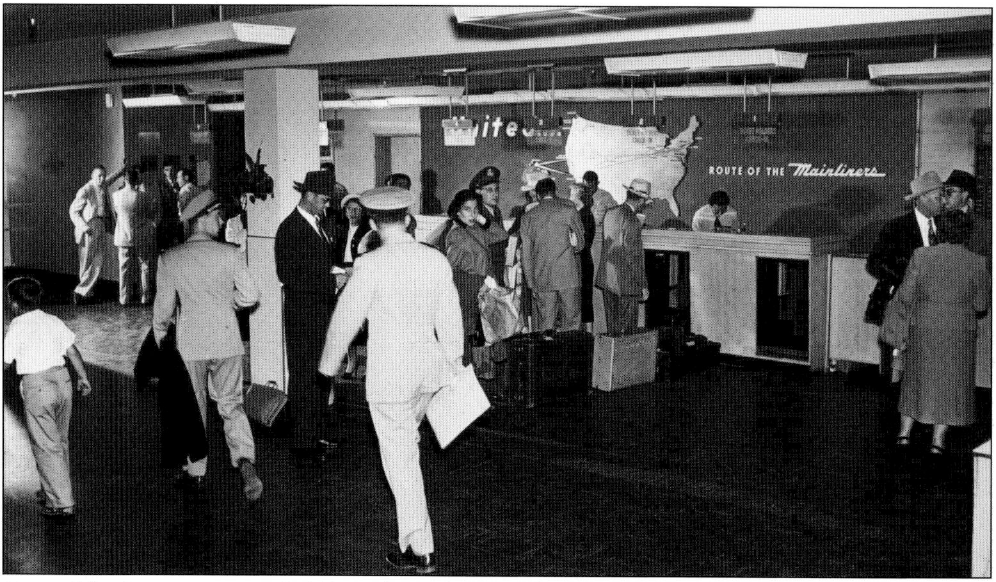

One of the busiest spots at LAX in the 1950s was this United Airlines check-in counter. After beginning service at the airport in 1946, United soon grew to become the largest air carrier in terms of number of flights and passengers boarded. The airline also established an aircraft maintenance facility at LAX.

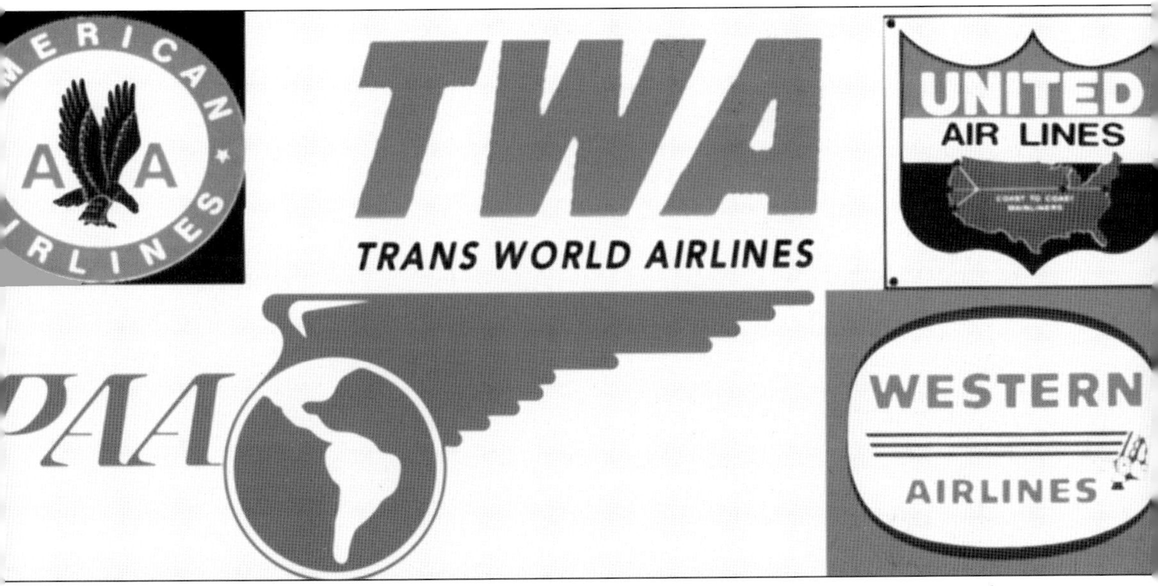

Public perception of Mines Field as an air show venue or aircraft manufacturing center was forever changed in late 1946 and early 1947. It was then that five major airlines at Lockheed Air Terminal in Burbank established operations at soon to be renamed Los Angeles International Airport. Logos pictured identified the new LAX airlines as American, United, Western, Pan American, and TWA. Mayor Fletcher Bowron and airport director Woodruff DeSilva were on hand for the first flights December 6, 1946.

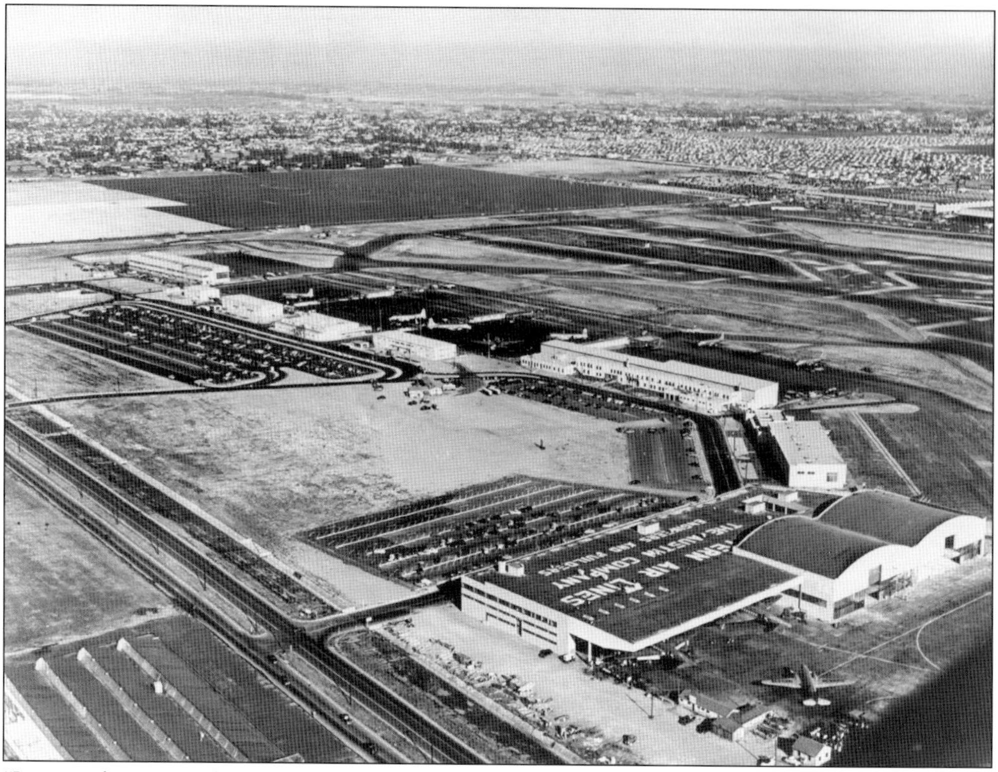

"Intermediate" was the name given these terminals, which served the five newly arrived airlines at Los Angeles Municipal Airport in 1947. The name signified the buildings' transitional status until the airport's new permanent Jet Age complex was dedicated in 1961.

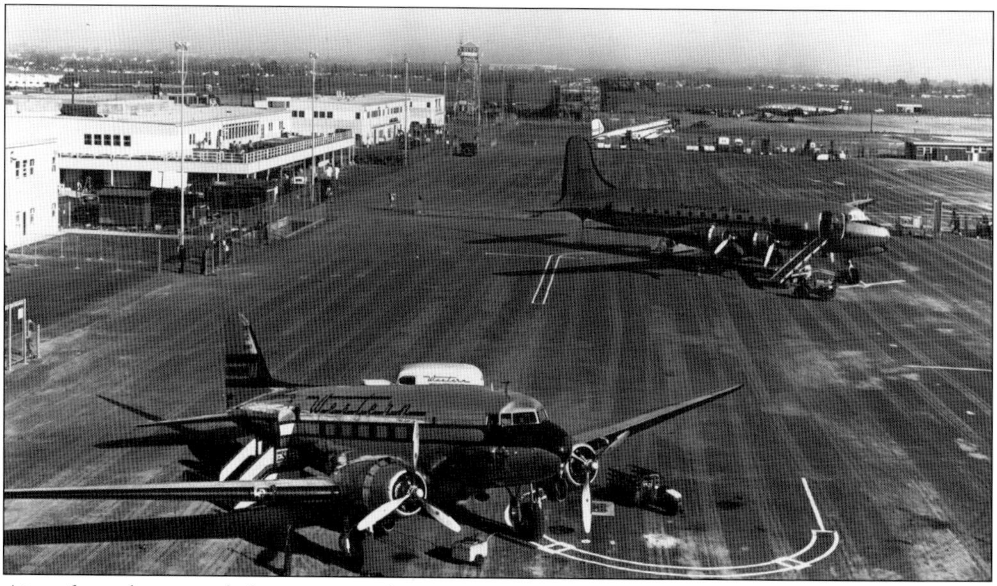

Aircraft are shown ready for service on the ramp at LAX in 1947. This area, behind the "intermediate" terminal buildings along Century Boulevard, later was converted to aircraft maintenance and cargo operations. Passenger operations were relocated west of Sepulveda Boulevard when a new central terminal area was opened in 1961.

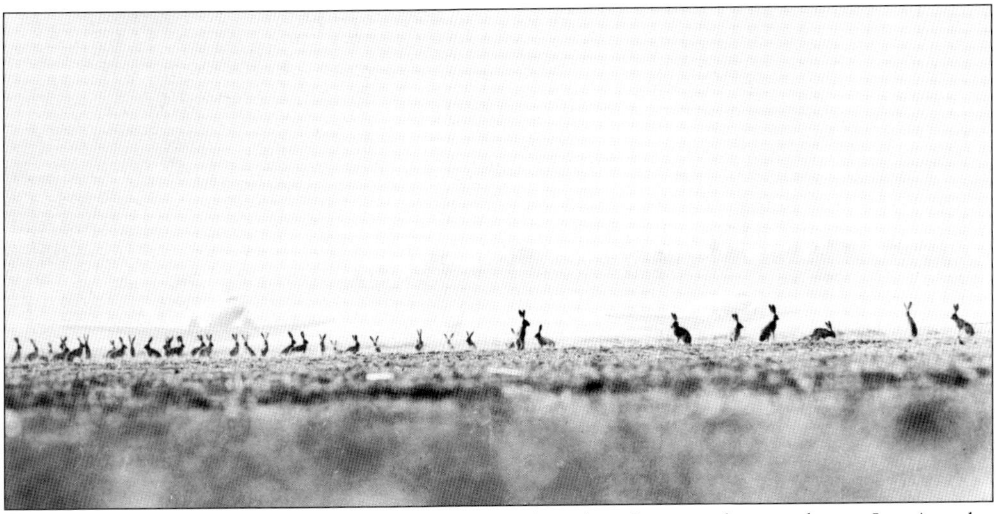

Jackrabbits were still a familiar sight on the airfield when this photograph was taken at Los Angeles Municipal Airport about 1947. Terminal and runway expansion during the 1950s and 1960s gradually reduced the population of rabbits and other wildlife on the airport's 3,500-acre site.

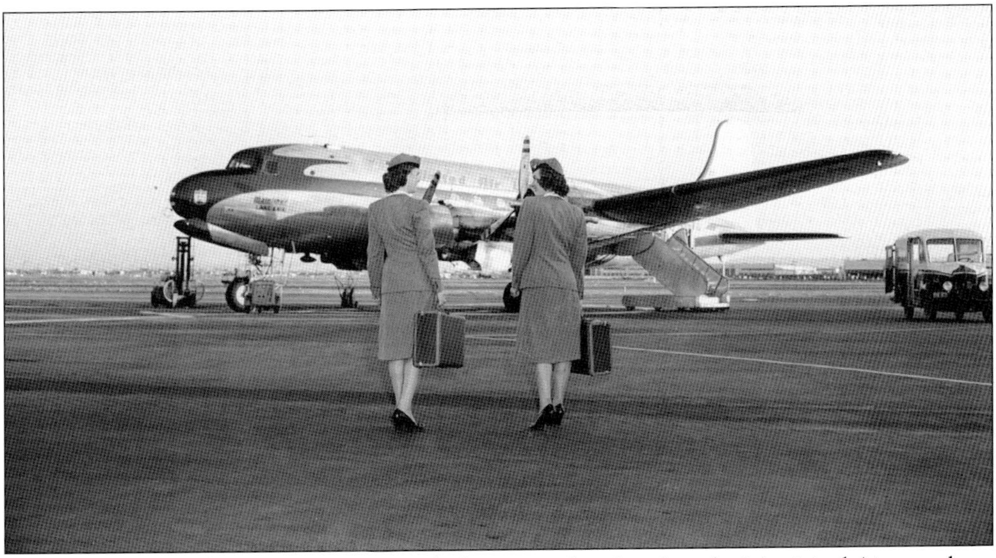

Two United Airlines stewardesses approach their aircraft at Los Angeles Municipal Airport about 1947. The first airline flight attendants were registered nurses. Later the ranks were restricted to unmarried women. Still later, married women were permitted and, finally, men.

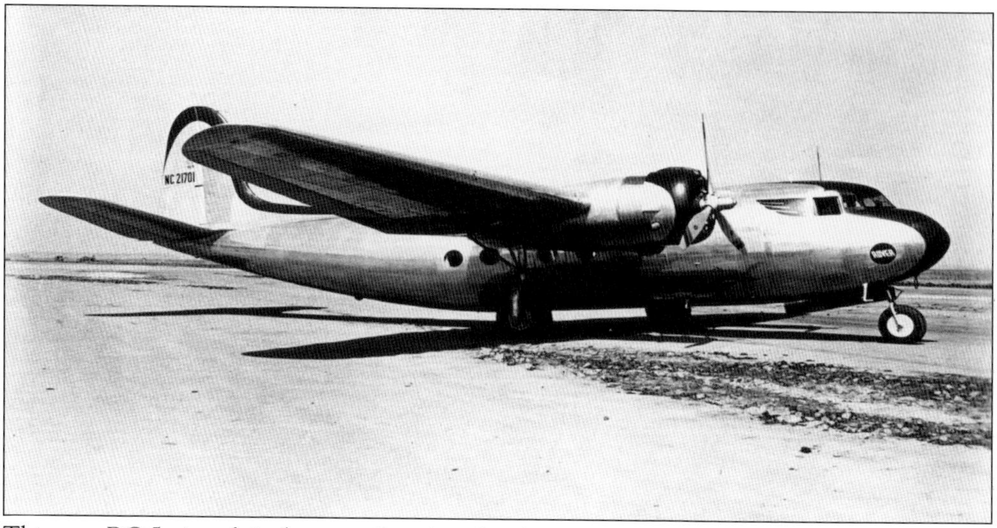

This rare DC-5 aircraft is shown at Los Angeles Airport in 1948. The DC-5, manufactured by Douglas Aircraft Company, never achieved the popularity of Douglas's DC-4 and DC-6 and is all but forgotten today. Douglas Aircraft later was merged to become McDonnell Douglas, which, in turn, was acquired by Boeing.

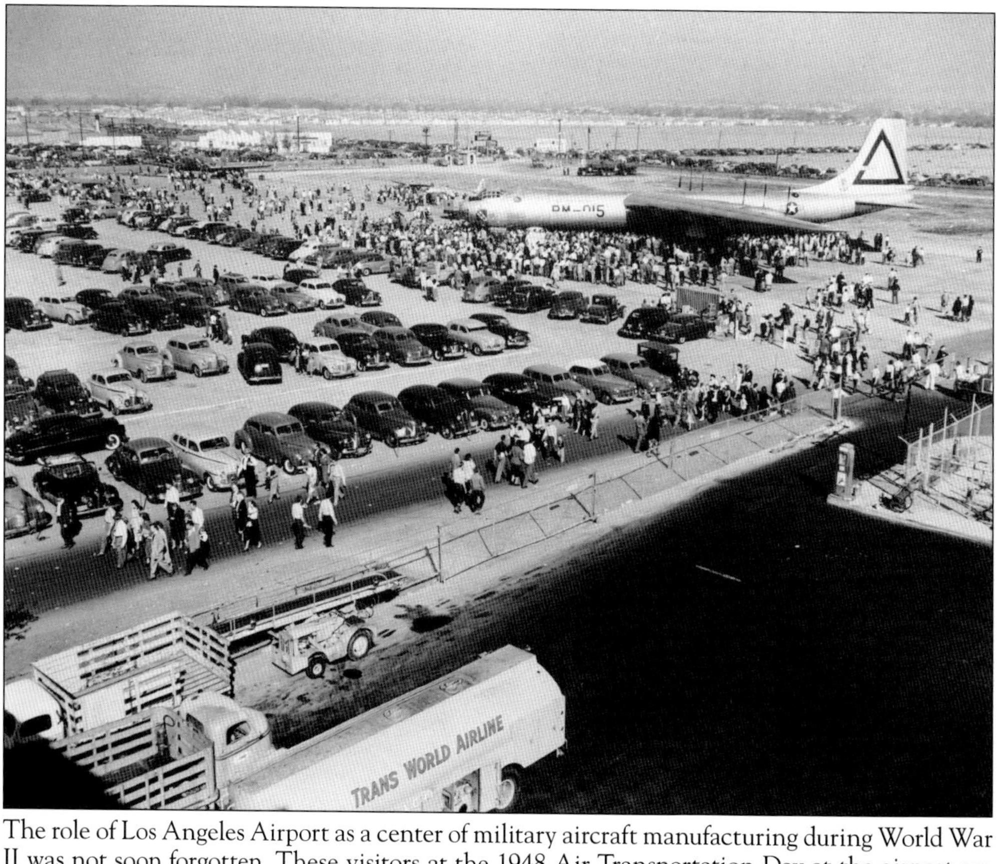

The role of Los Angeles Airport as a center of military aircraft manufacturing during World War II was not soon forgotten. These visitors at the 1948 Air Transportation Day at the airport are getting a close-up view of a U.S. Air Force B-36 bomber.

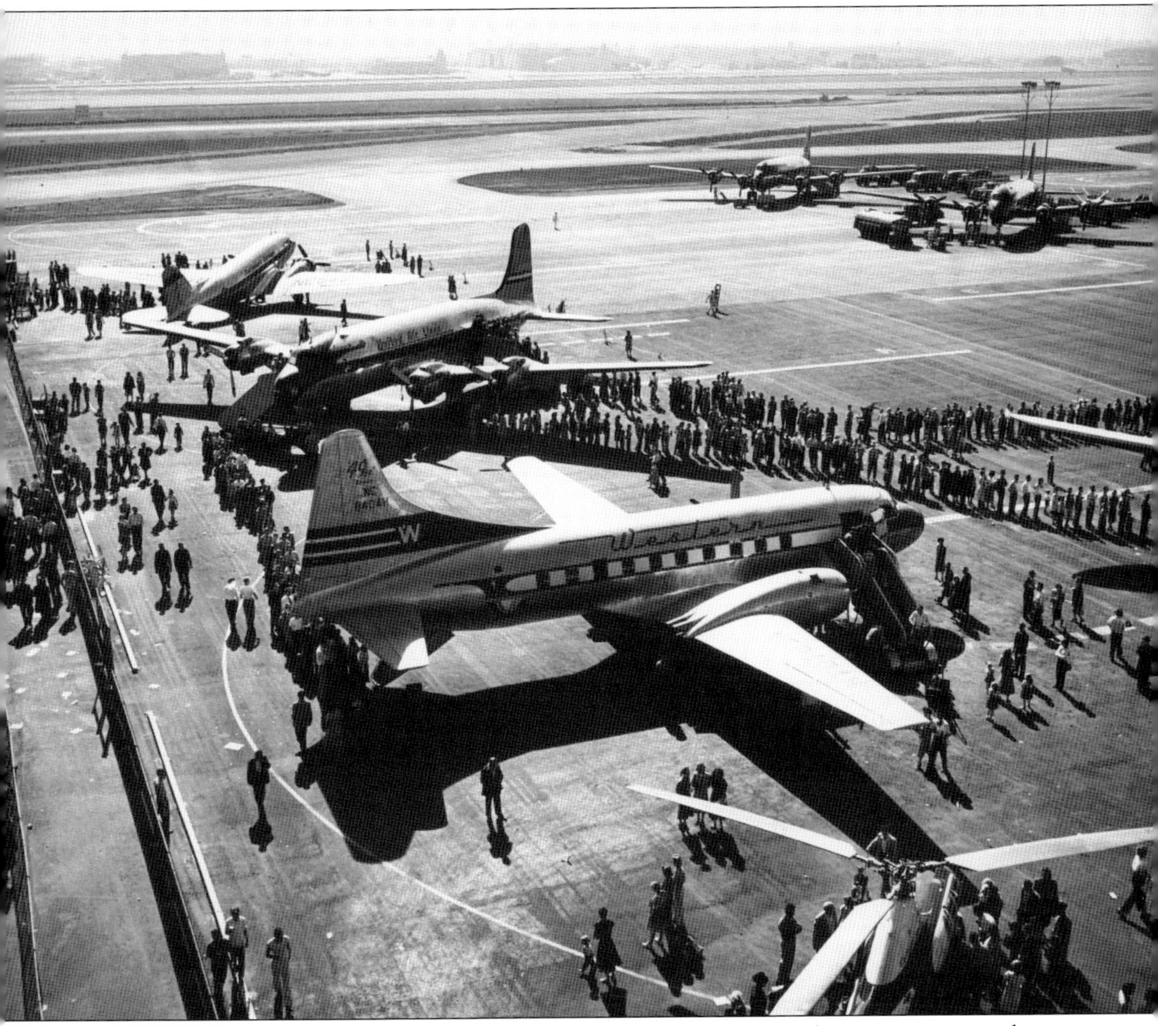

Los Angeles Airport was becoming Southern California's primary civil aviation center when this photograph was taken on November 14, 1948. The occasion was Air Transportation Day, an event that attracted hundreds of local families eager to view the modern aircraft of that post–World War II era.

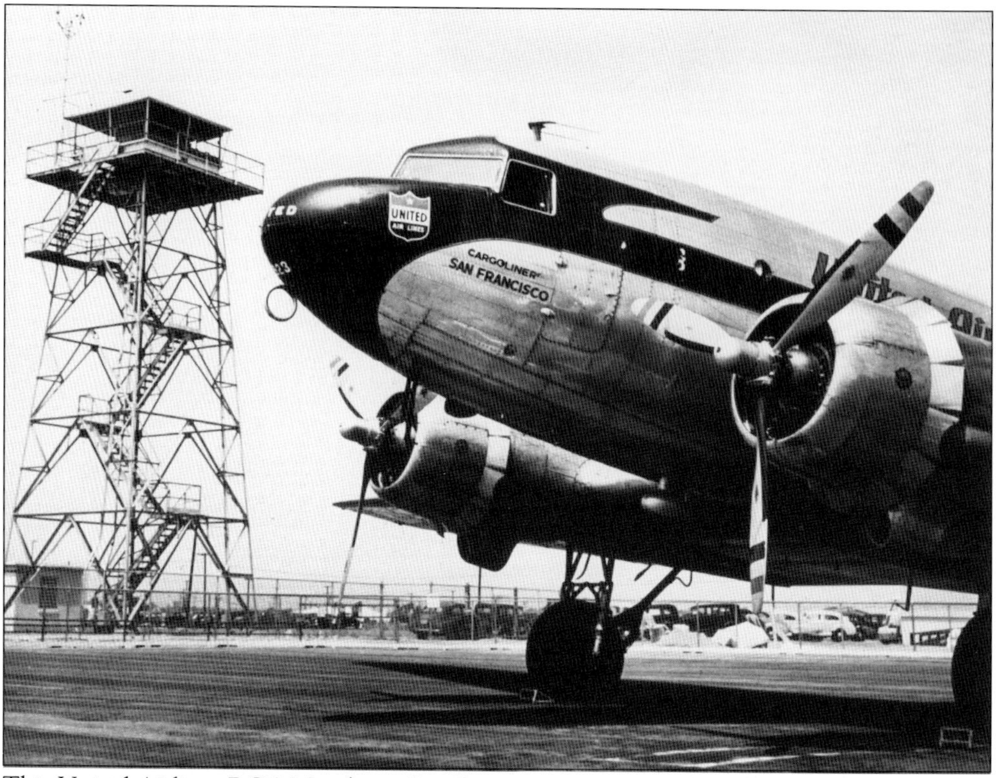

This United Airlines DC-3 Mainliner, *San Francisco*, is positioned on the ramp at Los Angeles Municipal Airport in the late 1940s. It was one of countless DC-3s in service at that time. The DC-3, manufactured by Douglas Aircraft Company, was noted for its versatility and durability. Many remain in service today. The second LAX Control Tower is in the background.

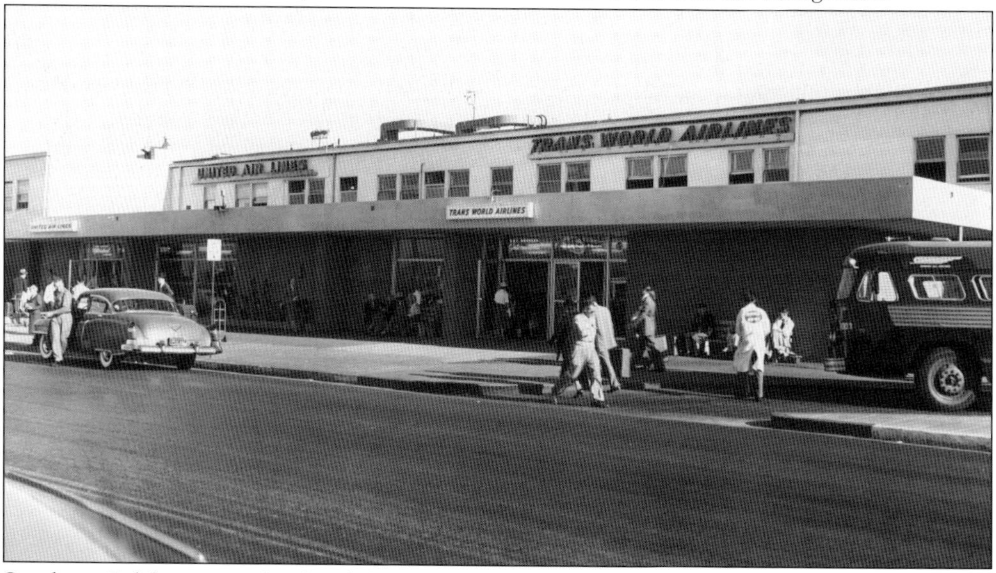

Southern California travelers headed for United Airlines or TWA flights in the late 1940s and the 1950s checked in at this terminal on Century Boulevard. This so-called "intermediate" terminal would remain in use until the LAX Jet Age terminal complex opened in 1961.

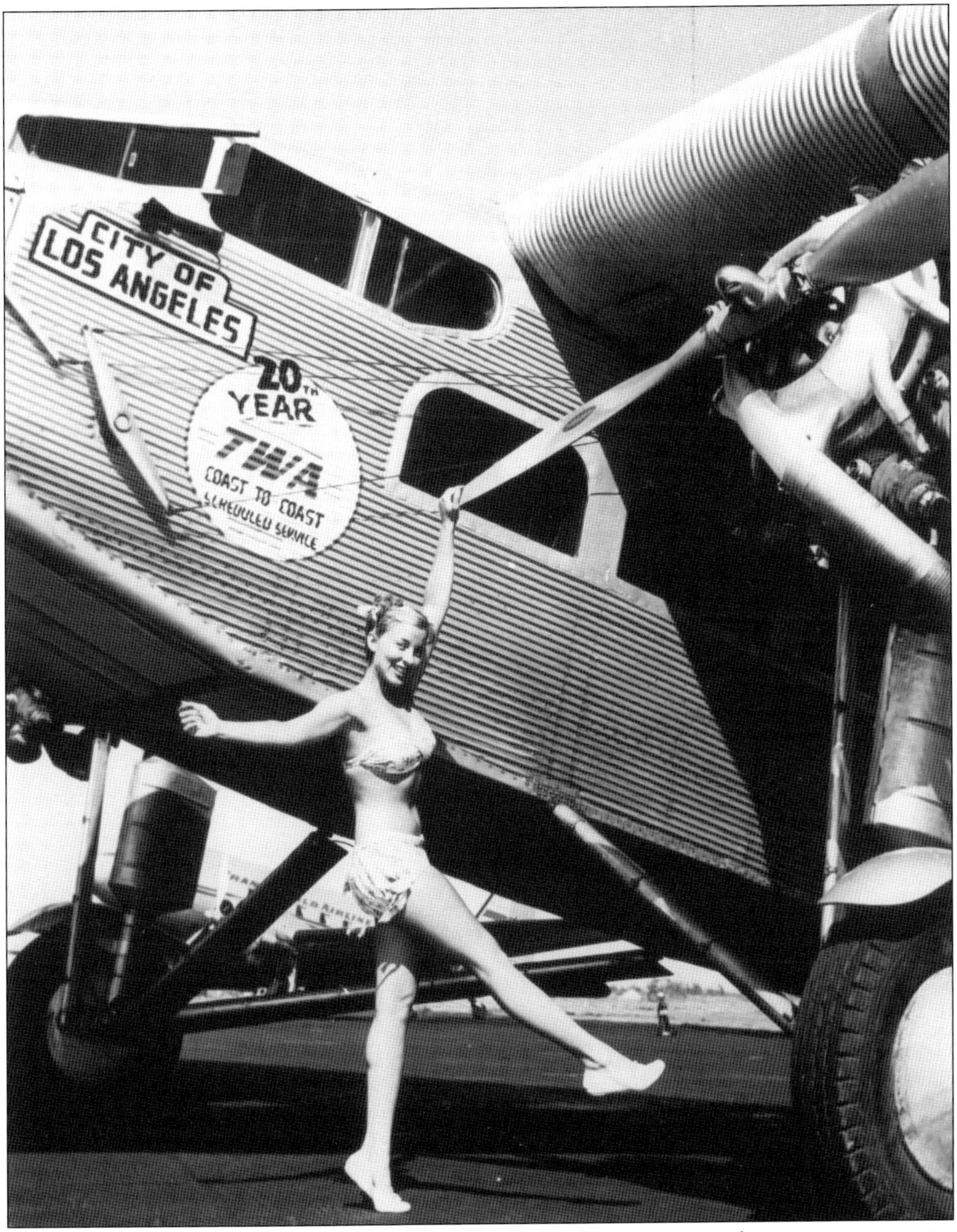

Actress Pat Hall helps Trans World Airlines salute the 20th anniversary of coast-to-coast service during this 1949 publicity event at Los Angeles Airport. The "City of Los Angeles" aircraft is a 1929 Ford Trimotor. The celebration continued with the trimotor retracing the 1929 route and a new TWA Constellation leading the way.

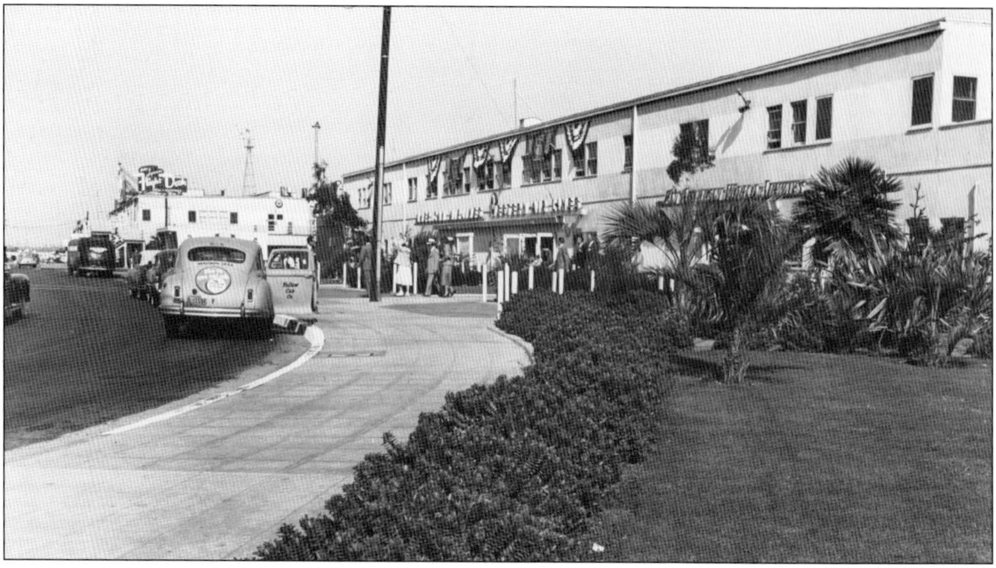

Western Airlines and American Airlines shared this terminal on Century Boulevard in the 1940s and 1950s. Western Airlines established its corporate headquarters at LAX and later constructed a large office building and maintenance hangar. These later were occupied by Delta Airlines when it acquired Western.

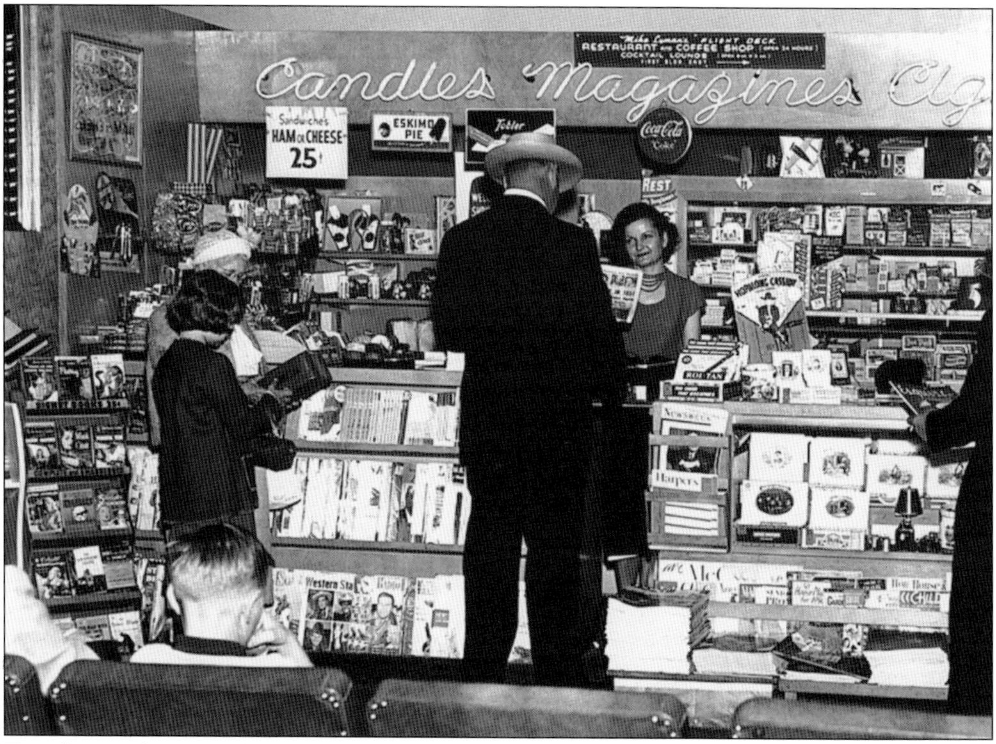

Travelers in the 1950s, like today, sometimes had a few minutes for shopping. This gift shop, on the second floor between two passenger terminals on Century Boulevard, was a favorite spot to buy a magazine, cigar, or even a 25¢ sandwich. For those with time to spare for lunch or a cocktail, there was Mike Lyman's Flight Deck and Cloud Room in the same building.

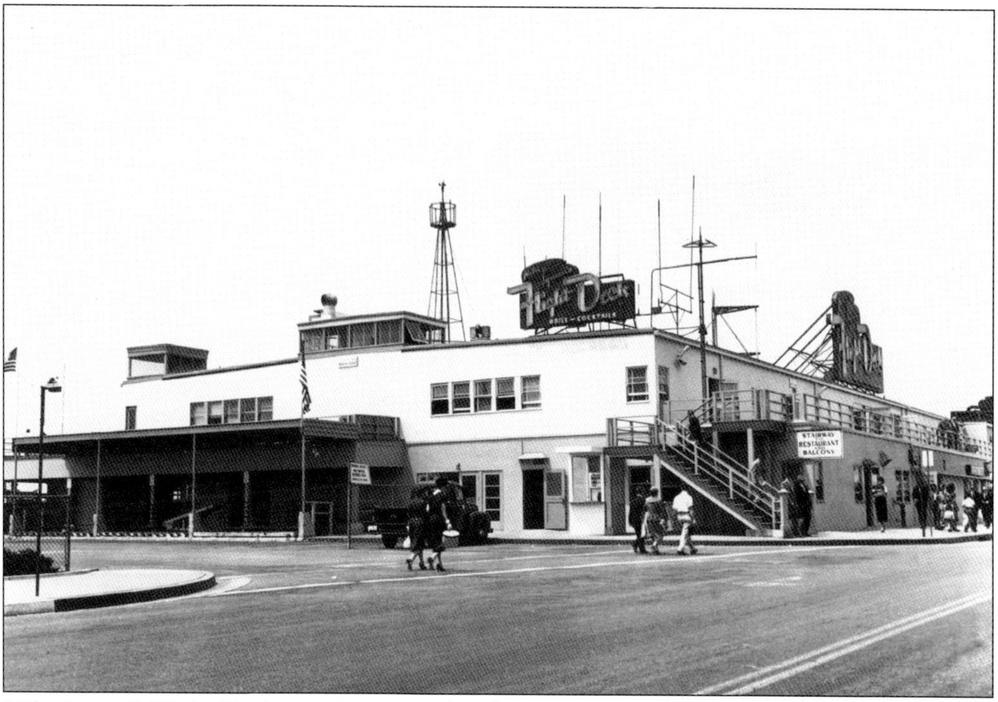

Mike Lyman's Flight Deck restaurant was the place to meet and greet when travelers were using the 1940s- and 1950s-era terminal buildings on Century Boulevard. The building also housed U.S. mail, a bank, coffee shop, and barbershop.

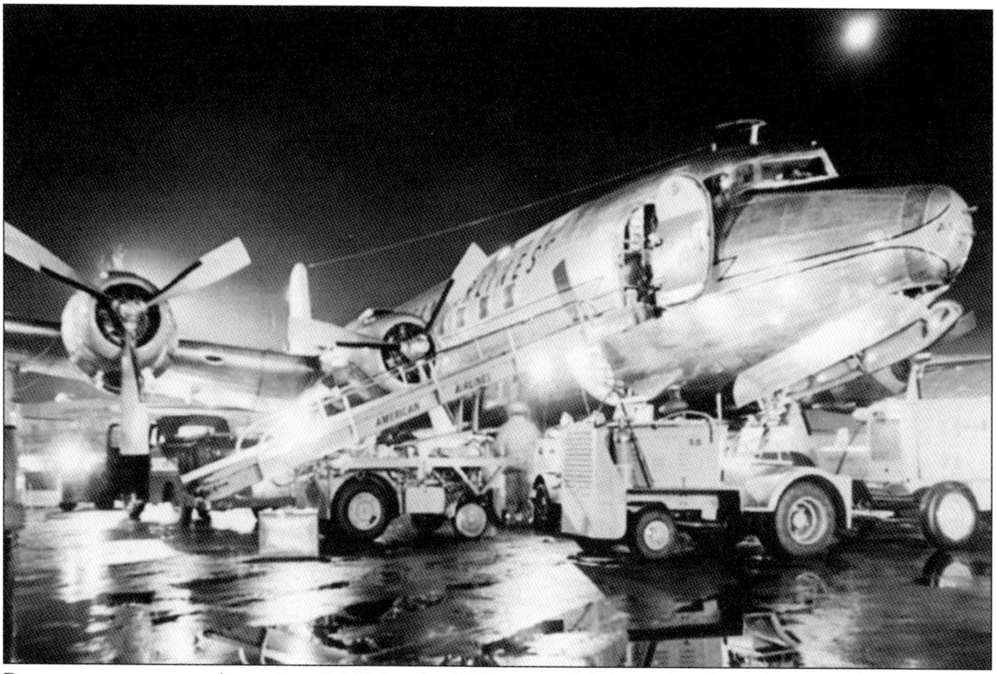

Passengers or cargo departing LAX in the 1950s were likely to be aboard a Douglas DC-6 like this American Airlines DC-6 pictured in preparation for flight. The popular aircraft was favored by airlines and travelers alike for its comfort and reliability.

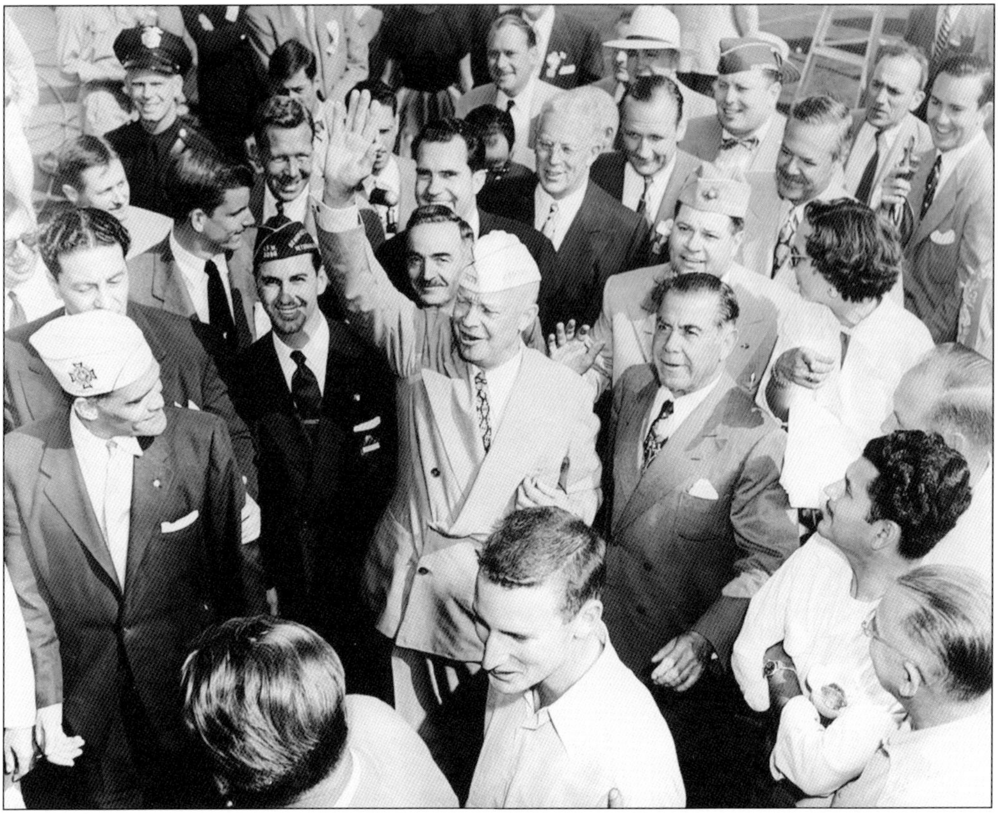

Gen. Dwight D. Eisenhower greets well-wishers as he passes through LAX in 1951, prior to his election as president. Among those pictured escorting the general is U.S. senator Richard M. Nixon of California, who was to become Eisenhower's vice president.

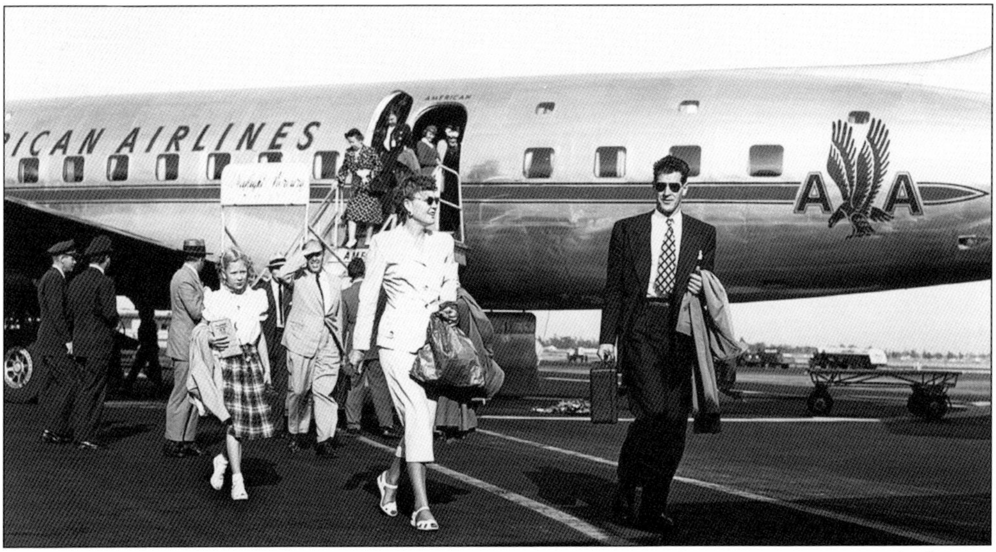

Passengers deplane from their American Airlines flight at LAX in the 1950s. Stair ramp deplaning gave travelers a good view of the airfield operations area as they walked to the terminal but, unlike modern loading bridges, offered no protection from wind and rain.

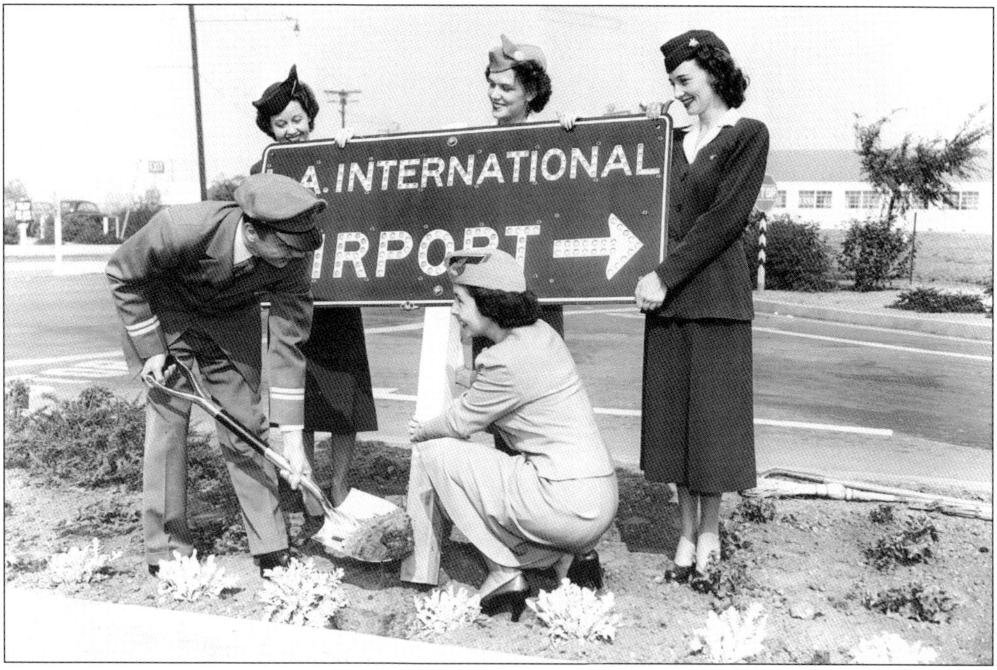

Many local residents continued to refer to Los Angeles International Airport by its original name of Mines Field, even as late as the 1950s when this new identification sign was installed. By the early 1980s, the name LAX was catching on with the public, the three letters having been assigned to the airport by the Federal Aviation Administration.

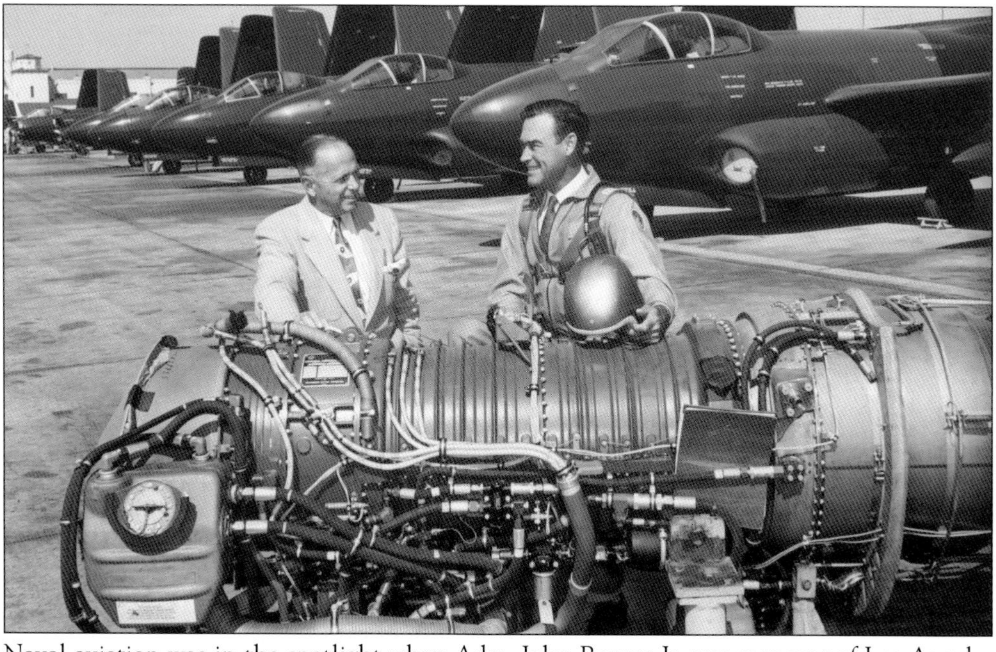

Naval aviation was in the spotlight when Adm. John Reeves Jr. was manager of Los Angeles International Airport. Here Reeves is shown a jet engine and Navy Skynight twin-jet fighters by LaVerne Browne, Douglas Aircraft flight operations manager, during the fourth annual Navy Air Transportation Day at LAX on September 28, 1951.

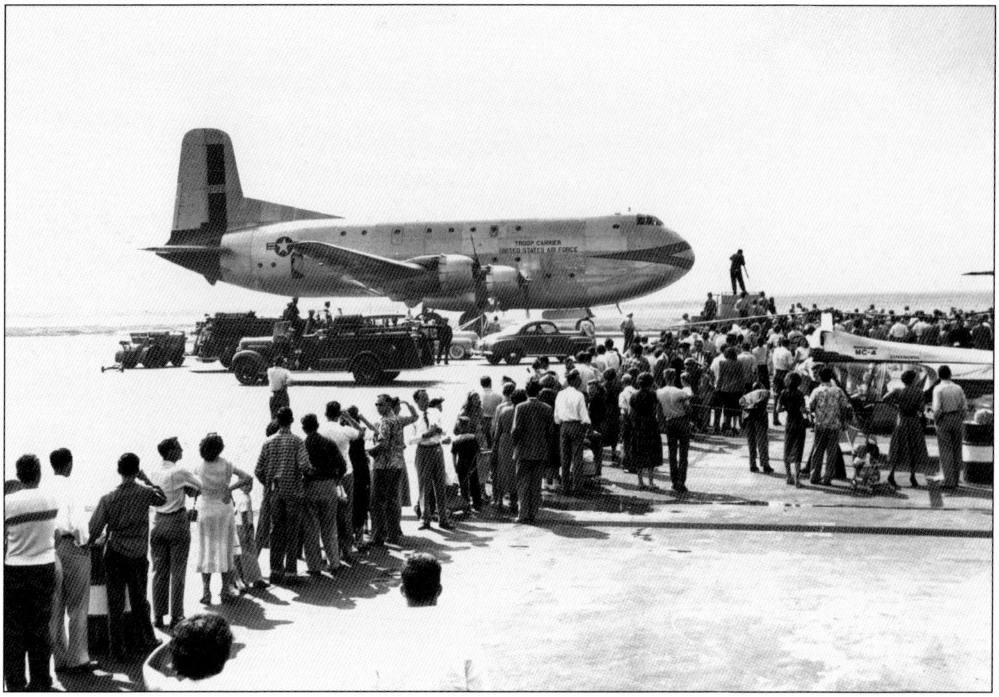

This Douglas C-124 was among the aircraft featured at the fifth annual Navy Air Transportation Day at Los Angeles International Airport on October 26, 1952. Many of the early administrators and operations staff at LAX had prior experience in military aviation.

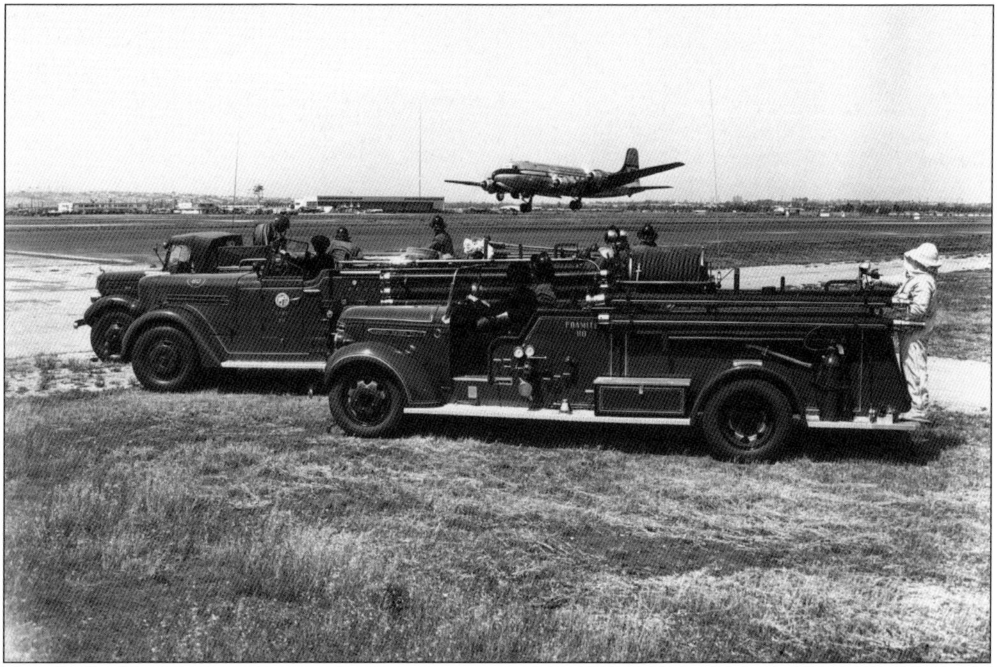

Los Angeles City firefighters observe the landing of a DC-4 at LAX in the early 1950s. The Los Angeles Fire Department has long served the needs of the airport with three stations staffed to provide rescue, property protection, and inspection services.

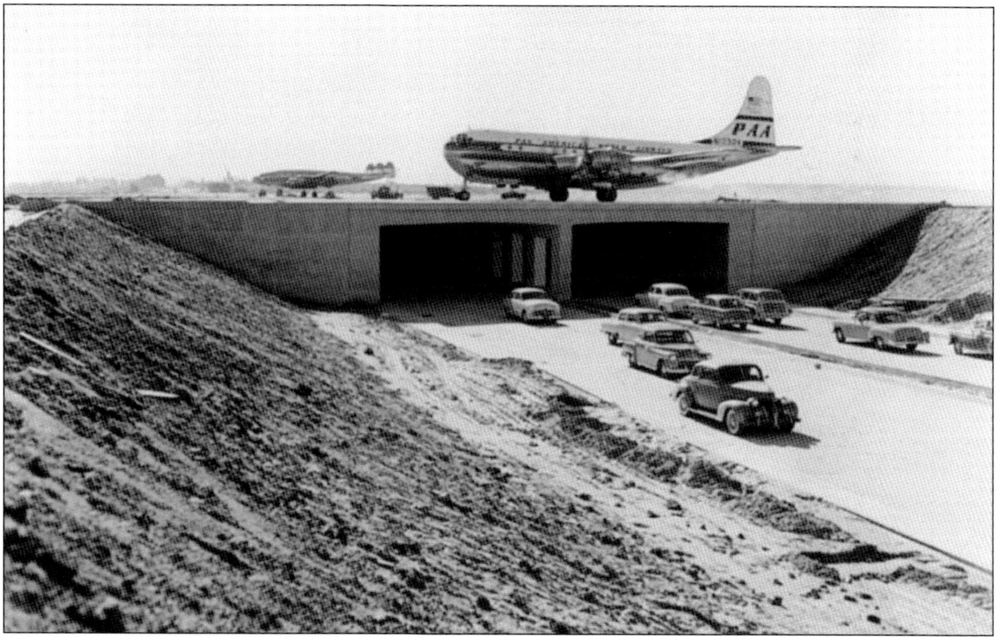

Larger aircraft required the lengthening of runways to the extent that they crossed Sepulveda Boulevard. A railroad-style crossing gate was used at first, but safety concerns necessitated a grade separation. The result was the Sepulveda Boulevard Tunnel, the first of its kind, completed in 1953 and still in service. Pictured in the foreground is a Boeing Stratocruiser.

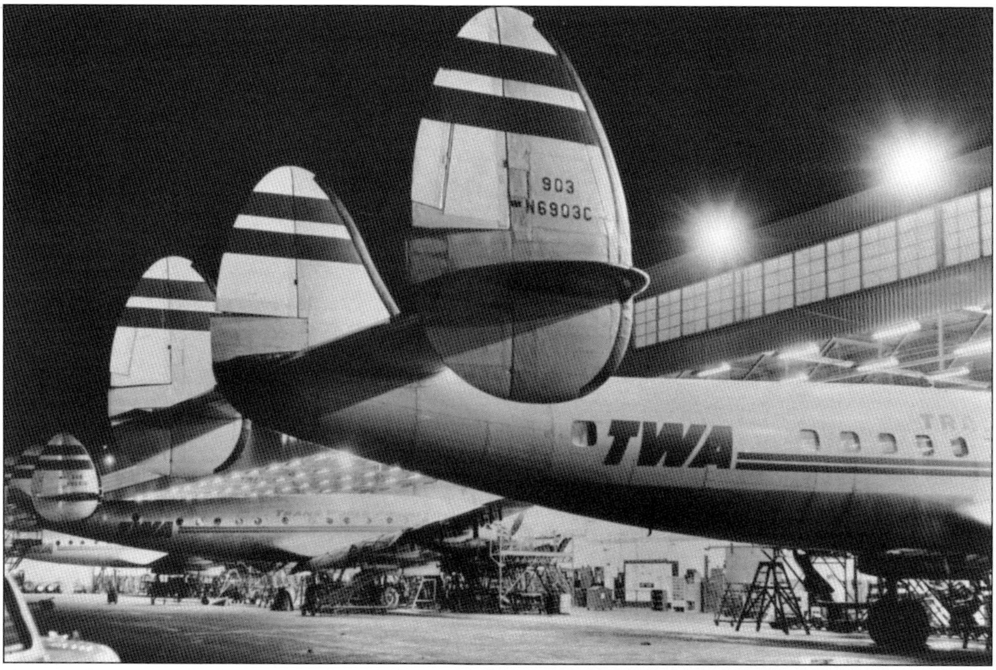

A popular aircraft choice in the 1950s, in addition to Douglas and Boeing models, was the Lockheed Constellation. These Constellations ("Connies") are shown in the TWA hangar at LAX in 1954. TWA, one of America's premiere international carriers and one of five original airlines at LAX, later was purchased by American Airlines.

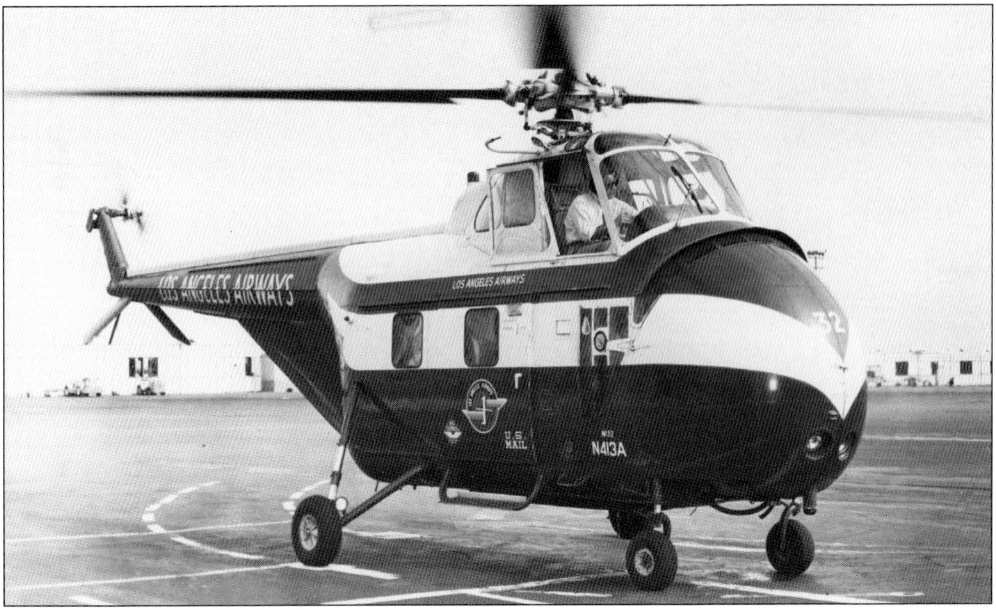

Los Angeles Airways inaugurated service at LAX in 1954 with this Sikorsky S-55 model. Helicopter travel expanded as many of the newer downtown high-rise buildings were equipped with helipads. Enthusiasm was tempered, however, when airport area residents raised concerns about noise, routing, and safety.

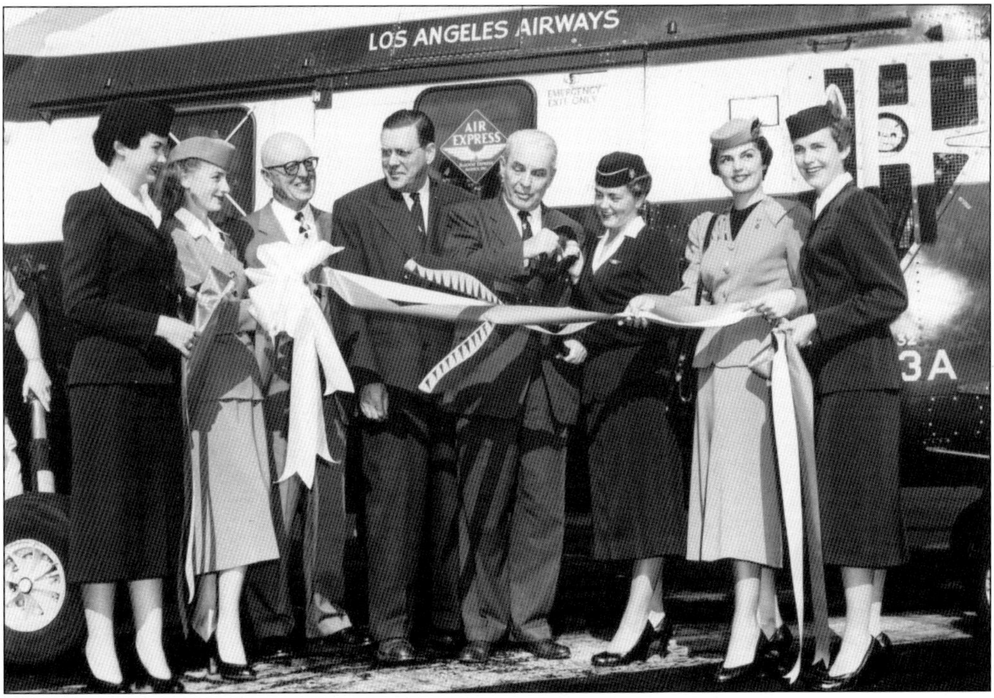

Officials of Los Angeles Airways and LAX were on hand for this 1954 ribbon-cutting ceremony for the airways' first helicopter flight, a trip to Disneyland. A high mark in helicopter service came during the 1984 Olympic Games, when numerous flights carried VIPs between the airport and sports venues throughout Southern California.

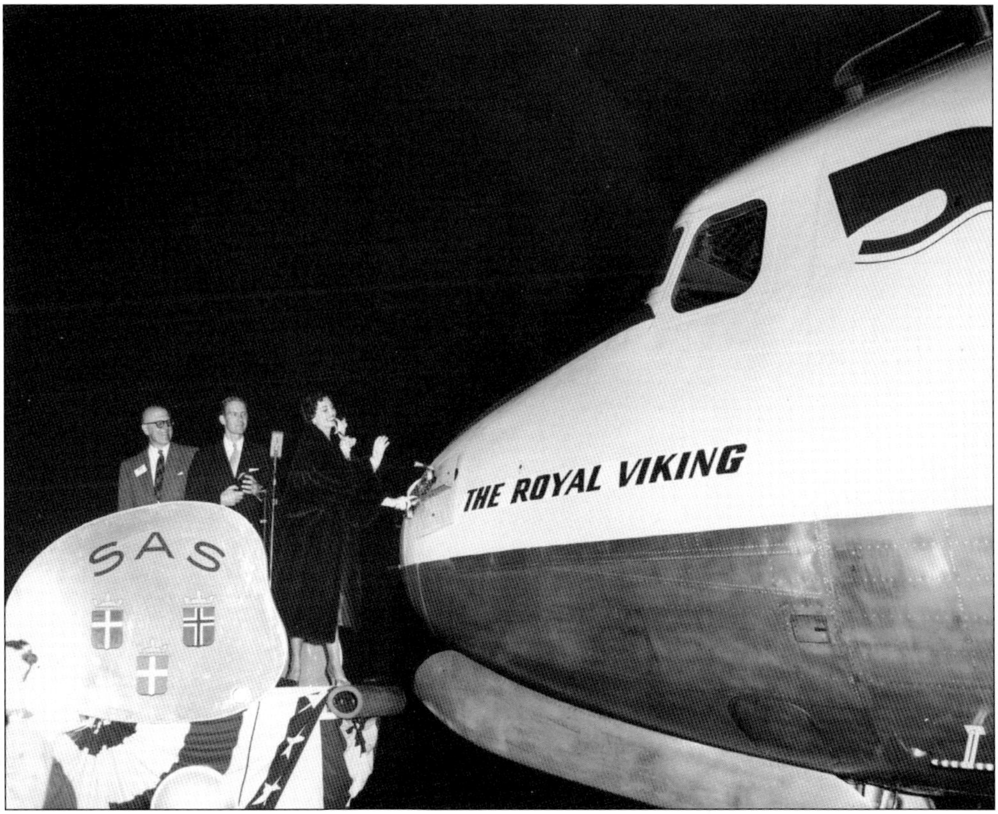

Actress Cyd Charisse christens Scandinavian Airlines Royal Viking airplane DC-6 minutes before it departed Los Angeles International Airport on the first eastbound polar route flight from California to Europe on December 8, 1954. Los Angeles Chamber of Commerce president Charles Detoy (left) and SAS regional manager Peter Tornquist look on. The polar route was important in greatly shortening travel time to Europe.

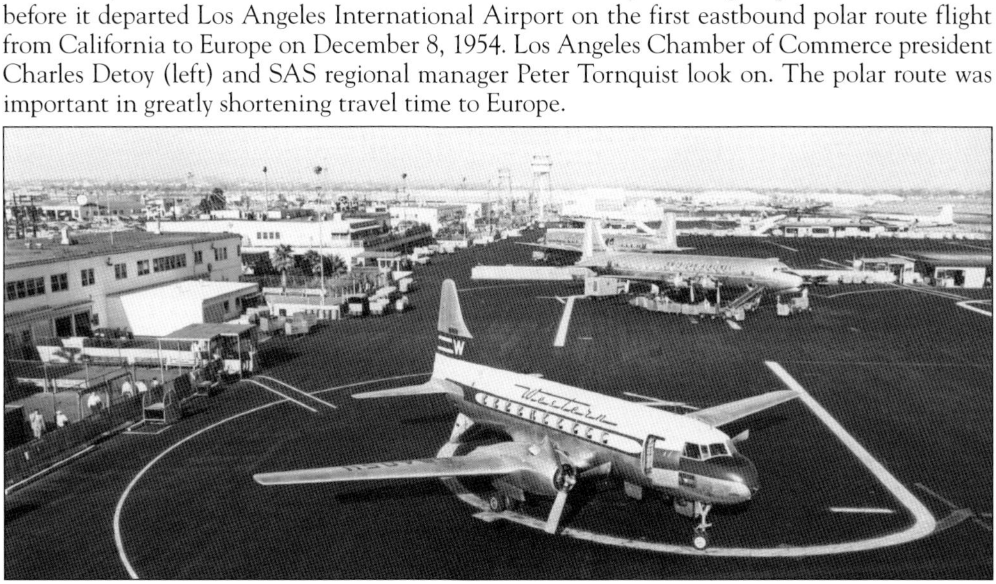

A visitor to Los Angeles International Airport on a day in the mid-1950s might have seen the following aircraft on the ramp: A Western Airlines Convair (foreground), awaiting the loading of passengers and cargo, and an American DC-6 and United Airlines passenger liner in the background.

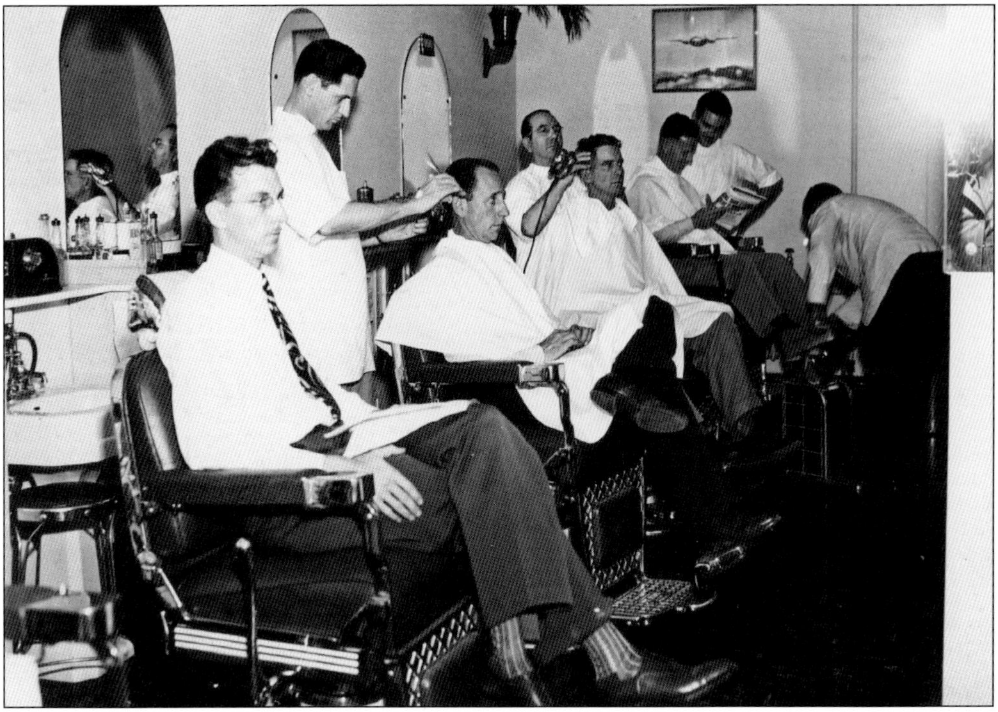

There often was time for a haircut at LAX during the more leisurely era of propeller-powered travel. This photograph taken in 1955 in a terminal barbershop shows business travelers being groomed to look their best.

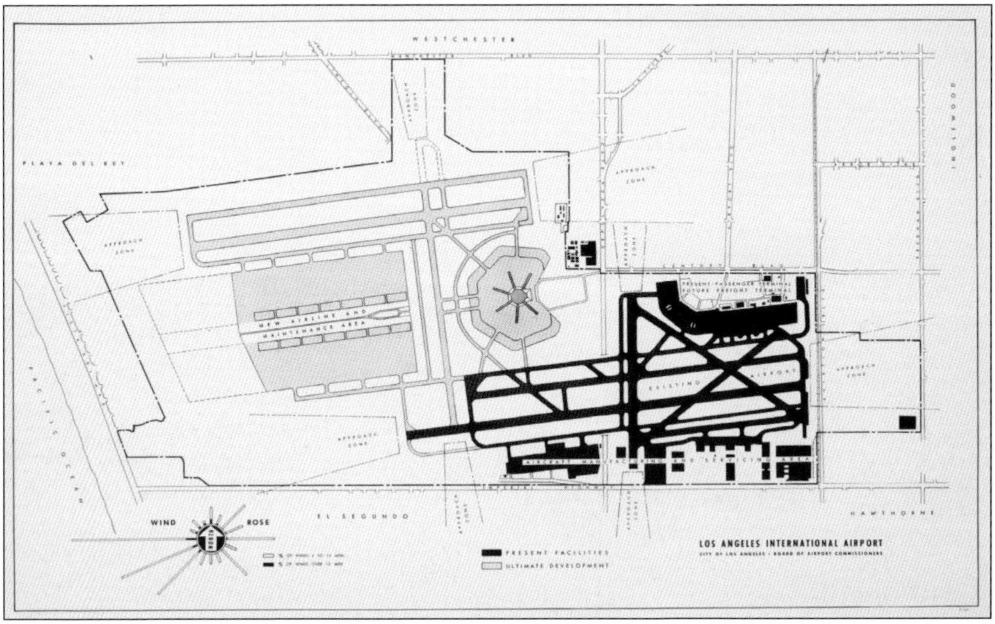

This artist rendering was unveiled on July 18, 1955, as plans moved ahead for a newly designed Los Angeles International Airport to meet the needs of passenger jet service. The airport's central terminal area was to be moved from the south side of Century Boulevard to land west of Sepulveda Boulevard.

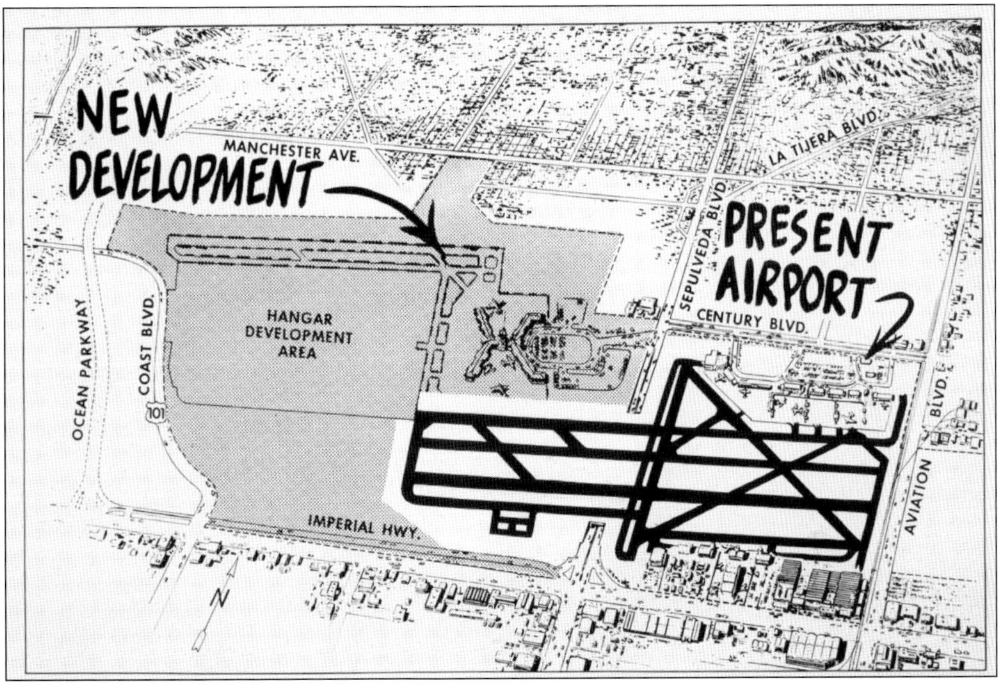

Artist renderings such as this one helped build public anticipation and support for a new terminal complex at LAX. When this concept was unveiled in 1955, it would be six more years before the new Jet Age airport was open and ready for service.

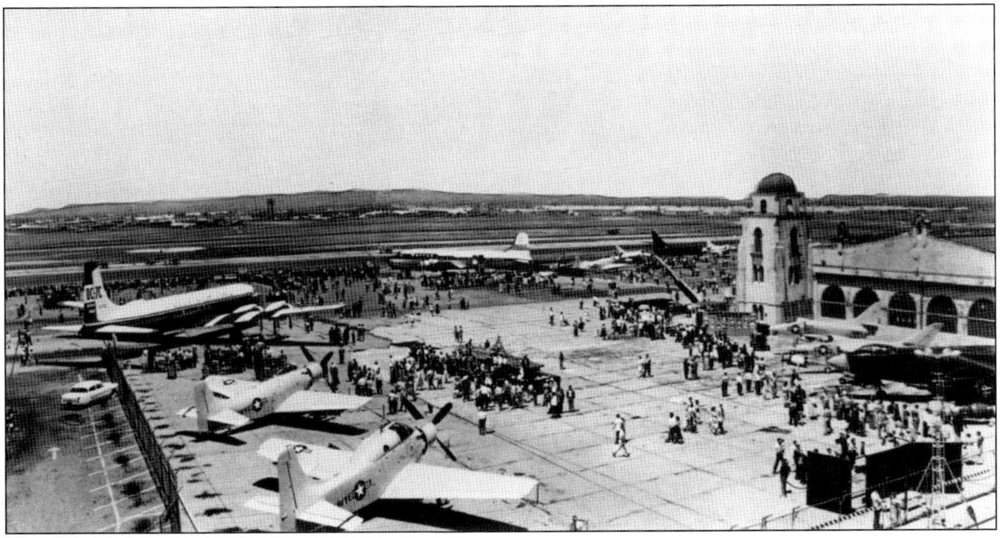

A visit to the airport was still a treat in the 1950s for many residents of Southern California. Peggy G. Hereford, the LAX public relations director, organized regular air fairs to showcase the airport and various aircraft. This 1956 Air Fair featured both civilian and military aircraft. Evoking memories of the airport's first years, Hangar No. 1 is on the right.

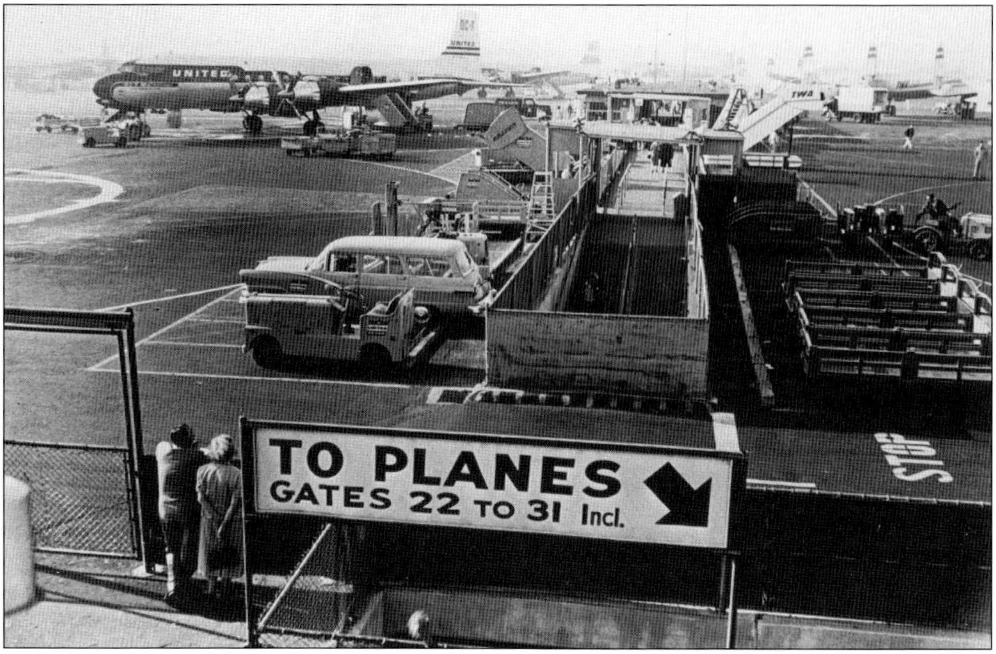

Passenger loading bridges, also known as jetways, were still on the drawing boards at LAX in 1956. Here, from that year, is a view of a passenger ramp and service road leading to the concourse for United Airlines and TWA flights. A United Airlines DC-7 and TWA Constellation are in the background.

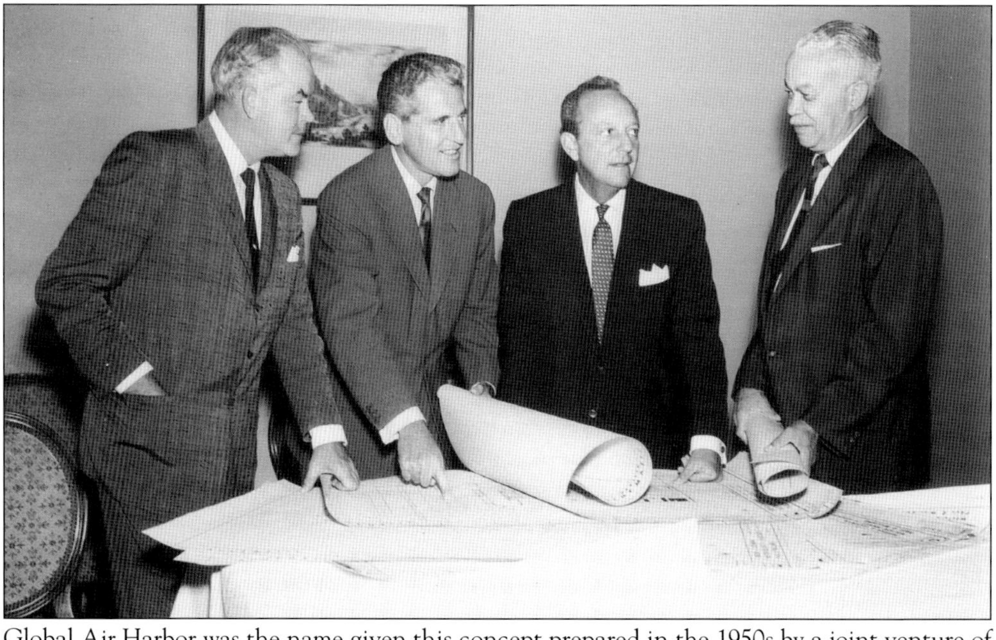

Global Air Harbor was the name given this concept prepared in the 1950s by a joint venture of leading architects, working with the LAX administration, to develop a plan to meet present and future requirements for passengers and aircraft. Shown in this September 14, 1956, photograph are, from left to right, architects Welton Becket, William Pereira, Charles Luckman, and Paul Williams. The LAX Jet Age Airport was dedicated in June 1961.

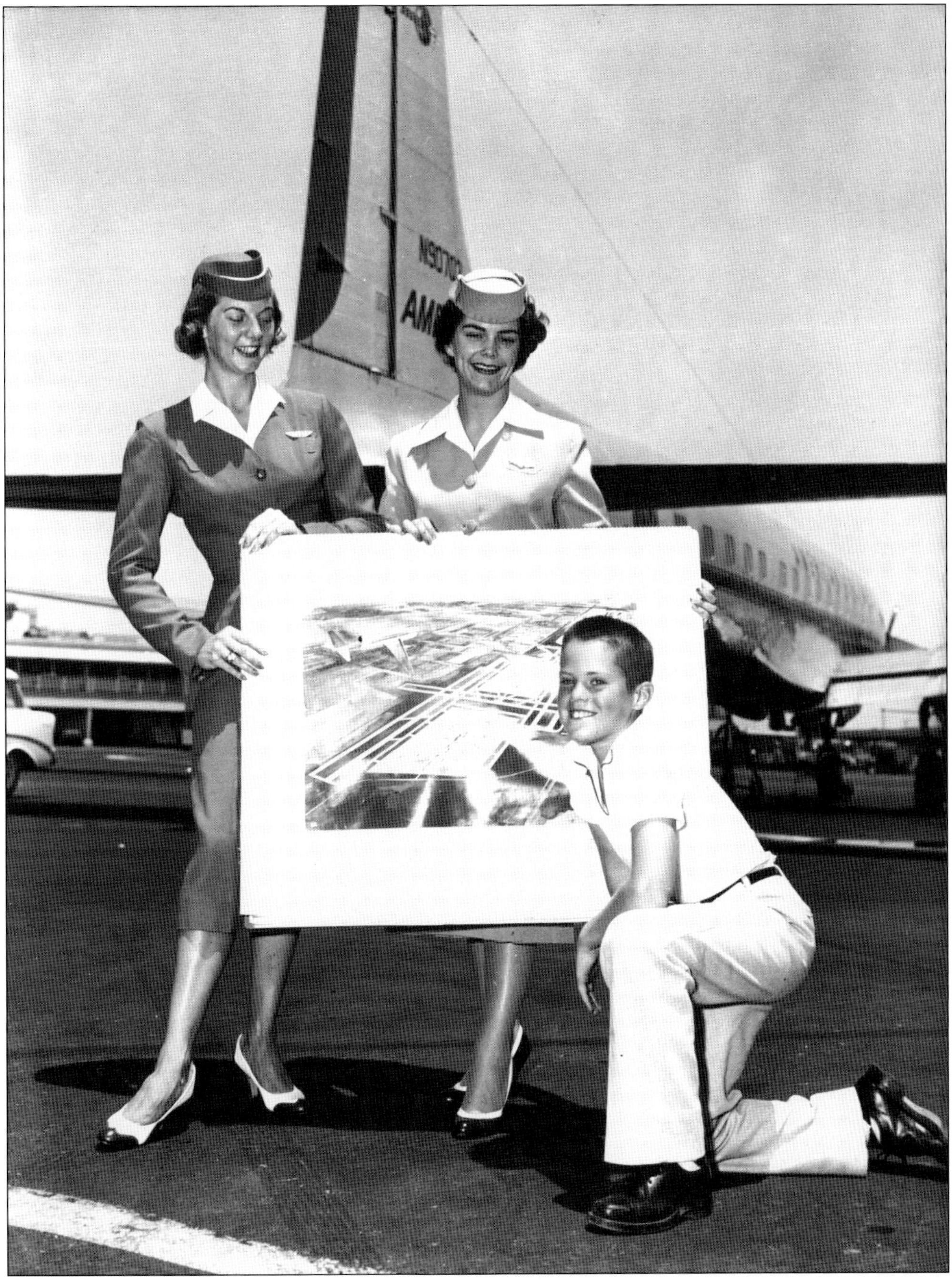

Air fairs of the 1950s were tamer than the air races of the 1920s and 1930s, but visitors still had a good time. Jeffrey Burden was proclaimed King for a Day on June 3 at the 1956 Air Fair. He is pictured with his escorts, stewardesses Hope Hively, left, from American Airlines and Dee Blackbourn from Western Airlines.

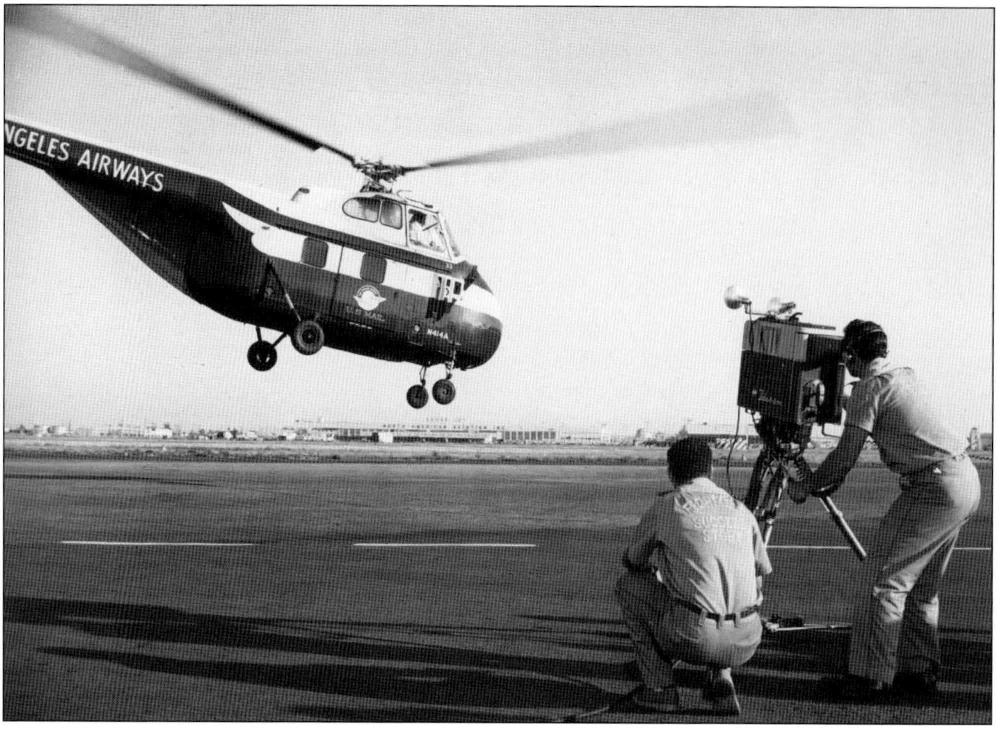

A film crew catches the landing of a helicopter at LAX in 1958. Commercial filming has long been an everyday occurrence at the airport. Film and television scenes supposed to take place at other U.S. airfields or even at foreign airports often are filmed instead at LAX because of favorable weather and proximity to studios.

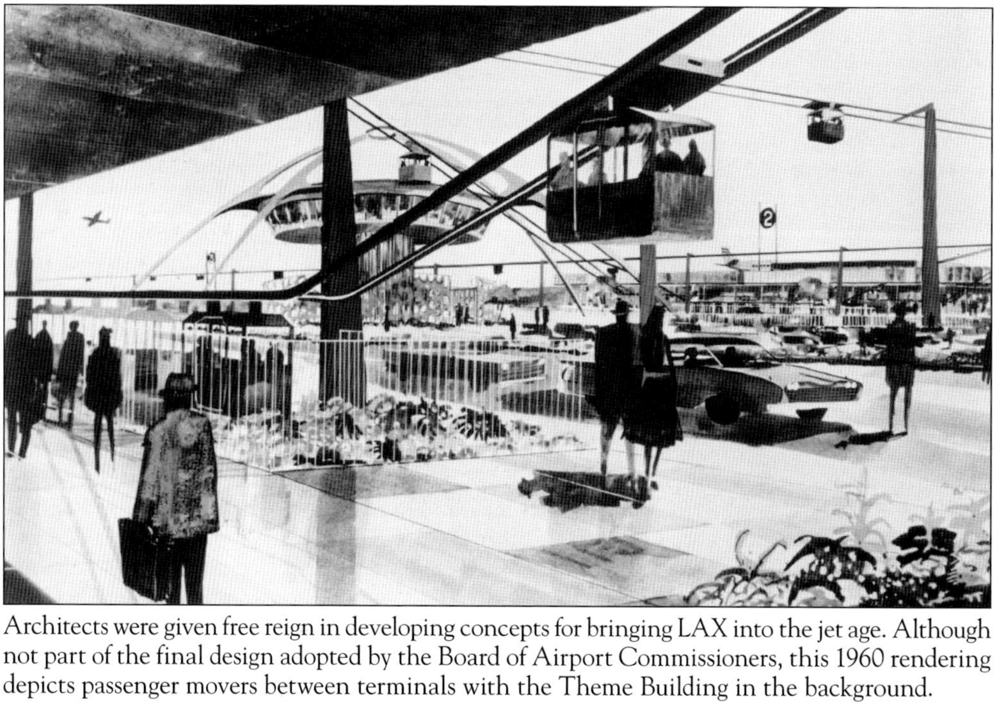

Architects were given free reign in developing concepts for bringing LAX into the jet age. Although not part of the final design adopted by the Board of Airport Commissioners, this 1960 rendering depicts passenger movers between terminals with the Theme Building in the background.

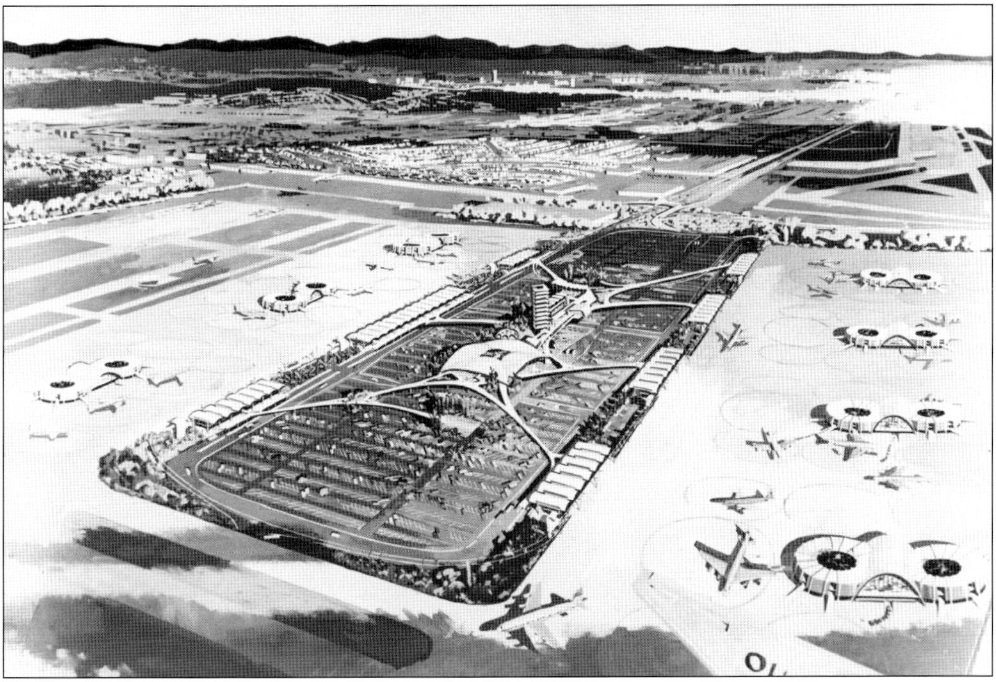

Comprehensive plans for the improvement of LAX had been on the drawing boards in the 1940s and even as early as the 1930s. It was in the 1950s that the future role of LAX as a center of jet age transportation became clear to airport administrators and planners. This rendering of the Master Plan for Los Angeles International Airport was prepared by the Joint Venture of Architects employed to design the new central terminal complex.

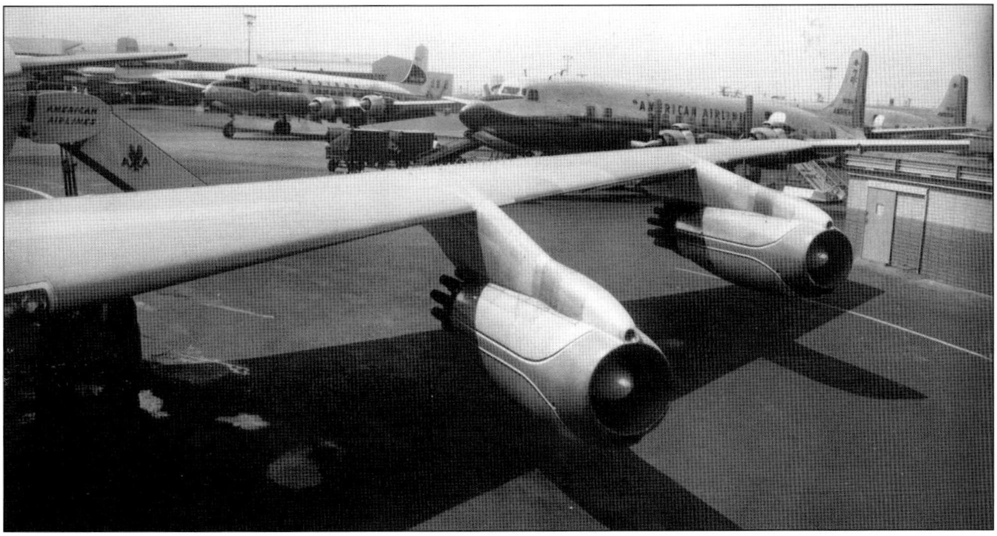

The late 1950s and early 1960s were years of transition, with propeller aircraft and hybrid prop-jets replaced by fully jet-powered aircraft. Shown at LAX are two jet engines of a new Boeing 707 (foreground) with propeller-powered DC-6s in rear. When noise issues arose, manufacturers worked to develop quieter "second-stage" jet engines and "hush kits" for the engines of early jets. Airport administrators established noise abatement and community relations offices as well as two community advisory committees to address noise and other concerns.

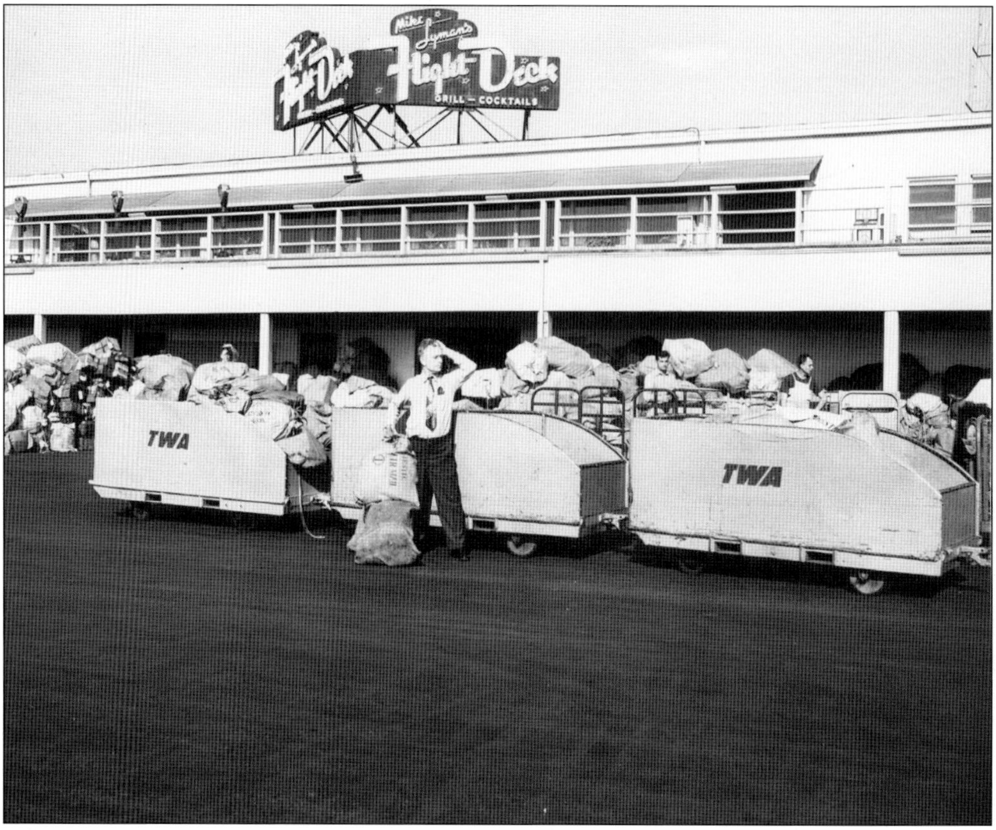

The role of LAX airlines in the processing and transport of airmail has grown dramatically through the years. Mail has been carried aboard passenger aircraft, cargo planes, and "combis" (combination passenger-cargo) as well as on aircraft devoted exclusively to mail.

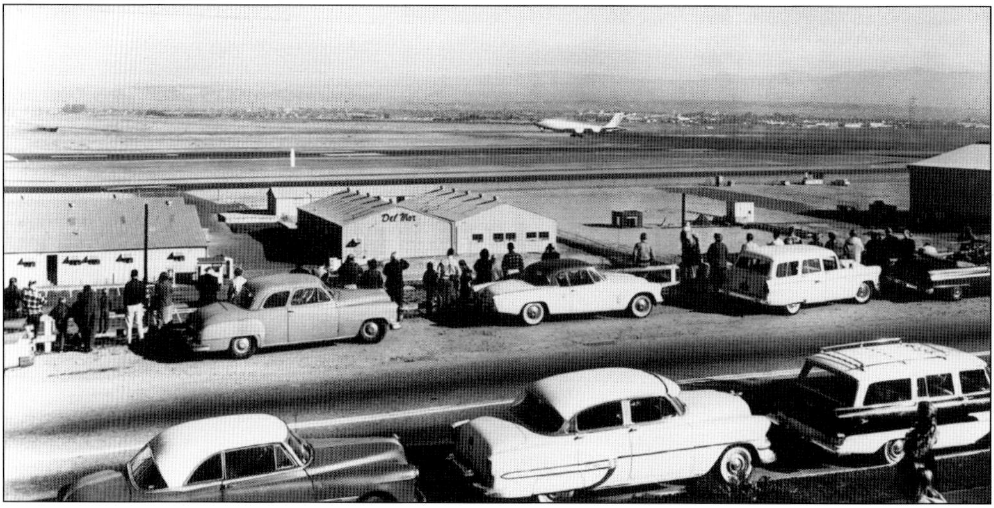

Spectators observe the first scheduled commercial jet flight, an American Airlines Boeing 707-123 at LAX on January 25, 1959. During the next few years, jets would replace the larger propeller-powered aircraft, dramatically reducing travel times to domestic and foreign destinations.

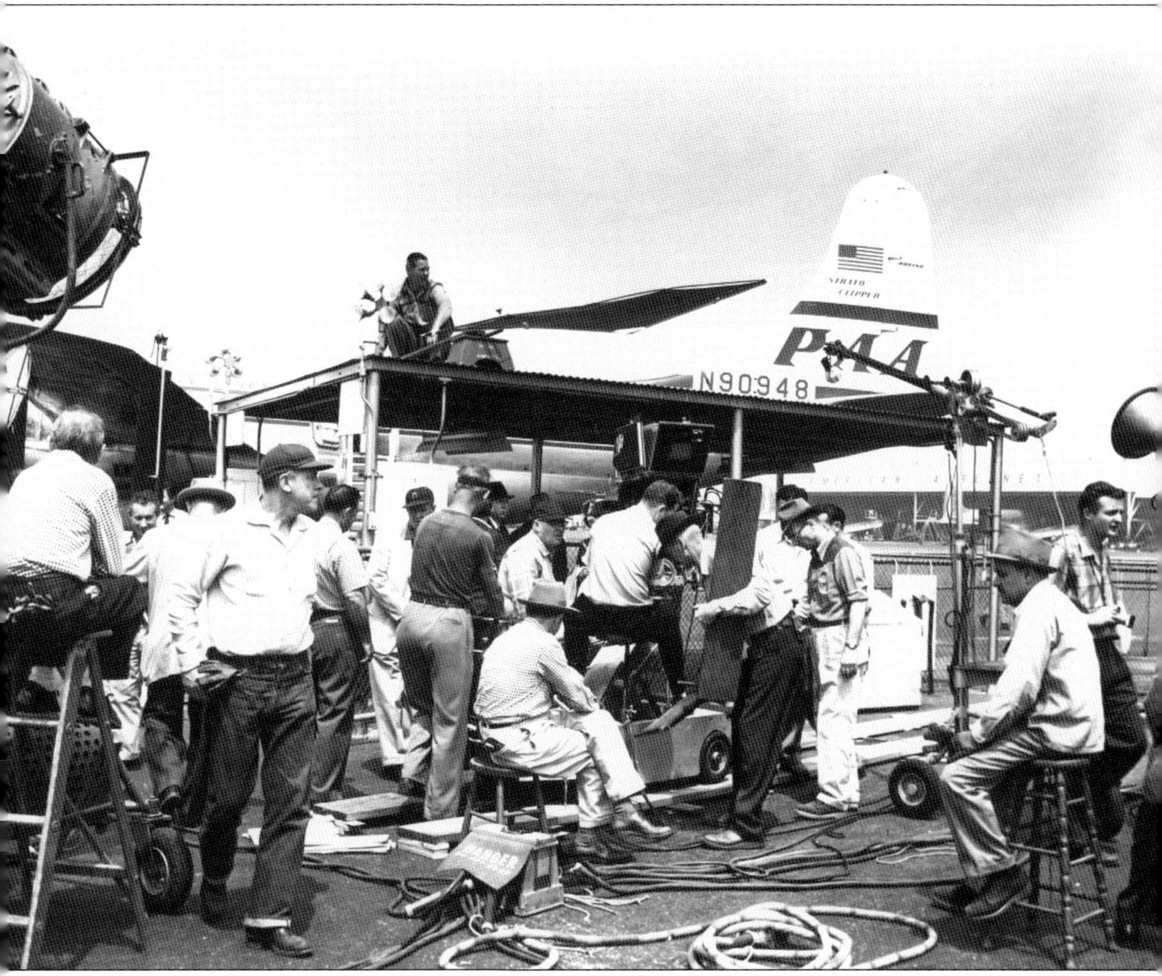

The proximity of LAX to Hollywood film and television studios has made the airport a popular location for production of many movies and television programs. Even as far back as the 1930s, production crews could be found at work on the airport. This photograph was taken in 1956.

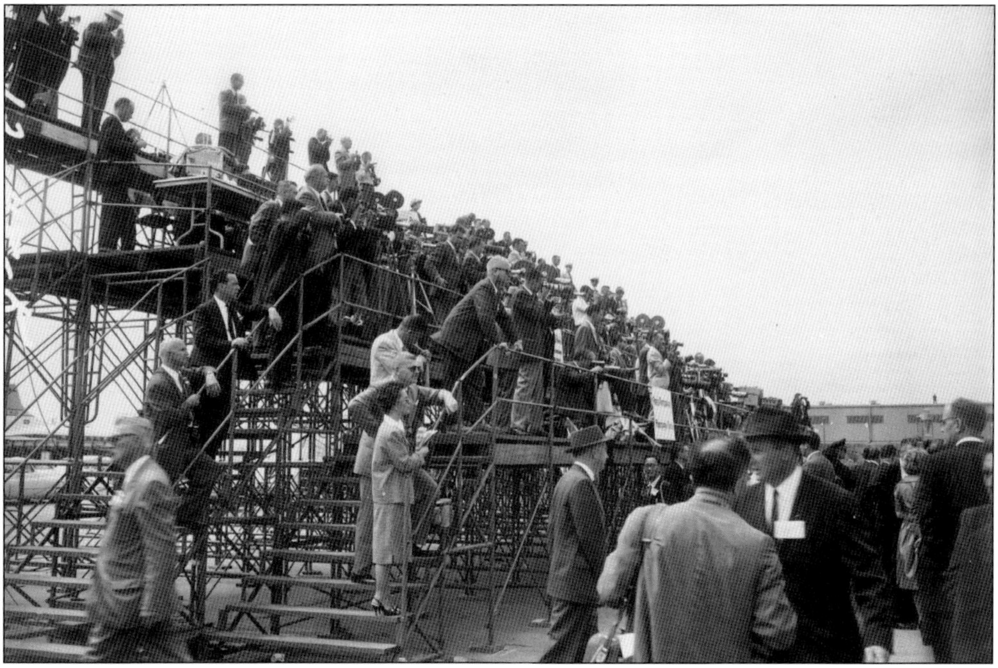

The arrival of Soviet premier Nikita S. Krushchev in Los Angeles in 1959 brought a crush of reporters and photographers to LAX. Krushchev was making headlines as the first head of the USSR to visit the United States, at the invitation of Pres. Dwight D. Eisenhower. A highlight of Krushchev's stay in Southern California was a visit to Disneyland.

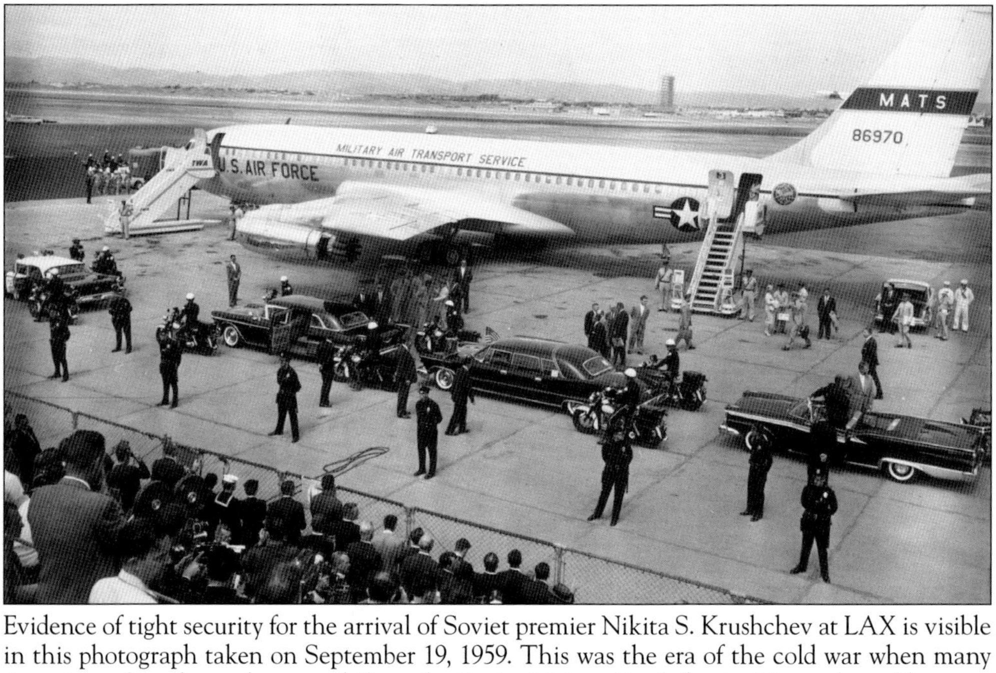

Evidence of tight security for the arrival of Soviet premier Nikita S. Krushchev at LAX is visible in this photograph taken on September 19, 1959. This was the era of the cold war when many Americans feared a nuclear attack from the Soviet Union. Krushchev's visit was hoped by some Americans to represent a thaw in the cold war. But to others, he was an unwelcome reminder of Soviet oppression.

Four

The Jet Age

Despite the continued operation by leading airlines of a host of piston-powered, propeller airplanes, by 1961, more than one million jet flights were logged at LAX.

The decade was marked by significant airport expansion. In 1961, U.S. vice president Lyndon Johnson officially dedicated the new airport. All new were the main terminal complex (Central Terminal); additional ticketing and satellite buildings; and a 12-story, 172-foot-tall combination airport administration building and air traffic control tower housing all Federal Aviation Administration (FAA) operations and offices.

By June 1962, a full 21 airlines served LAX, including 11 international carriers. Airmail increased 400 percent from 1947 to 1962, air express 200 percent, and air cargo an astounding 1,300 percent. The new Cargo City began operations in 1964, with several airlines building their own cargo facilities in 1965–1966. A $10-million postal center in Cargo City began operations in June 1968.

The city's Department of Airports furthered the concept of regional air service with the 1967 acquisition of Ontario International Airport in an agreement with the City of Ontario in San Bernardino County. In 1969, the department began acquiring 17,500 acres of land in northern Los Angeles County that would eventually become Palmdale Regional Airport (PMD).

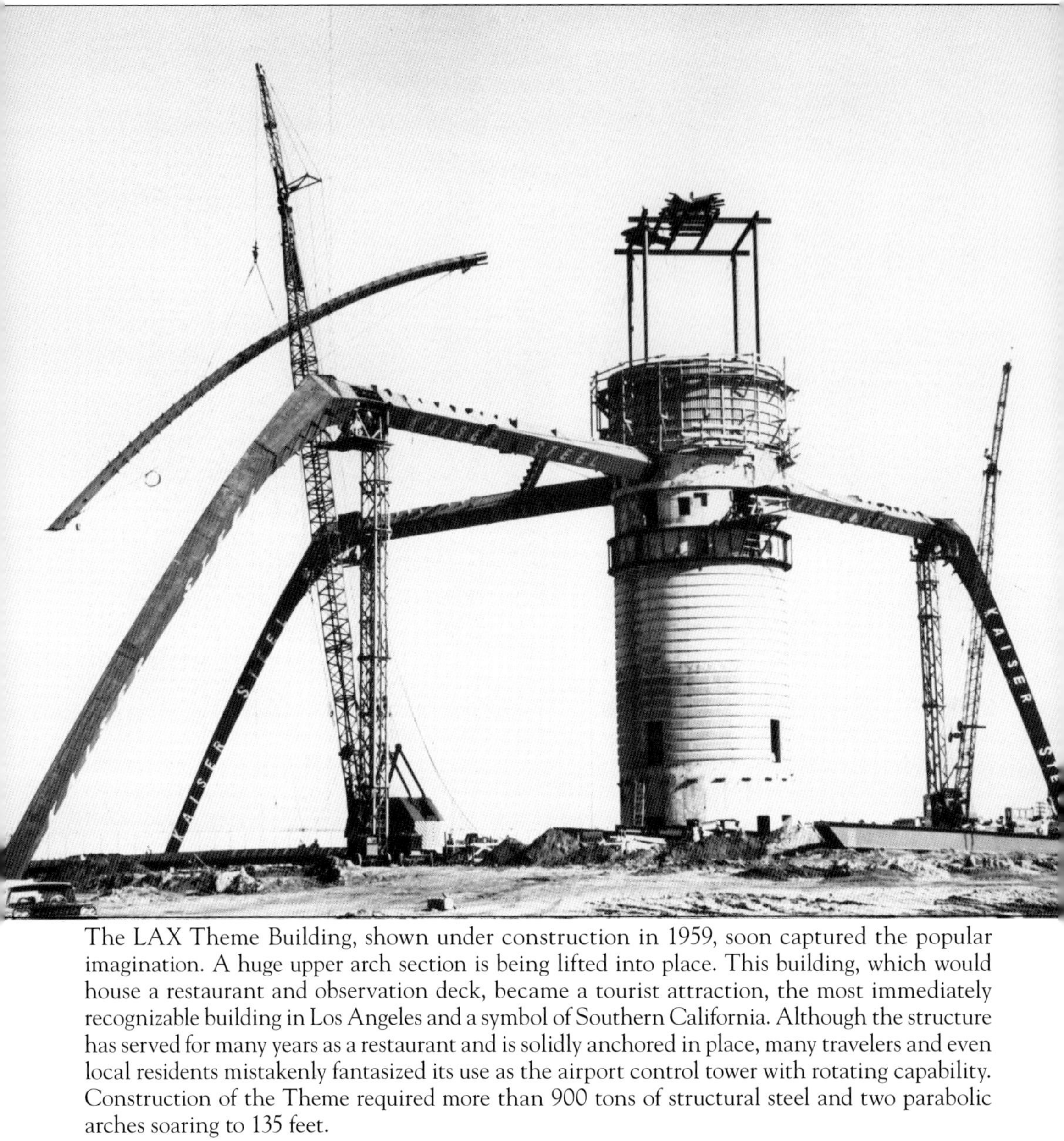

The LAX Theme Building, shown under construction in 1959, soon captured the popular imagination. A huge upper arch section is being lifted into place. This building, which would house a restaurant and observation deck, became a tourist attraction, the most immediately recognizable building in Los Angeles and a symbol of Southern California. Although the structure has served for many years as a restaurant and is solidly anchored in place, many travelers and even local residents mistakenly fantasized its use as the airport control tower with rotating capability. Construction of the Theme required more than 900 tons of structural steel and two parabolic arches soaring to 135 feet.

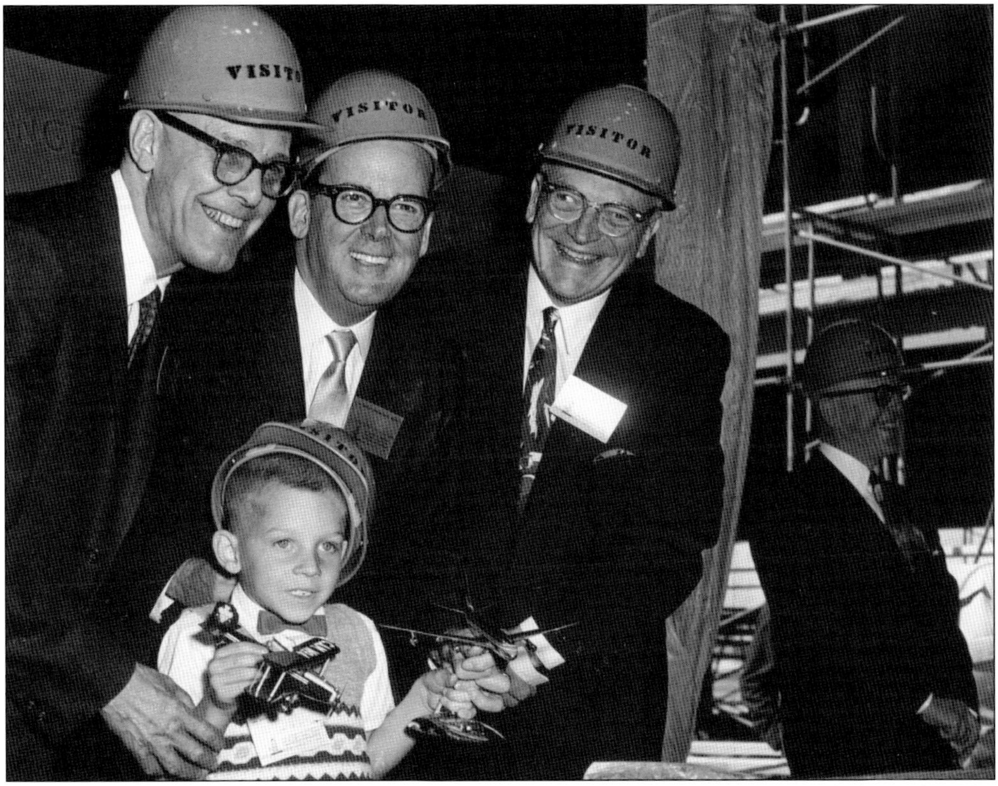

The new LAX Control Tower/Administration Building was the first structure dedicated in the airport's Jet Age complex. Among VIPs on hand for the March 25, 1959, ceremony were, from left to right, Los Angeles city councilman L. E. Timberlake, Mayor Norris Poulson, and Airport Commission president Don Belding, pictured with five-year-old Jackson "Joe" Seay, grandson of pioneer airline pilot Jimmy James.

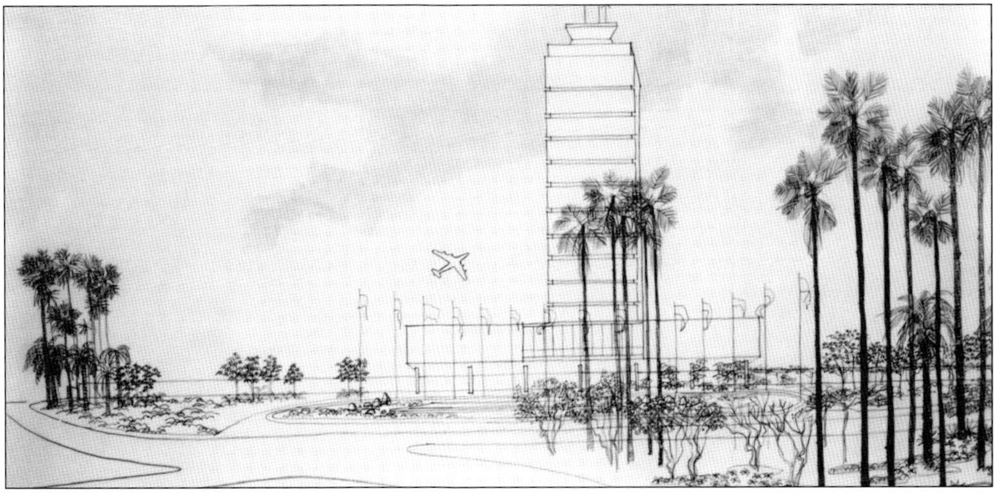

This concept for the new LAX Control Tower/Administration Building emphasized the simplicity of the structure's architectural design and landscape setting. The 12-story tower stood 172 feet above the runways and gave air traffic controllers an unobstructed view of surface traffic up to two miles distant.

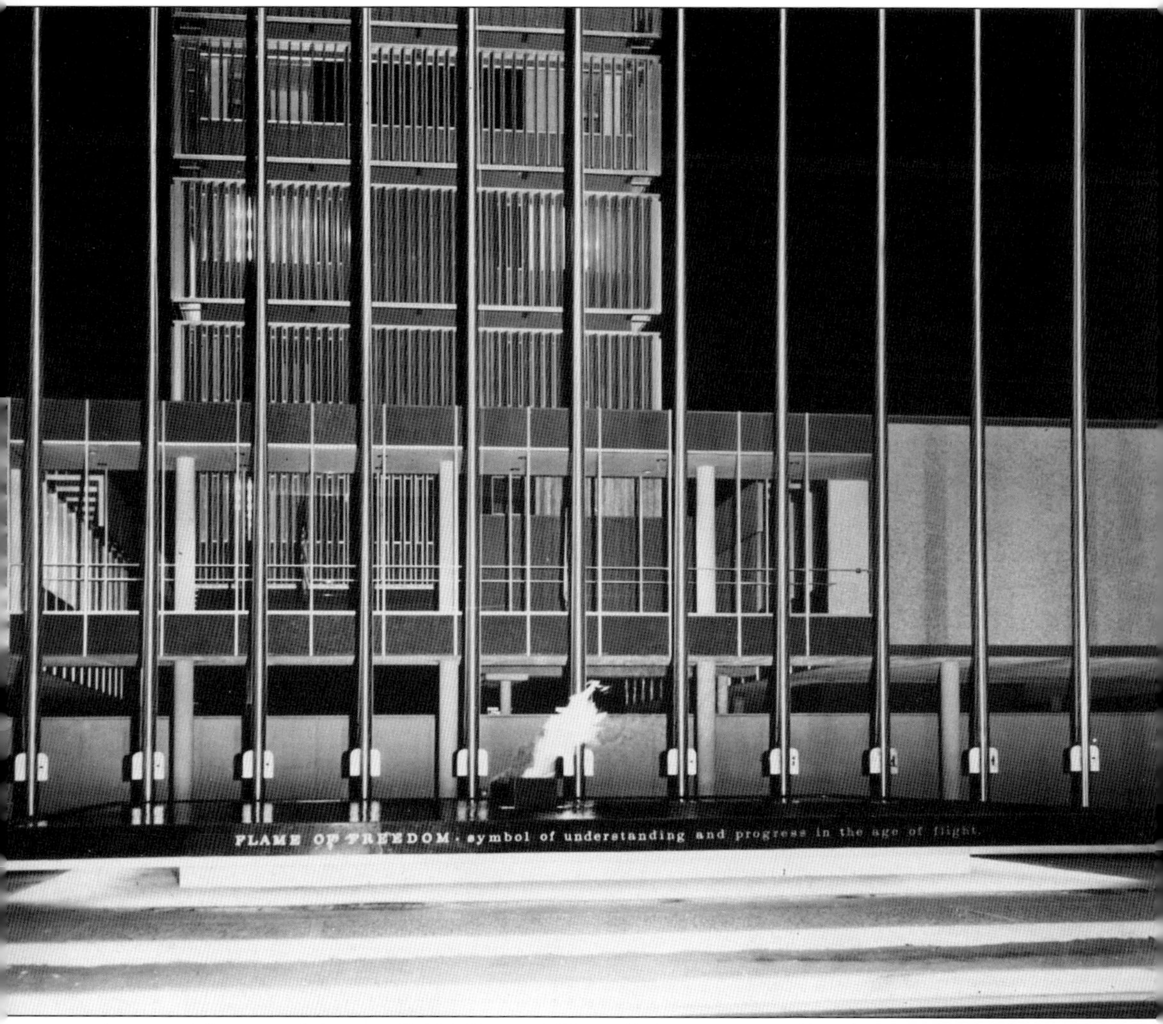

A special feature of the new LAX Control Tower/Administration Building was the Flame of Freedom, pictured above amid the airport's new flag court. Flags of all international carriers serving LAX were flown there for many years.

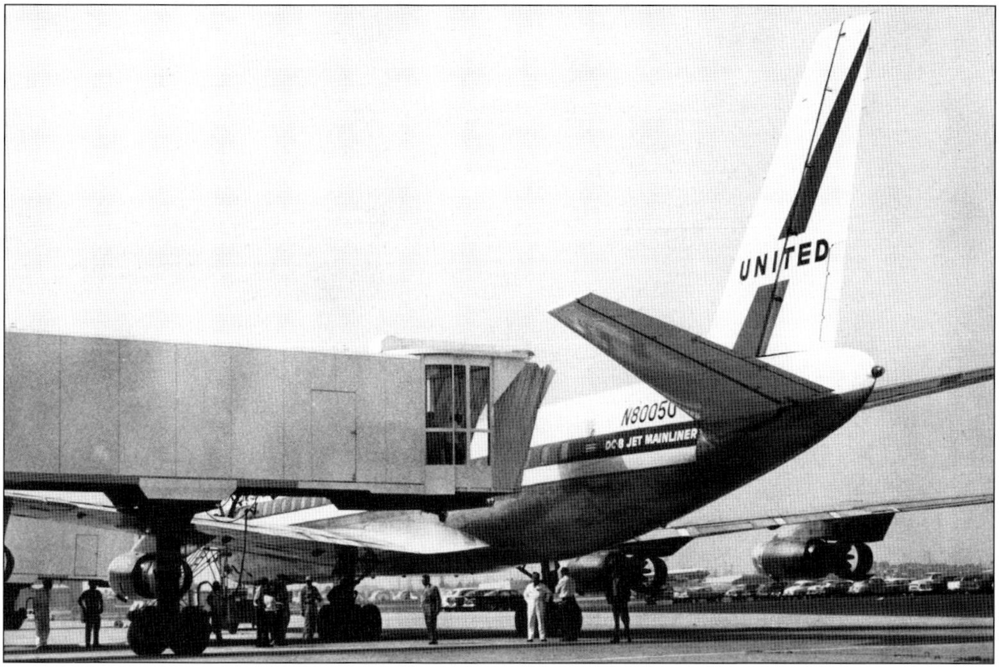

A welcome change from the old LAX terminals, where passengers climbed stair ramps to reach aircraft, the Jet Age complex featured loading bridges, also known as jetways, which gave travelers direct access to their flights. Pictured above is a United Airlines DC-8 boarding passengers via jetway on July 10, 1961.

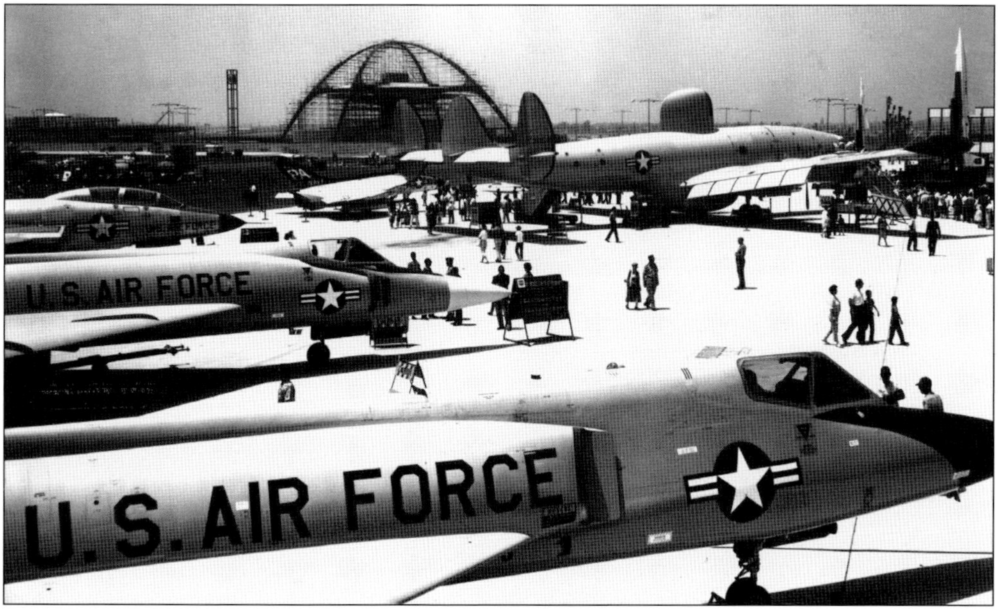

Prior to the opening of the new Jet Age terminal complex, a preview day was conducted on June 22, 1961, planned by longtime LAX Public Relations director Peggy G. Hereford. Featured was an array of NORAD air defense equipment. These included an F-106, F-102, F-101, RC-121, and Navy F-4D. At right, pointing skyward, are the Nike Ajax and Nike Hercules missiles. Nike missiles were positioned in defensive posture immediately north of the airport for many years.

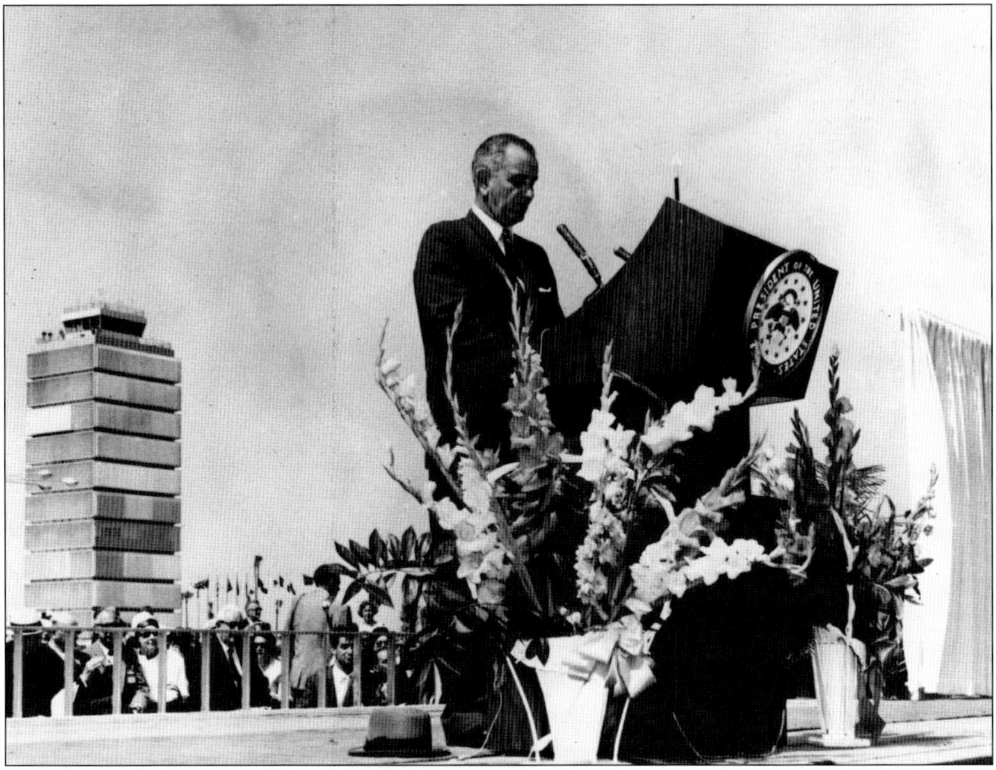

Keynoting the official dedication ceremony for the new Jet Age LAX on June 25, 1961, was Vice Pres. Lyndon Baines Johnson. Johnson had served during World War II as a pilot in the U.S. Army Air Corps.

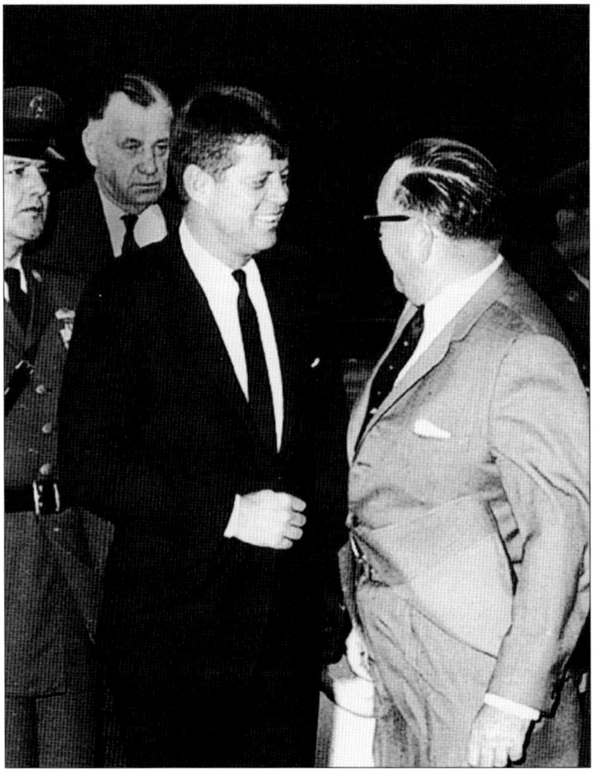

California governor Edmund G. "Pat" Brown welcomes Pres. John F. Kennedy at LAX in 1961. Presidential arrivals at the airport became increasingly frequent in the jet travel era. Air Force One, with the president aboard, typically arrived and departed from the Continental Airlines hangar, a secure area at the west end of the airport.

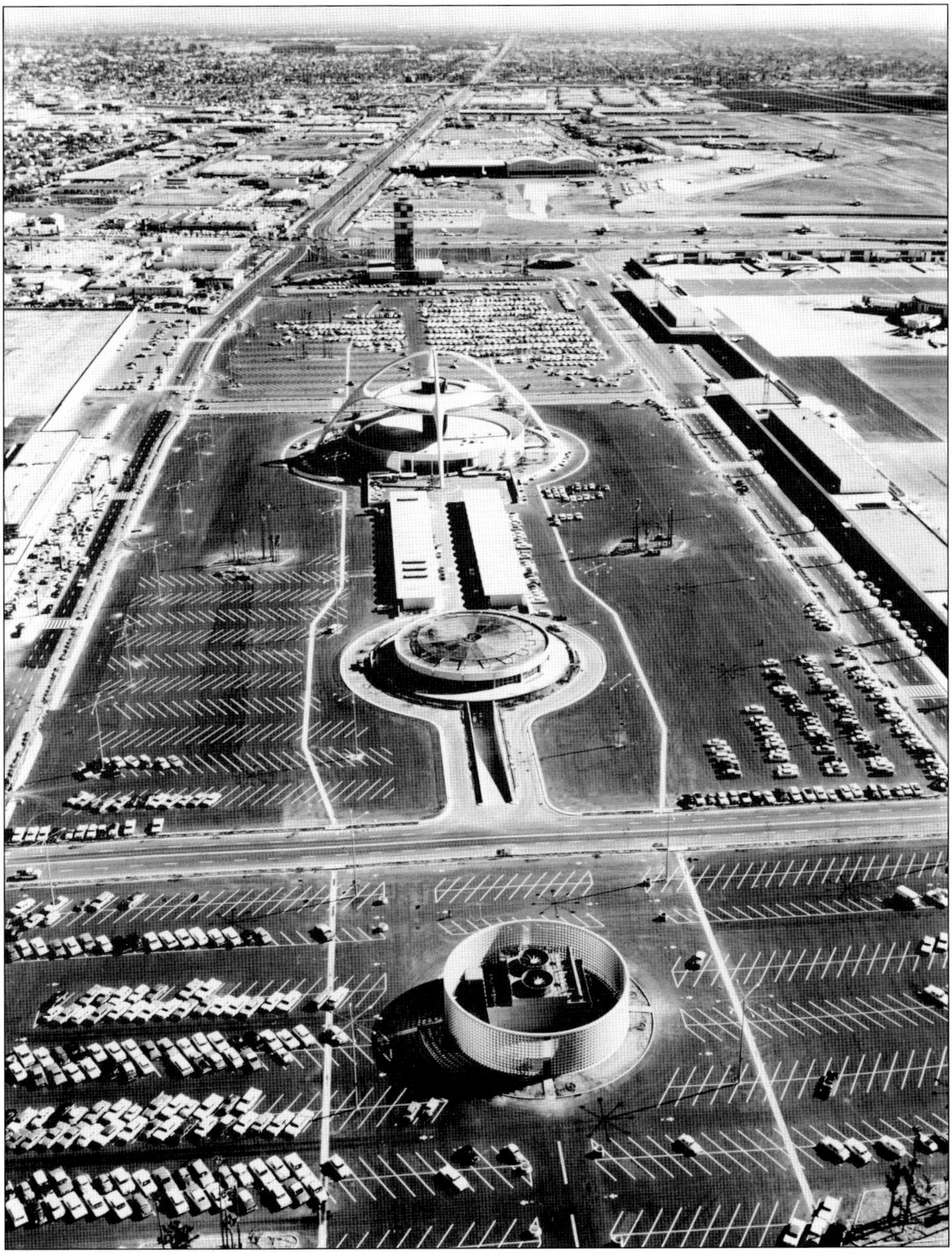

Concern for the automobile was a close second to the airplane in planning for the Jet Age LAX. This aerial view of the new Central Terminal Complex on November 21, 1961, clearly depicts the significant space devoted to auto parking. The development plan was a joint venture of Pereira and Luckman, Welton Beckett and Associates, and Paul R. Williams.

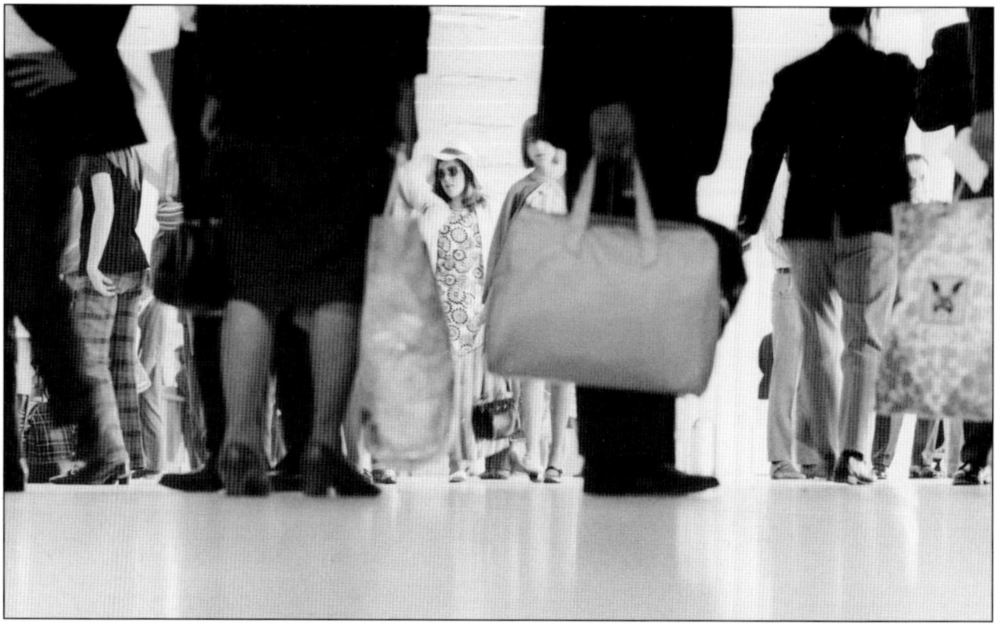

The 1960s were an exciting time for passengers at LAX. Jet travel was becoming more common, ticket prices were declining on many routes as airline competition increased, and new terminals at LAX and other airports were geared to greater comfort and convenience of travelers.

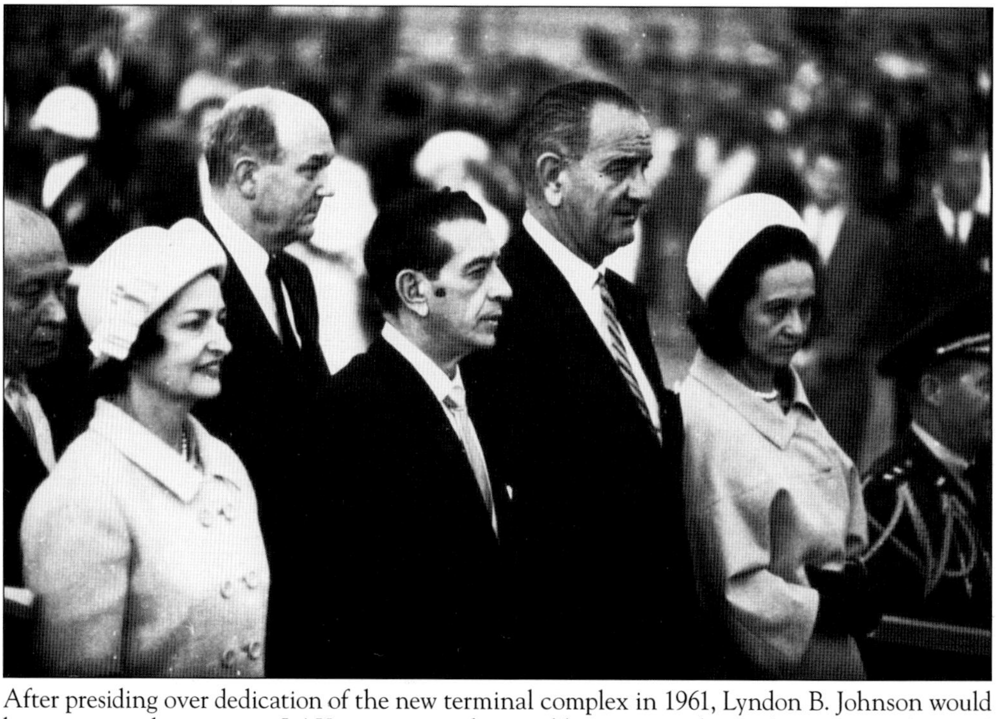

After presiding over dedication of the new terminal complex in 1961, Lyndon B. Johnson would become a regular visitor at LAX as vice president and later as president. The vice president and Lady Bird Johnson (left) are pictured on October 3, 1962, during a meeting at LAX with Mexican president and Mrs. Adolfo Lopez Mateos. Secretary of State Dean Rusk is in the background. The leaders were en route to an official visit in Asia.

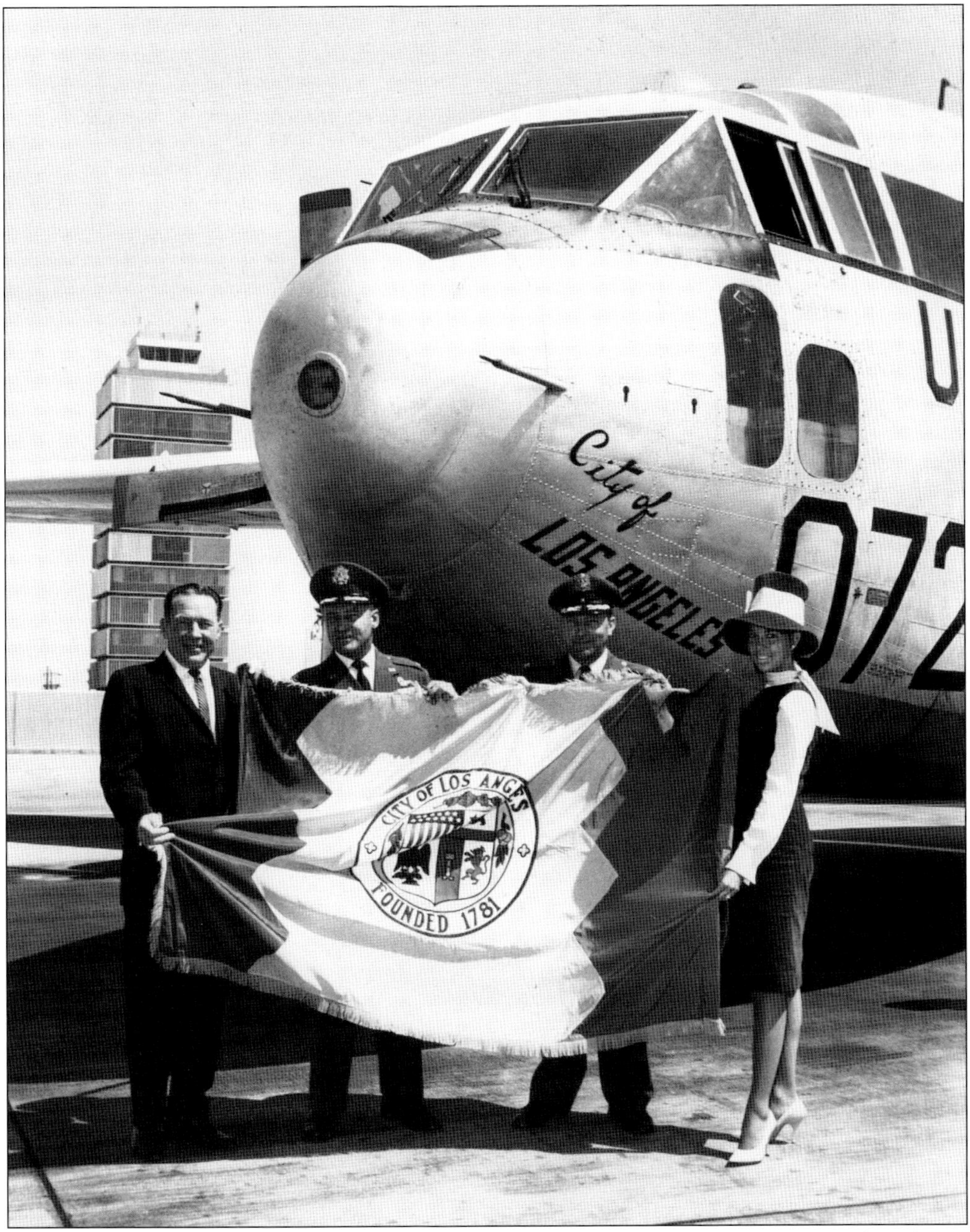

This unique ceremony at LAX on August 12, 1963, featured leaders from city government, the military, and show business. Pictured at the dedication of a C119 military transport plane in honor of the city of Los Angeles are Mayor Sam Yorty, Col. E. O. Anderson, Col. M. E. Larson, and vocalist Dodie Stevens, whose recording of "Tan Shoes and Pink Shoe Laces" was a Top 40 hit of that era.

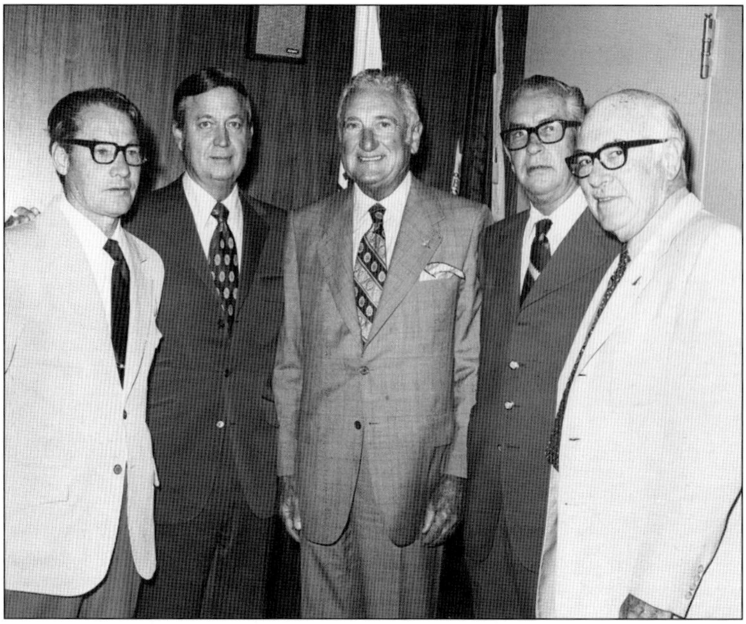

Airport Commission president Stephen C. Bilheimer, pictured in center with fellow commissioners, was a key leader as LAX transitioned into the jet era of passenger travel. Bilheimer, a merchandising executive, brought his business expertise and important civic contacts to his work at LAX.

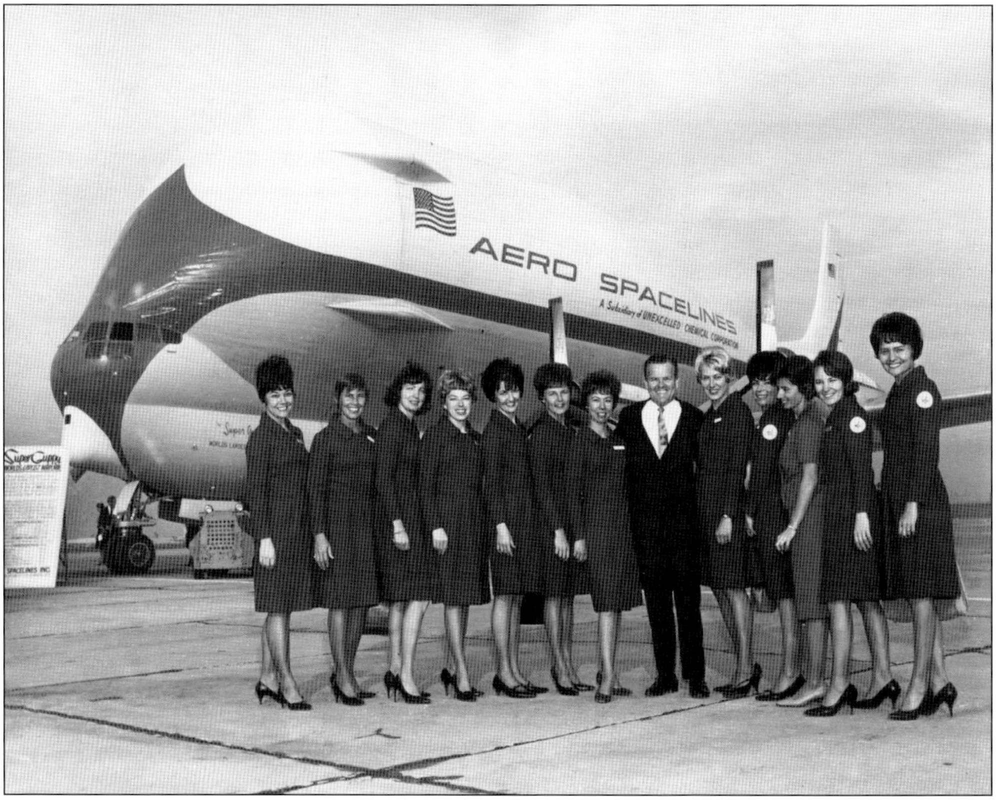

Jack Conroy of Aero Spacelines previews the Super Guppy in 1965 for LAX Airport Guides. Dubbed the "pregnant guppy," the curious aircraft now is all but forgotten. The Airport Guides remain active in their mission of educating students of all ages about LAX, its airlines, aircraft, and history. The group now is based at the Flight Path Learning Center in the airport's Imperial Terminal.

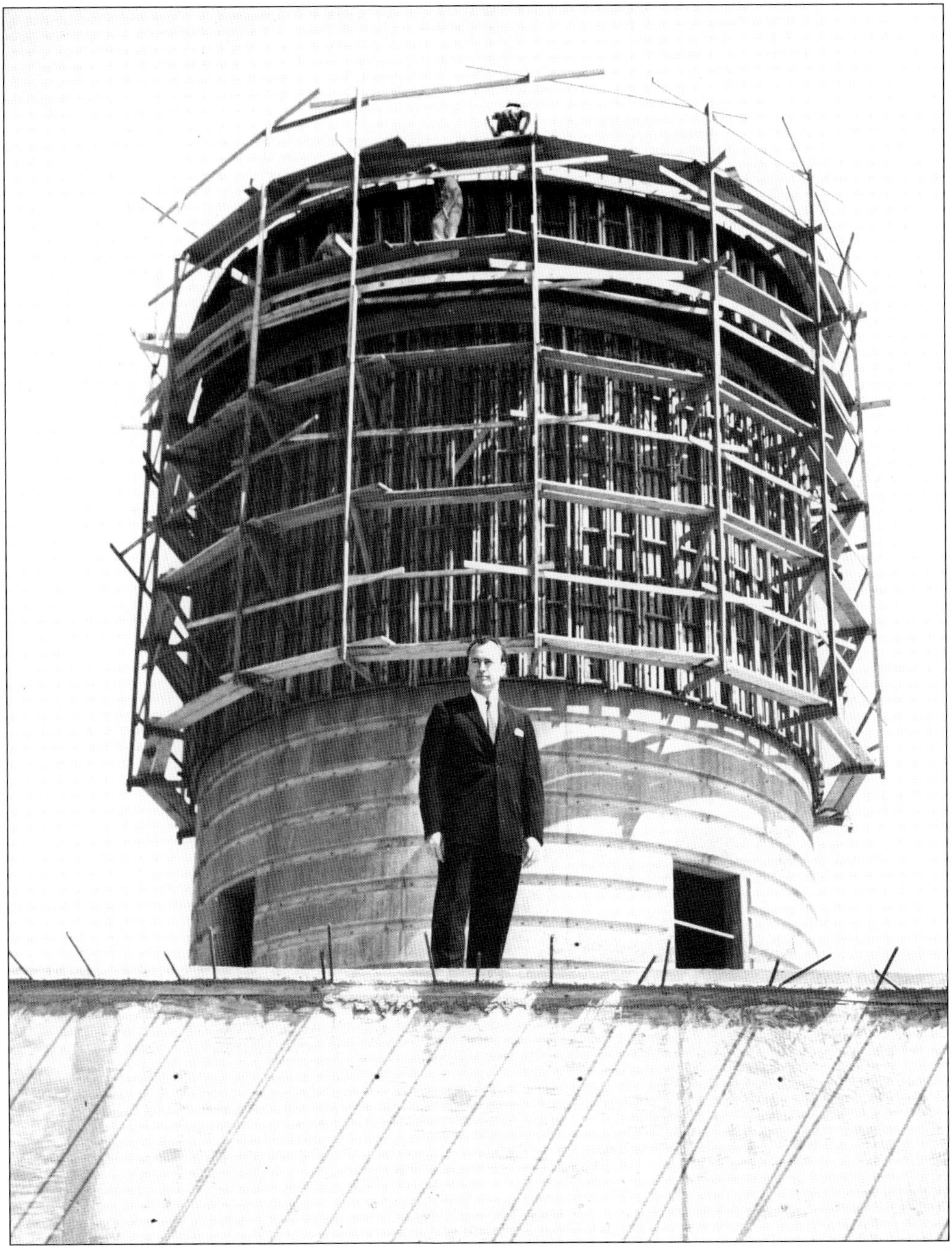

Francis T. Fox, Los Angeles Department of Airports general manager from 1958 to 1968, is pictured checking progress on construction of the LAX Theme Building. Fox, who oversaw development of the Jet Age airport, was a member of President Kennedy's Project Horizon, an advisory group on federal aviation policy. He played a significant role in national and international airport planning. Fox also is remembered as a hands-on administrator who could greet most airport employees by their first names.

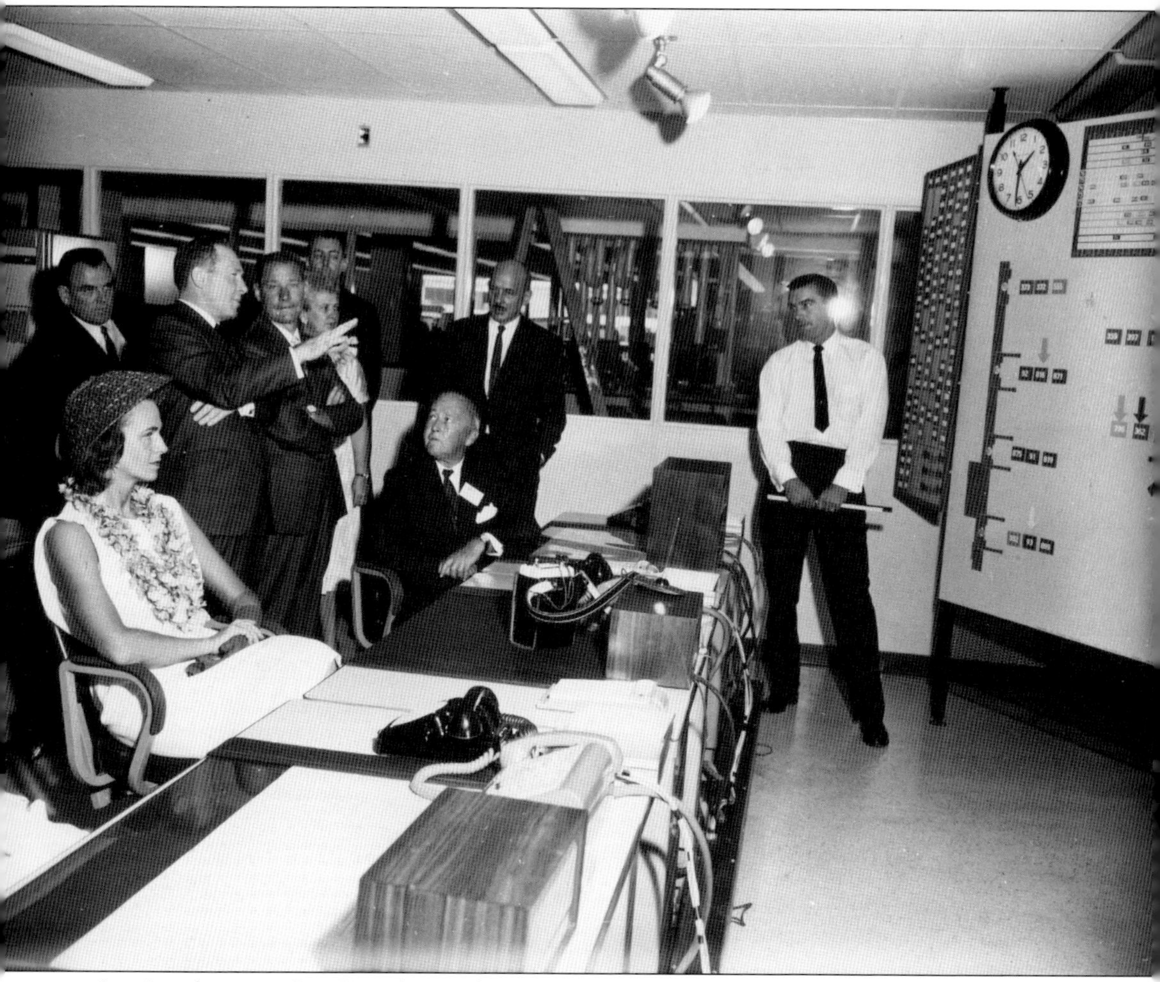

Los Angeles mayor Sam Yorty kept a close watch on operation of the new Jet Age terminal complex at LAX during the 1960s. Yorty (left) meets here with airport staff for an update. Yorty, a former congressman and state legislator, was elected mayor in 1961 as the first of the new terminals were beginning service. He often represented Los Angeles overseas during his three terms in office, retiring in 1973.

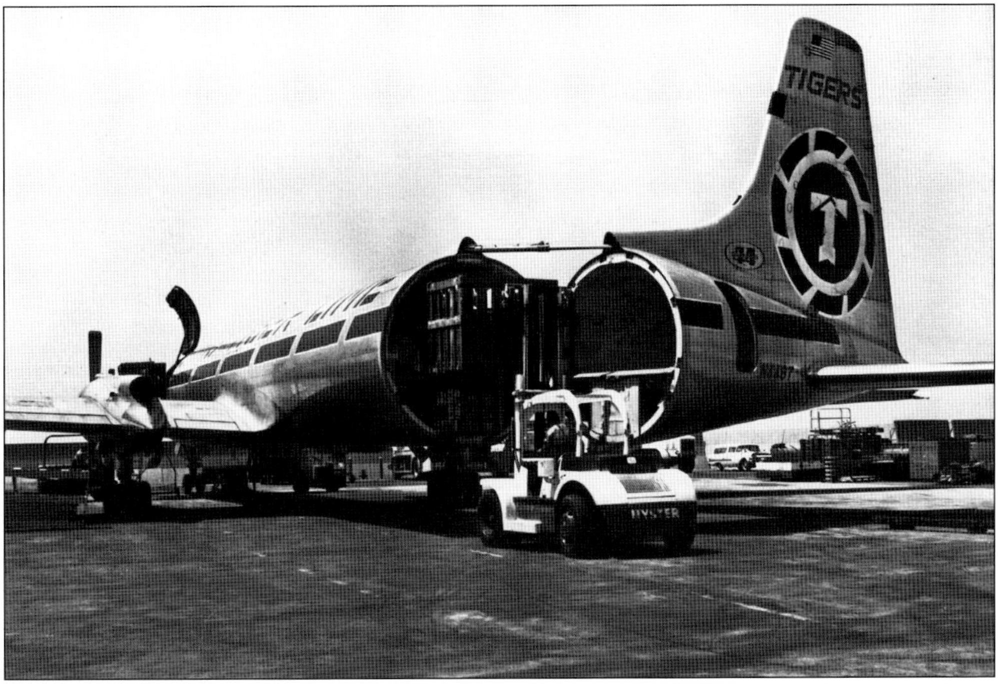

Less visible than its passenger terminals, the air cargo areas of LAX are a vital link to Southern California's Pacific Rim trading partners. During many years, the dollar value of the airport's cargo has surpassed that of the Port of Los Angeles and Port of Long Beach. Pictured is a swing-tail aircraft of the Flying Tiger Line taking on cargo on the south side of the airport on August 23, 1963. Flying Tigers now is part of Federal Express, one of the busiest cargo carriers at LAX.

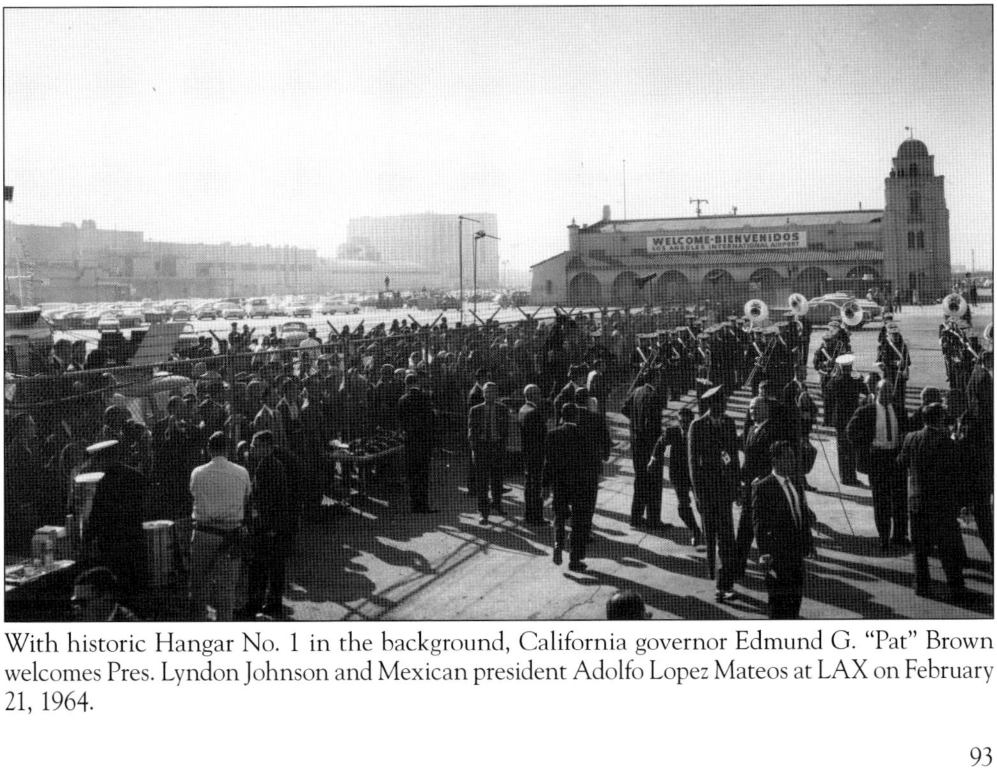

With historic Hangar No. 1 in the background, California governor Edmund G. "Pat" Brown welcomes Pres. Lyndon Johnson and Mexican president Adolfo Lopez Mateos at LAX on February 21, 1964.

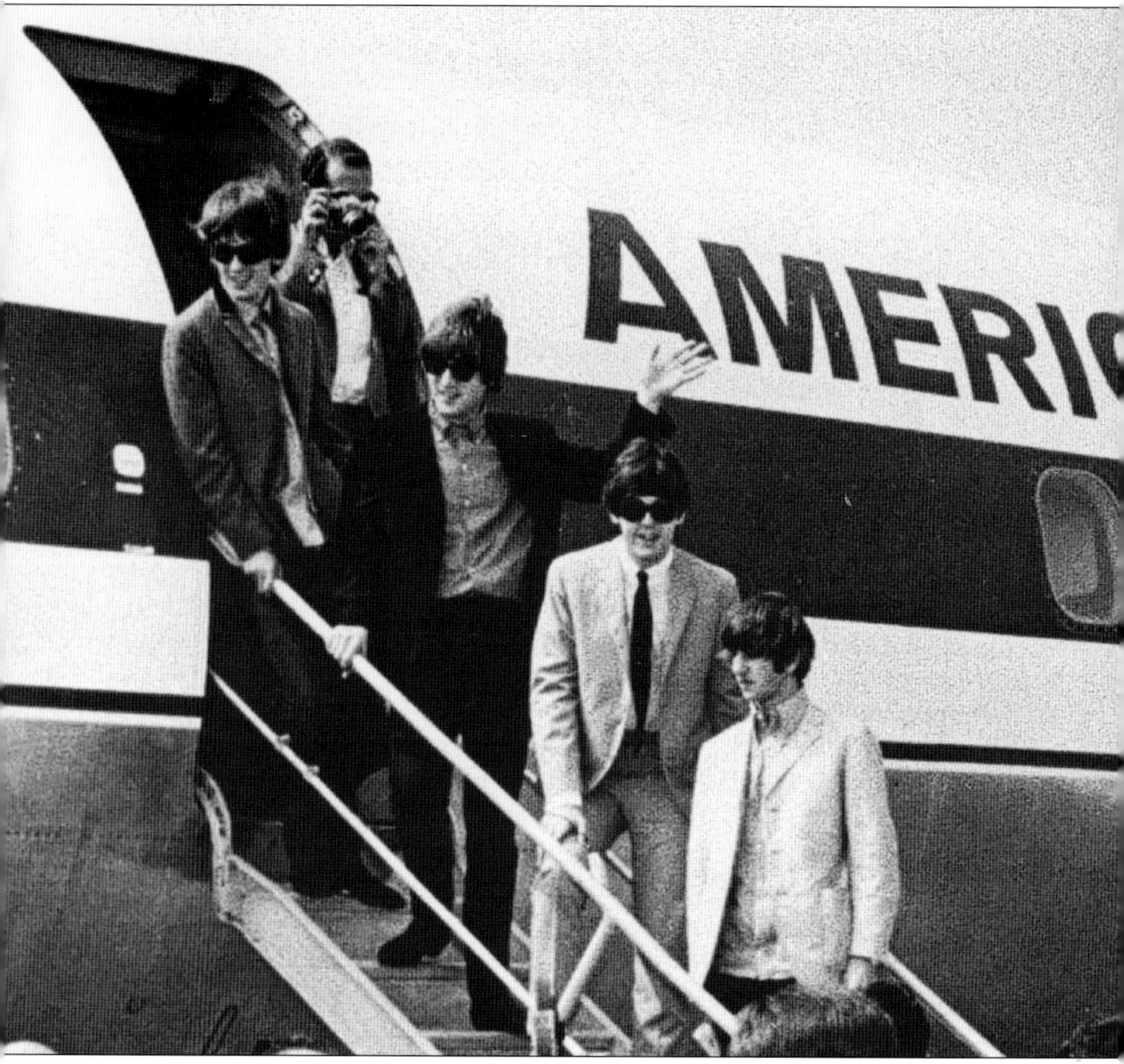

Among the most celebrated arrivals at LAX in the 1960s were the Beatles. The British pop group had made their first American television appearance on CBS's *The Ed Sullivan Show* on February 9, 1964, and received heavy radio airtime on Los Angeles stations KFWB and KRLA. A hysterical mob of fans greeted the songsters on their arrival at LAX.

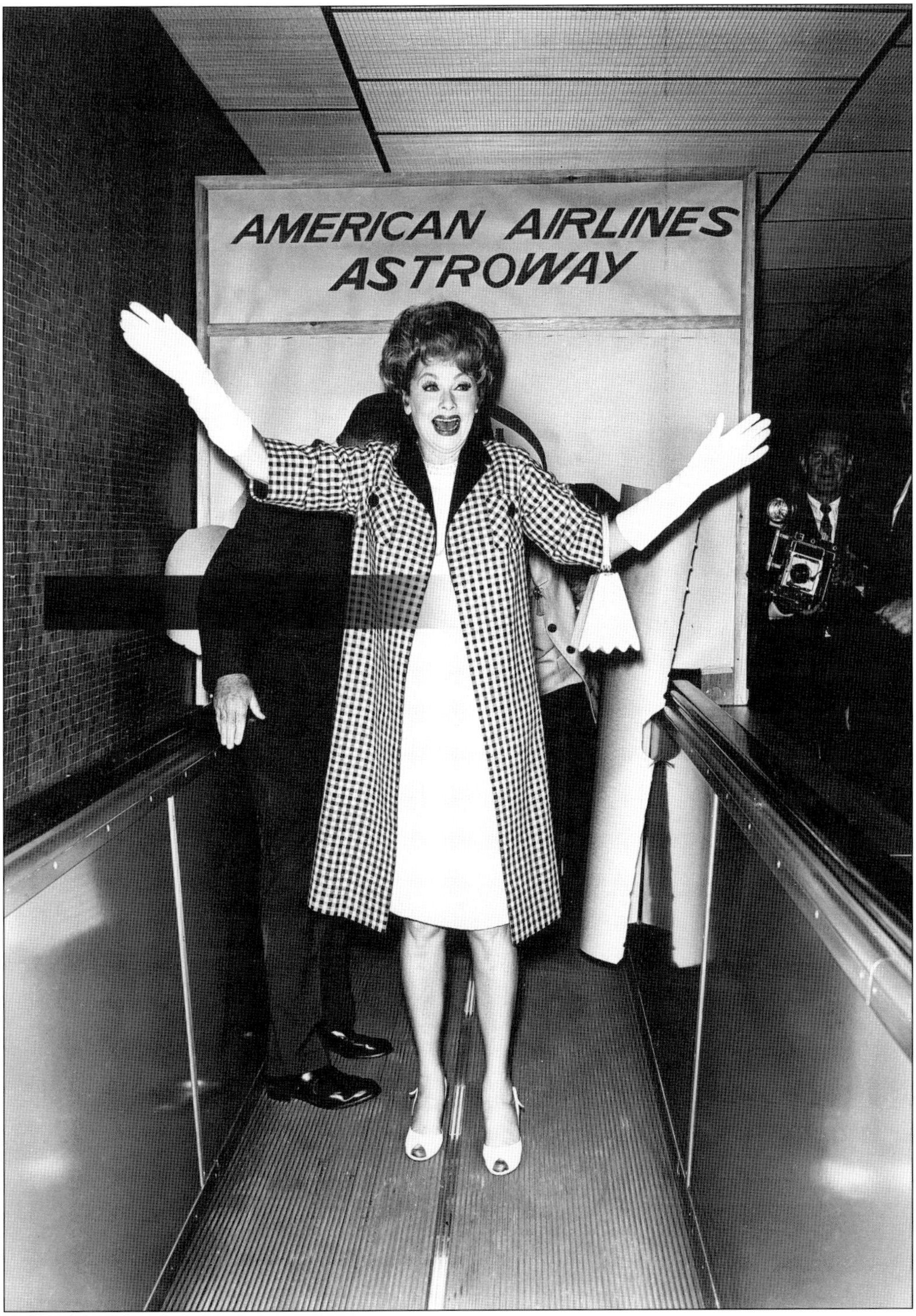

The proximity of LAX to Hollywood and its celebrities provided many mutual promotional opportunities. The stars often used their airport departures and arrivals as photo ops. In turn, the airport and airlines incorporated celebrities into their own promotions. Here television star Lucille Ball dedicates a new "Astroway" moving sidewalk in the American Airlines terminal.

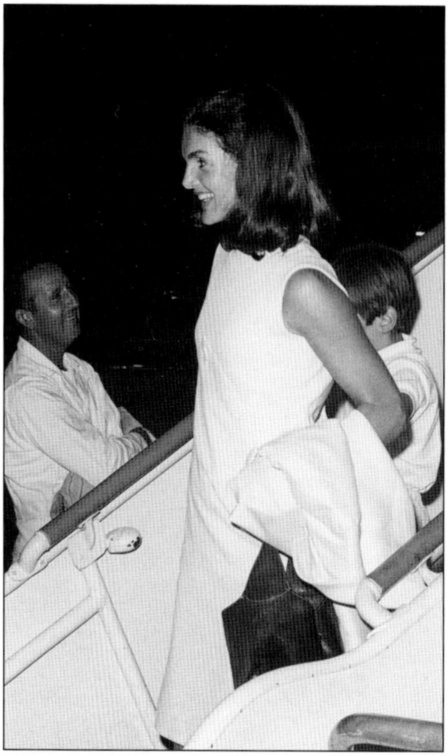

Former First Lady Jacqueline Bouvier Kennedy arrives at LAX in 1966 accompanied by young John F. Kennedy Jr.

Space-age astronauts vied with Hollywood stars and major-league athletes as the most popular celebrities during the 1960s. Here Apollo II astronaut Neil Armstrong is greeted by Mayor Sam Yorty (second from right) and others on his arrival at LAX on August 13, 1969.

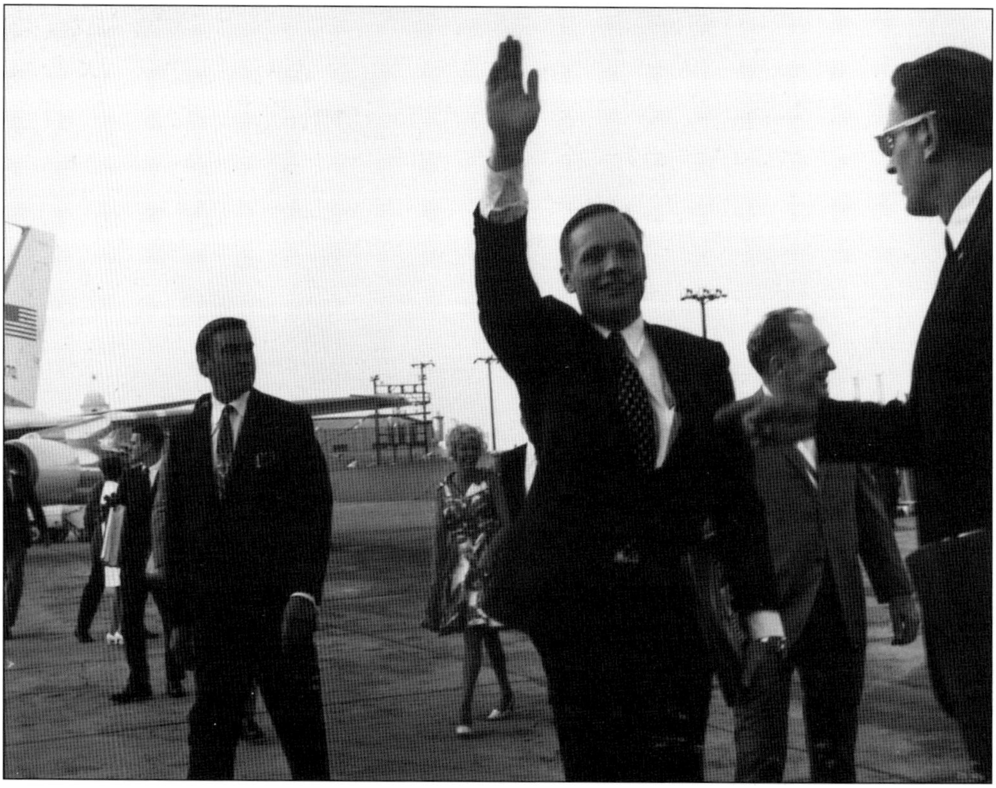

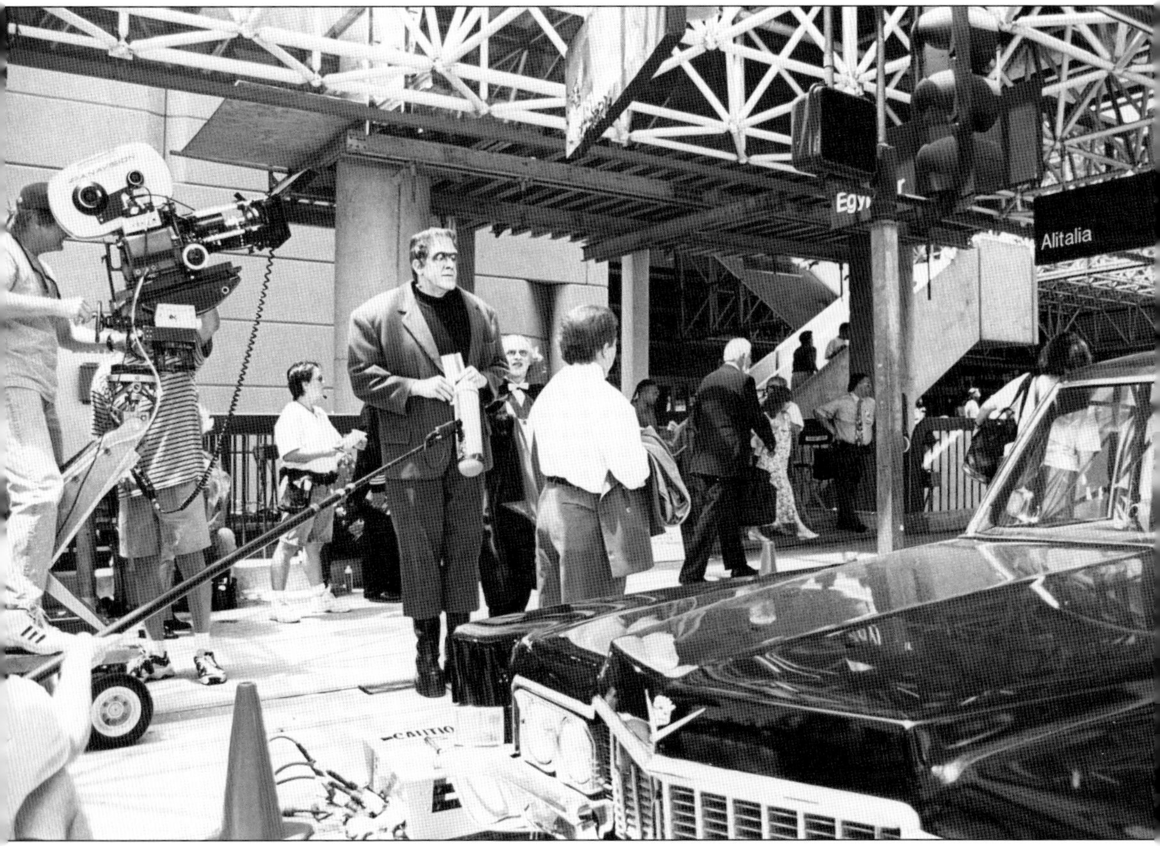

LAX travelers, particularly those from out of town, were thrilled to see their favorite motion picture and television stars working at the airport. Here the cast of *The Munsters* prepares for a scene for the film version of the television show in front of the Tom Bradley International Terminal.

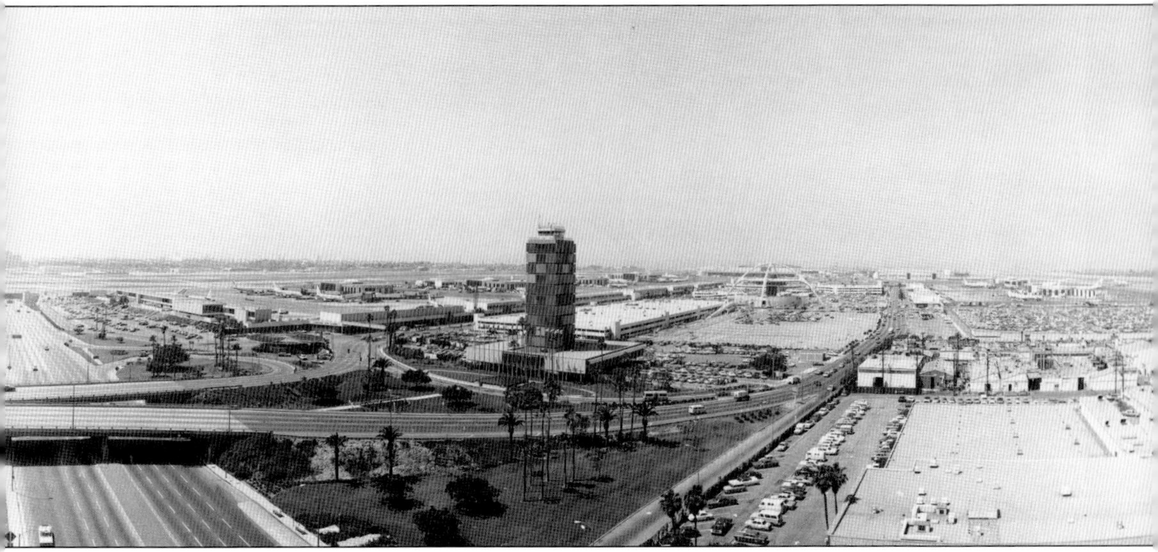

The 1960s LAX passenger terminal complex was a design unique both in function and appearance. Favorable comparisons were made by travel writers with other major domestic and international airports. However, most Southern Californians simply knew it was a vast improvement over the "old" terminals on the south side of Century Boulevard.

Five

Wide-Body Jets and the New LAX

The era of wide-body jets—B-747s, DC-10s, L-1011s—began in the 1970s. TransWorld Airlines inaugurated Los Angeles–New York service with Boeing 747s. The McDonnell Douglas DC-10, built in Long Beach, 20 miles south of Los Angeles, was the first aircraft to meet new federal standards for reduced noise and emissions. The British/French Concorde, the world's first supersonic transport, made a courtesy visit to Los Angeles on October 24, 1974. When the city celebrated 25 years of commercial passenger service in 1971, LAX had served more than 200 million passengers. In 1978, LAX and Van Nuys Airport marked their 50th anniversaries, Ontario International Airport its 55th.

The 1980s could very well be designated the "international decade." The Tom Bradley International Terminal was built in time to host thousands of athletes and officials from around the world arriving for the Los Angeles–hosted 1984 Olympics. The 963,000-square-foot Bradley Terminal housed 11 aircraft gates.

The second-level roadway was also completed in time for the Olympics, doubling curb space in front of each passenger terminal, speeding vehicles through the airport. Parking for LAX increased with completion of three new structures in the Central Terminal Area, and the addition of Lots C and D. A total of 26,550 parking spaces are available at LAX today.

In December 1989, the Department of Airports presented a $59.7-million check to the city to retire bonds originated in 1956. The bonds financed the Jet Age airport, including the Theme Building. Repayment of the bond issue was made without imposing any expense to Los Angeles taxpayers.

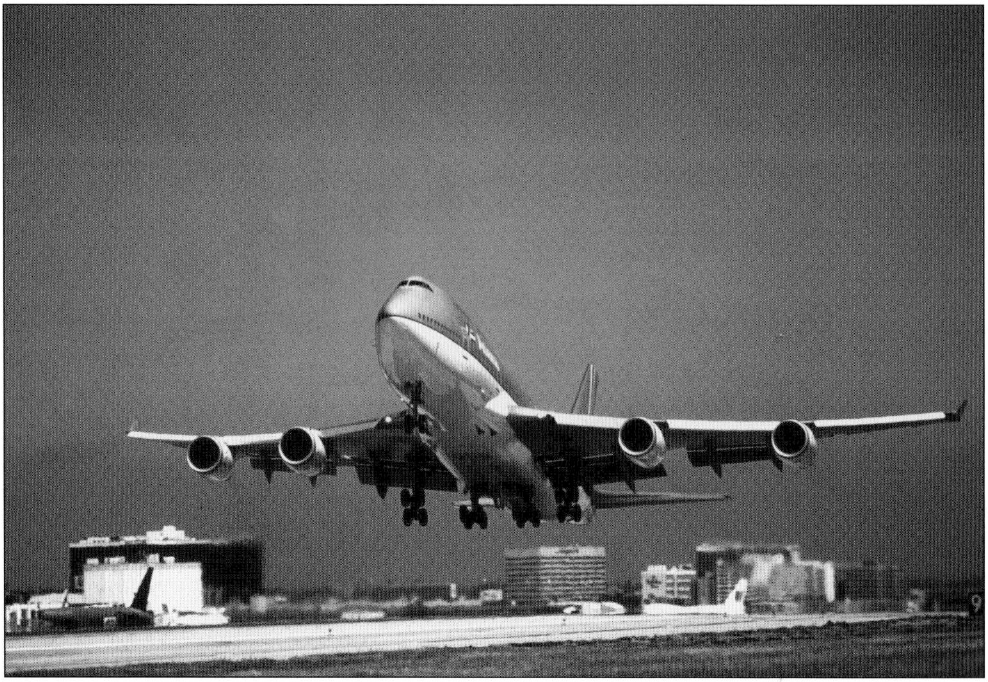

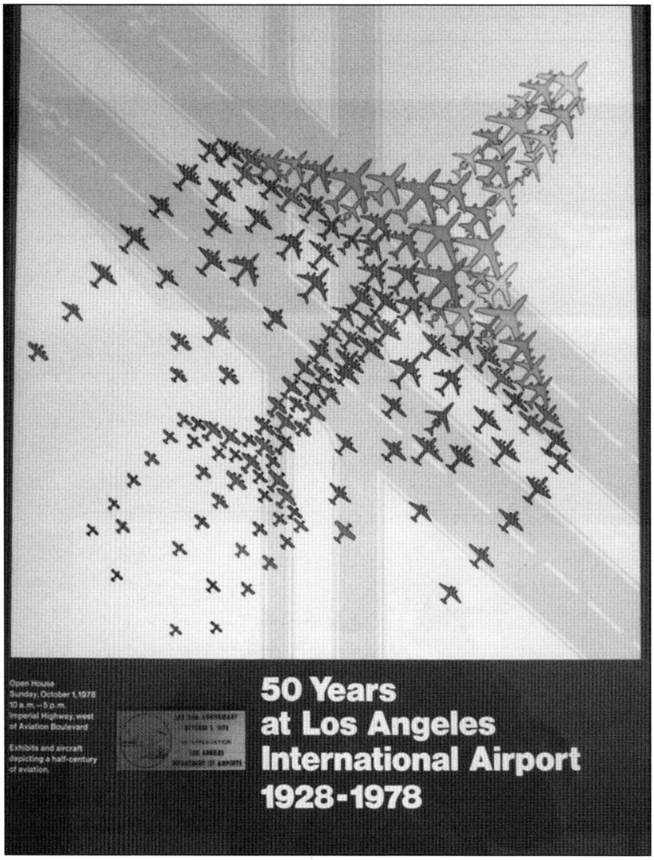

A Boeing 747-400 is caught here in a classic takeoff shot at LAX about 1990. Commonly called the Jumbo Jet, the Boeing 747 was developed at Paine Field near Everett, Washington, and was first flown commercially in 1970.

Los Angeles International Airport celebrated its 50th anniversary in 1978. The milestone came during a time of government deregulation of airlines, resulting in a vastly increased number of air carriers and new travel routes. The increased competition often meant lower ticket prices for travelers.

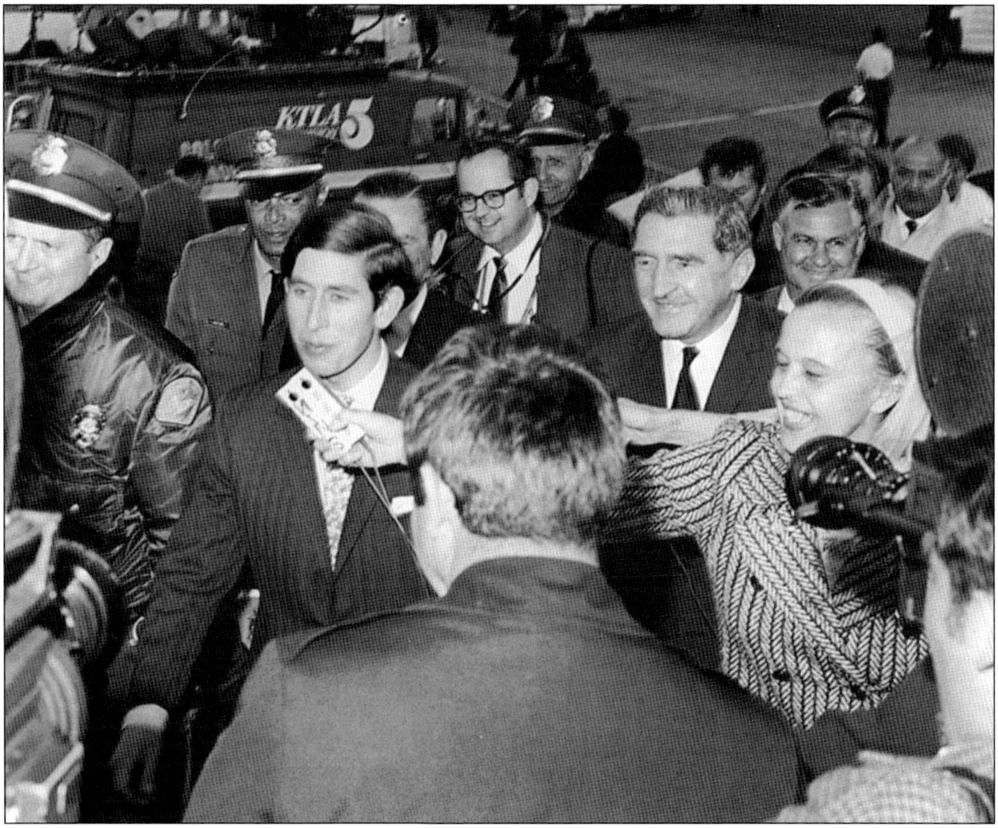

Great Britain's Prince Charles arrives at LAX in 1970, the year after his investiture as the Prince of Wales and the Earl of Chester on July 1, 1969. The prince was 22 years old in 1970. He and other members of the royal family often fly to North America to promote international goodwill and British economic interests.

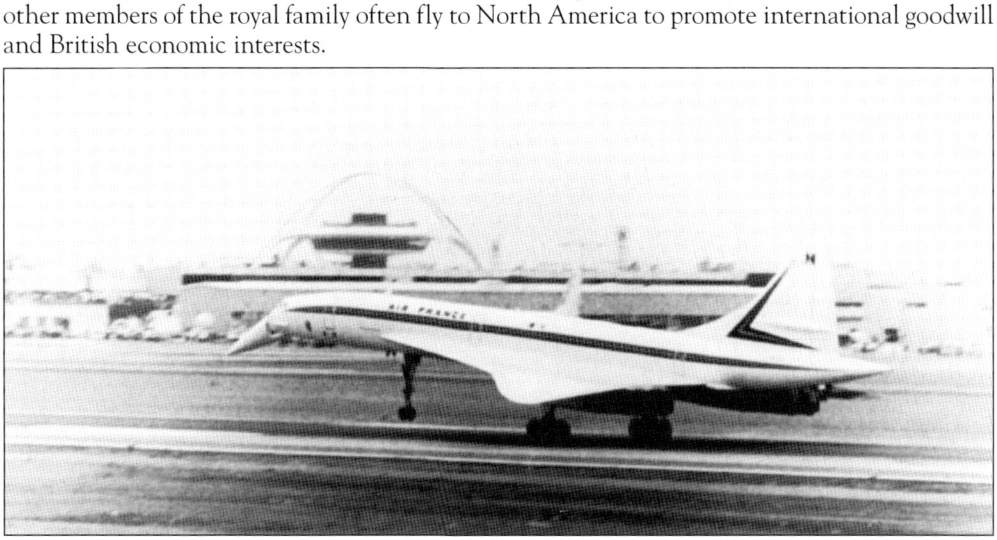

An Air France Concorde SST is seen arriving at LAX on October 23, 1974. The SST stood for "supersonic transport." These aircraft could cross the Atlantic Ocean in half the time of regular airliners. Both Air France and British Airways operated Concorde service from Paris's Charles De Gaulle Airport and London's Heathrow to New York's JFK and Washington, D.C.'s Dulles.

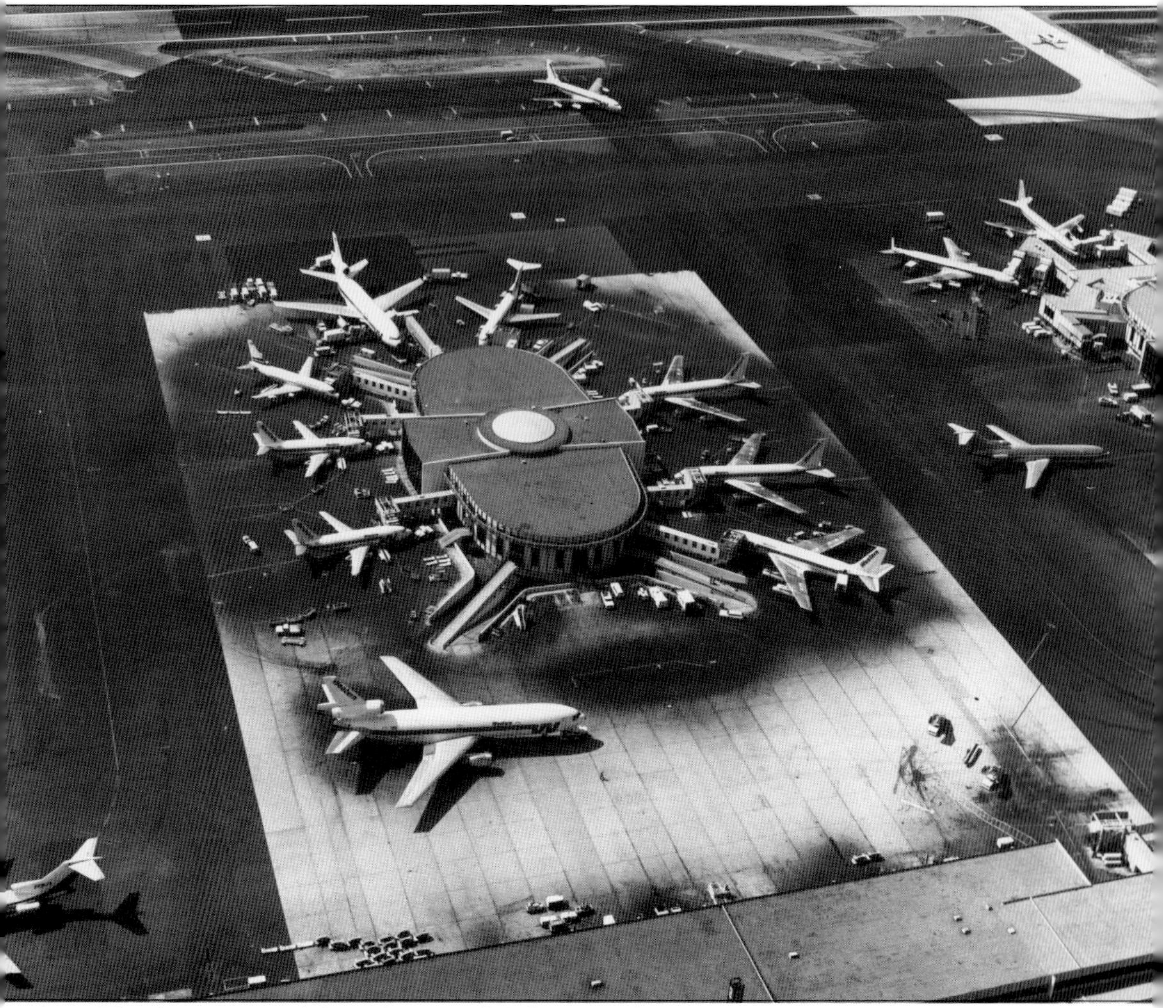

This dramatic aerial shot of Terminal 5 illustrates the traffic when a full house of jets loads at once. This photograph from the 1970s depicts the activity of dozens of support vehicles that are needed to service and load and offload the varyingly sized behemoths of the skies.

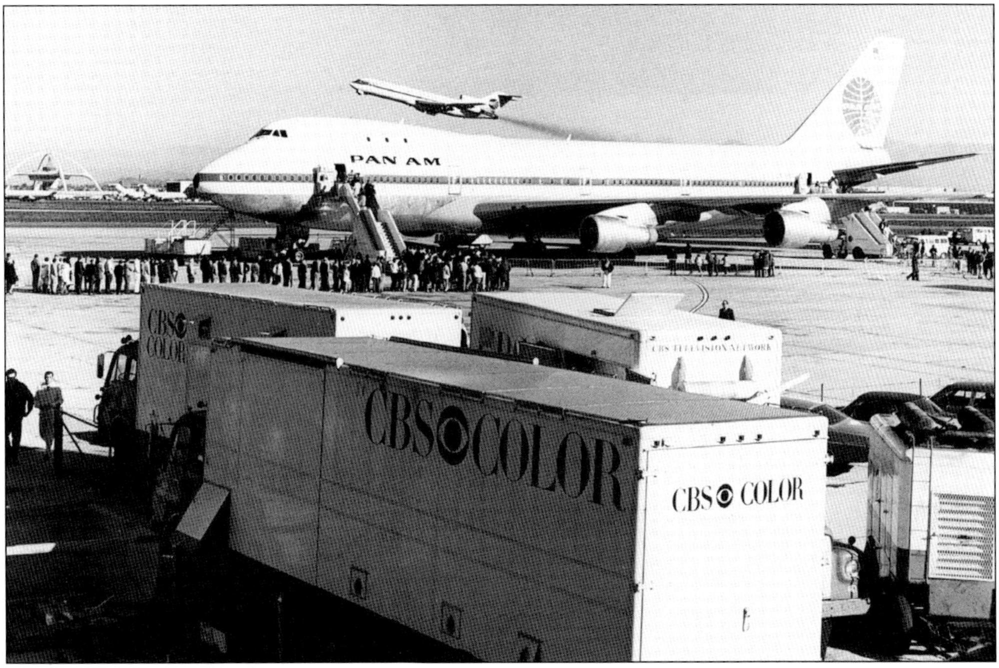

Television coverage has been a consistent aspect of life at LAX. As a flight takes off in the background, the press converges at the foot of the mobile steps on the tarmac to cover a visiting dignitary's arrival on a Pan Am 747 in 1976. Note the CBS News control trucks in the foreground.

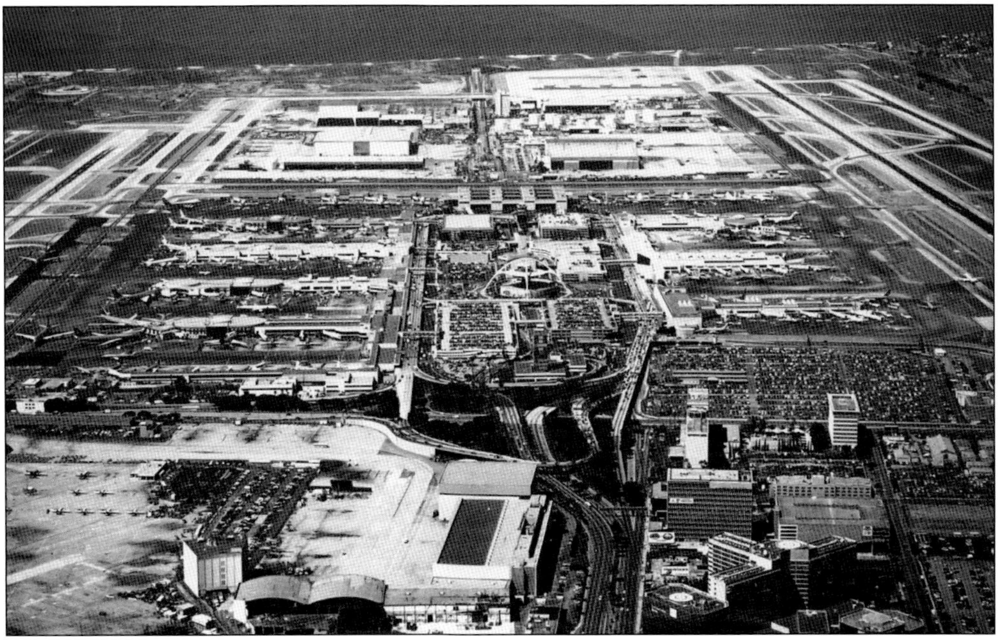

The LAX Central Terminal Complex is immediately recognizable as airborne travelers approach the airport. This contemporary view includes the Century Boulevard approach in the foreground, arched Theme Building, parking structures, administrative offices, and control tower at center, and terminal buildings around the perimeter of the second level roadway. The Pacific Ocean is visible in the distance.

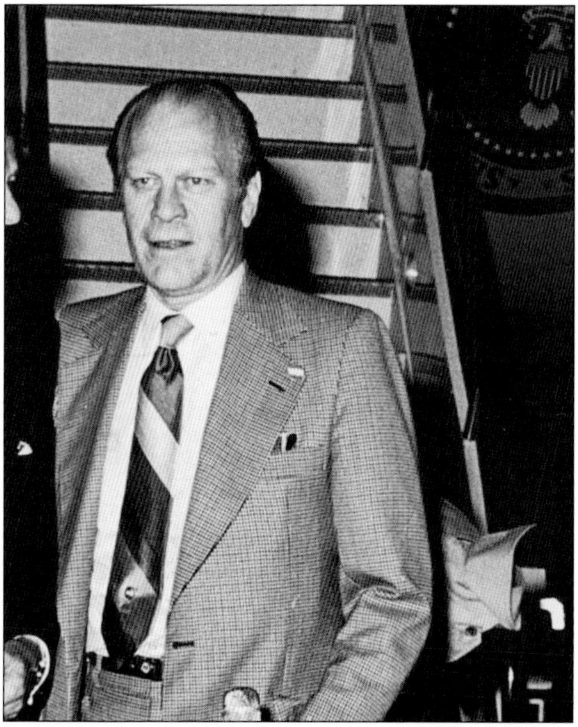

Pres. Gerald Ford was also a frequent traveler through LAX. He is seen here in 1974, the year he assumed the presidency from Richard Nixon, who relinquished the post after the Watergate scandal. President Ford's wife often arrived and departed through LAX as she founded and oversaw her namesake substance abuse clinic, the Betty Ford Center in Rancho Mirage, near Palm Springs.

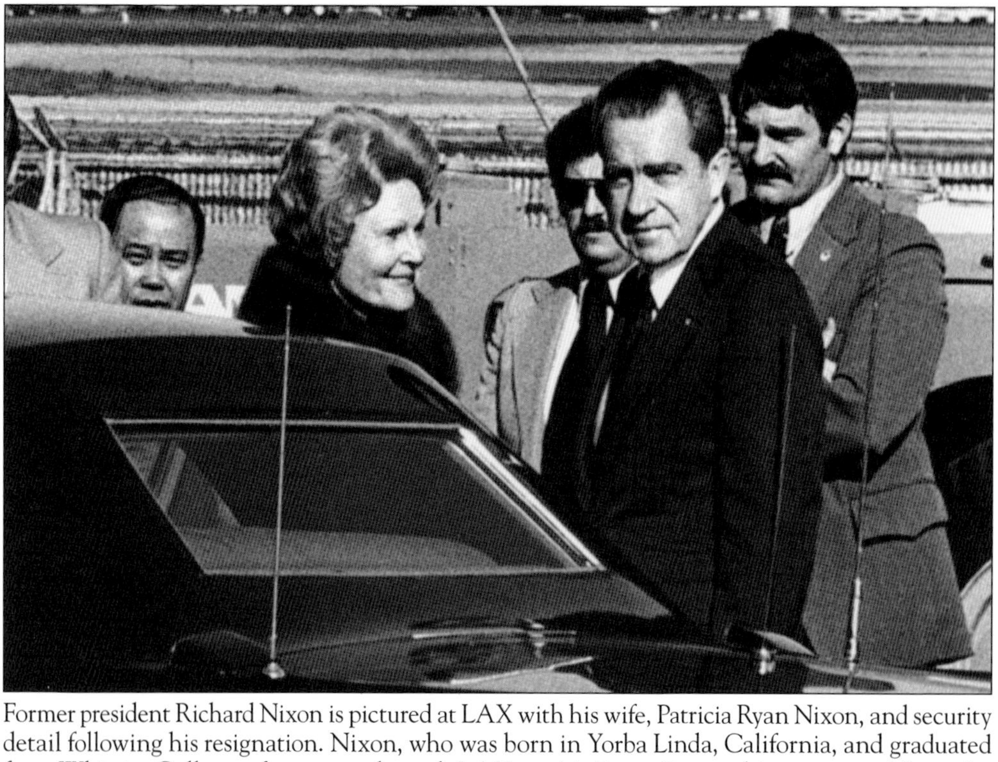

Former president Richard Nixon is pictured at LAX with his wife, Patricia Ryan Nixon, and security detail following his resignation. Nixon, who was born in Yorba Linda, California, and graduated from Whittier College, often came through LAX on Air Force One on his way to and from the Western White House on the bluff overlooking San Clemente, in Orange County.

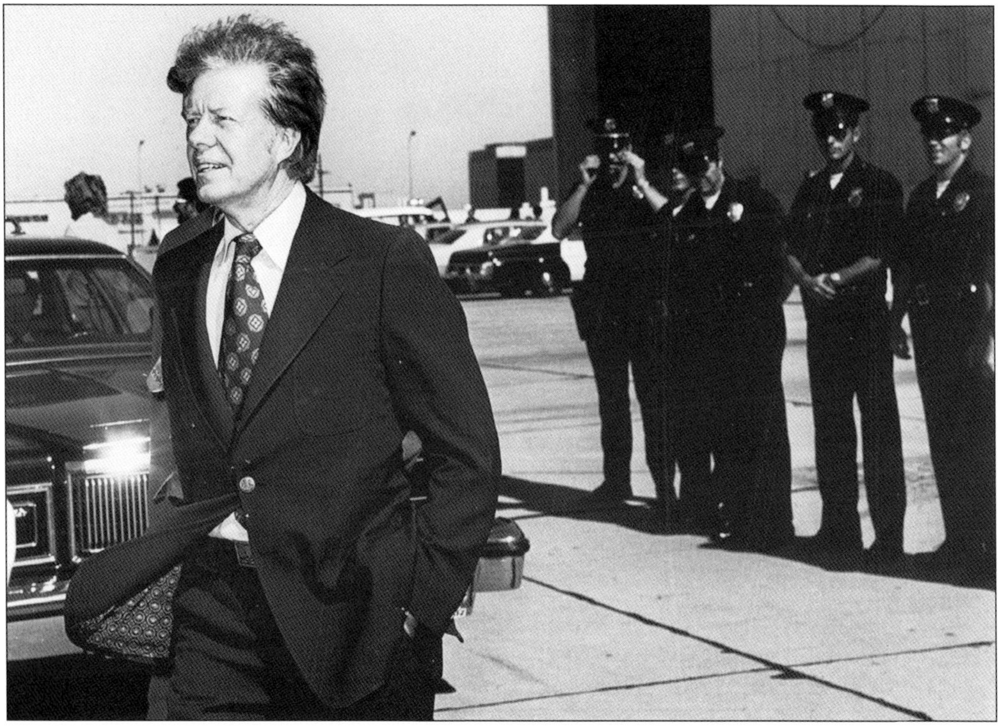

Jimmy Carter arrives at LAX in 1976 as the president-elect. The former governor of Georgia served in the Oval Office from 1977 to 1981. One of his many trips through LAX included travel to a Los Angeles taping of the TV show *What's My Line?*, when panelist Soupy Sales guessed the secret guest's identity.

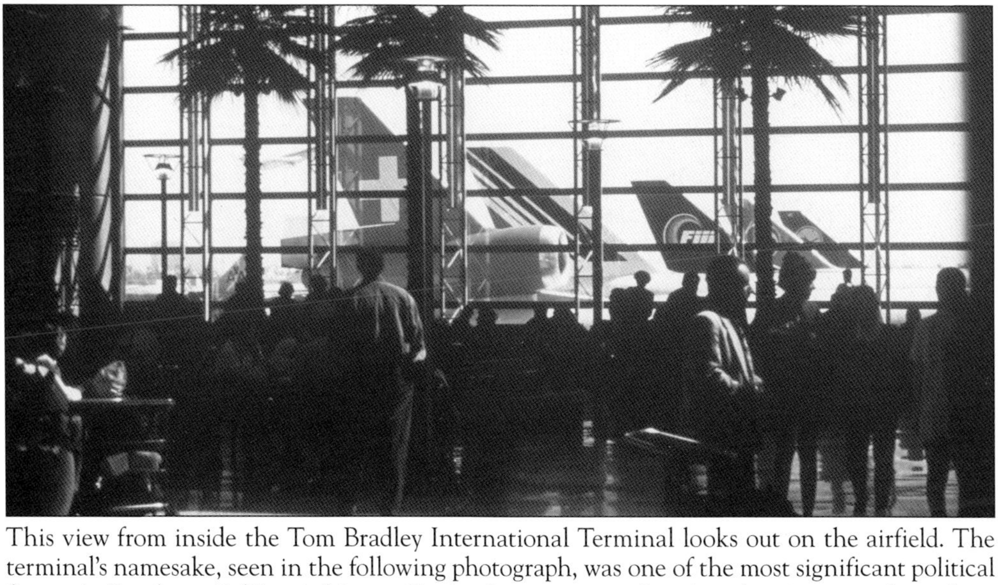

This view from inside the Tom Bradley International Terminal looks out on the airfield. The terminal's namesake, seen in the following photograph, was one of the most significant political figures in Southern California history. During his tenure as a Los Angeles city councilman from 1963 to 1973, and especially during his influential two decades and five terms (1973 to 1993) as the mayor of Los Angeles, Bradley was an unceasing advocate of transportation gains and especially of the needs of LAX.

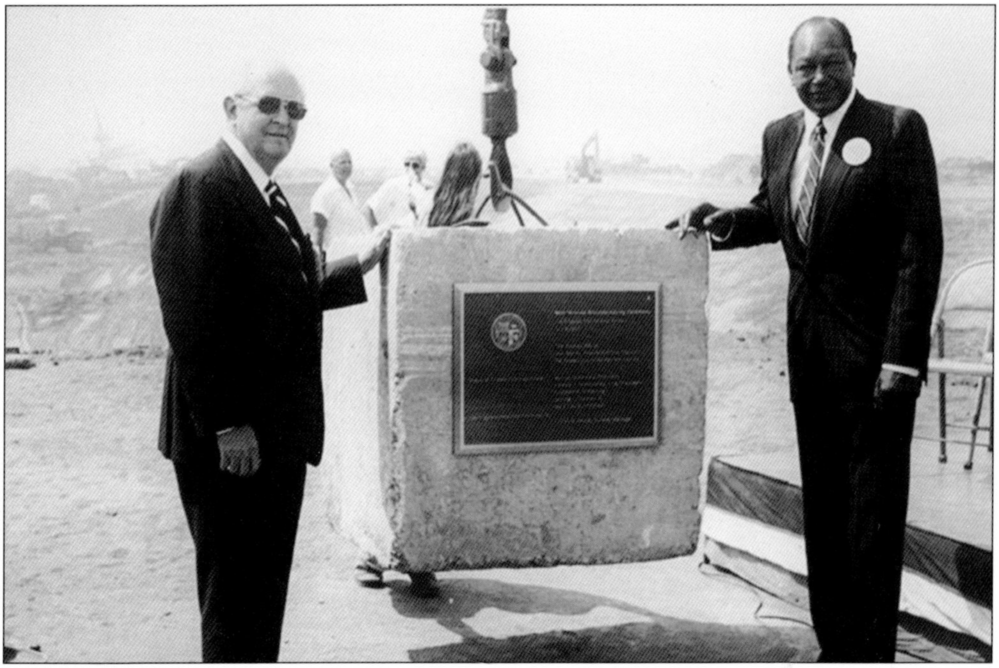

Department of Airports executive director Clifton Moore, left, and Los Angeles mayor Tom Bradley pose with the cornerstone of the new Tom Bradley International Terminal in 1982. The terminal was completed with the forthcoming 1984 summer Olympic Games in mind. Bradley was among the first African Americans to be elected as the mayor of a major U.S. city.

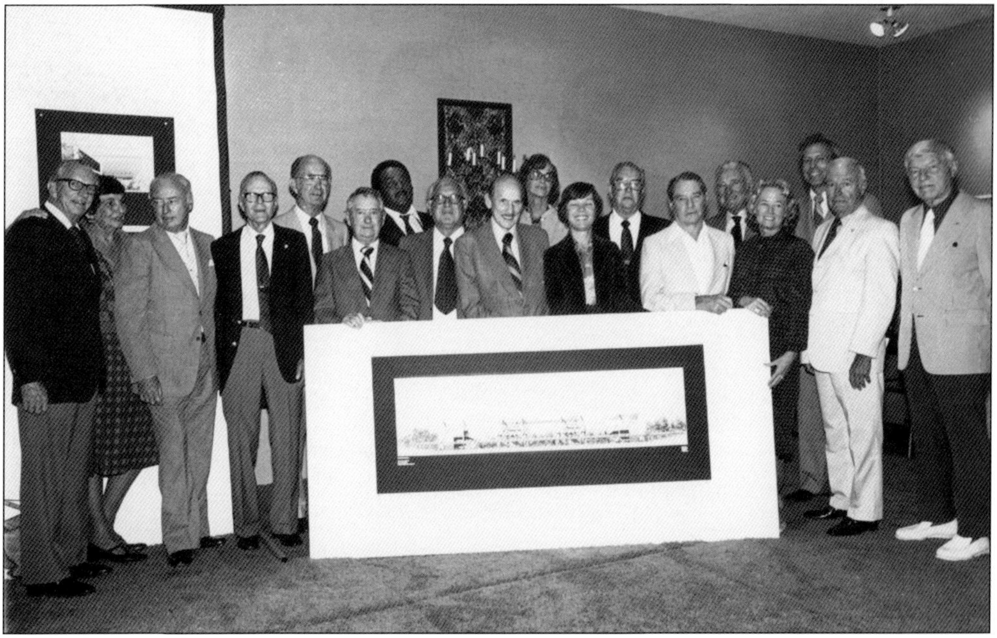

Completion of "The New LAX" just ahead of the 1984 Olympic Games in Los Angeles was marked by numerous special events. Here former members of the Board of Airport Commissioners tour expanded facilities, which included the new Tom Bradley International Terminal, remodeled domestic terminals, a second-level roadway, and other improvements.

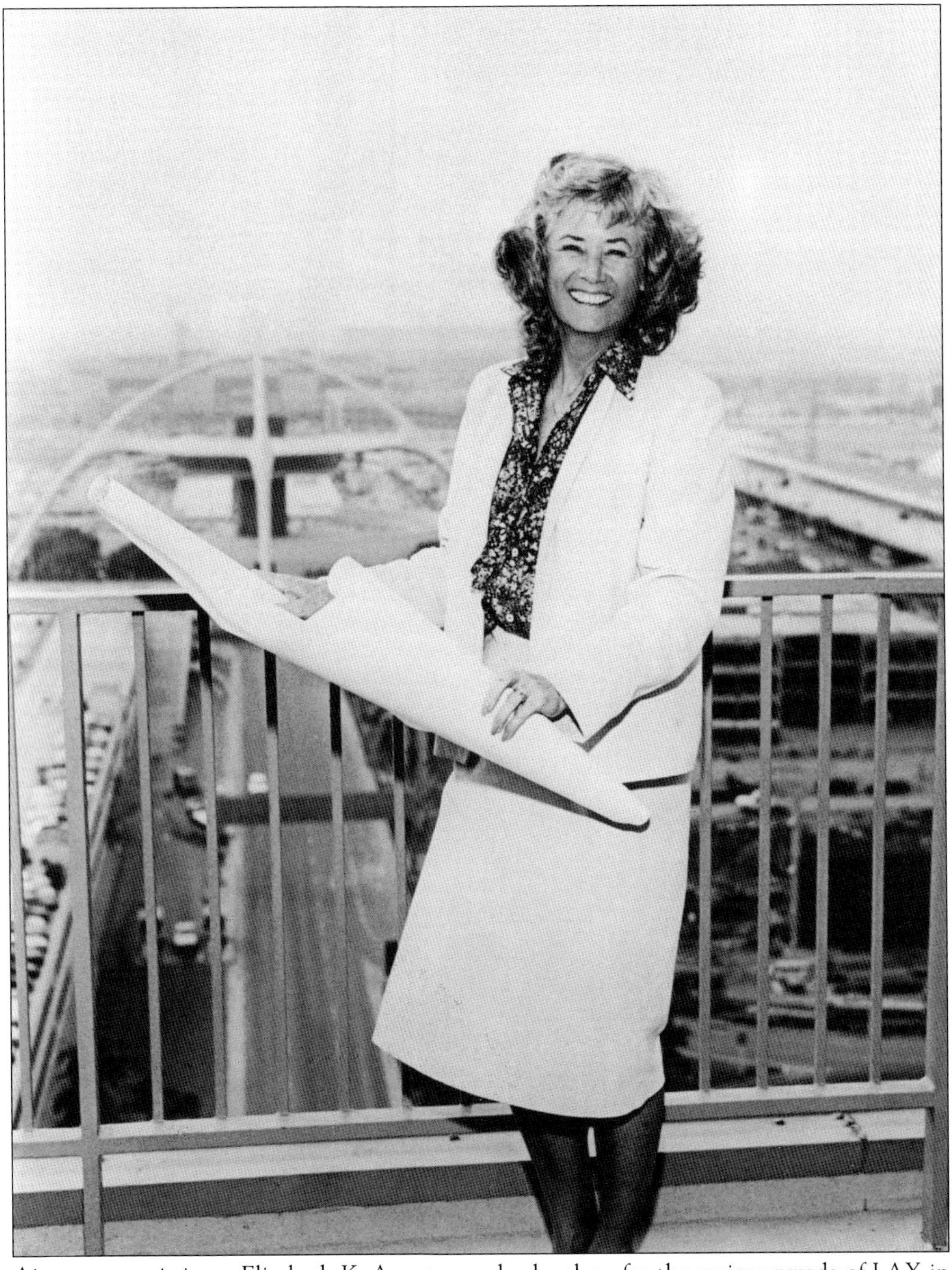

Airport commissioner Elizabeth K. Armstrong checks plans for the major upgrade of LAX in preparation for the 1984 Olympic Games. Armstrong served as commission president for several years during the 1980s. She made special efforts to see that airport employees were recognized for their contributions to LAX.

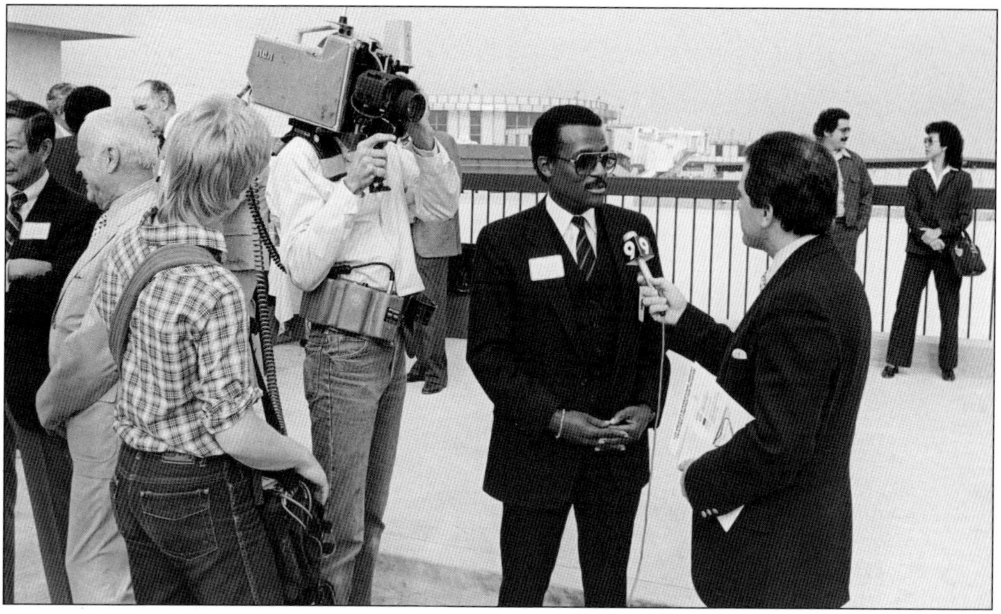

Attorney Johnnie L. Cochran Jr. is interviewed by news media as LAX prepares for the coming of the 1984 Olympic Games to Los Angeles. Cochran was appointed by Mayor Tom Bradley in 1981 to serve on the Airport Commission during the critical years of LAX modernization. Cochran was elected to several terms as commission president.

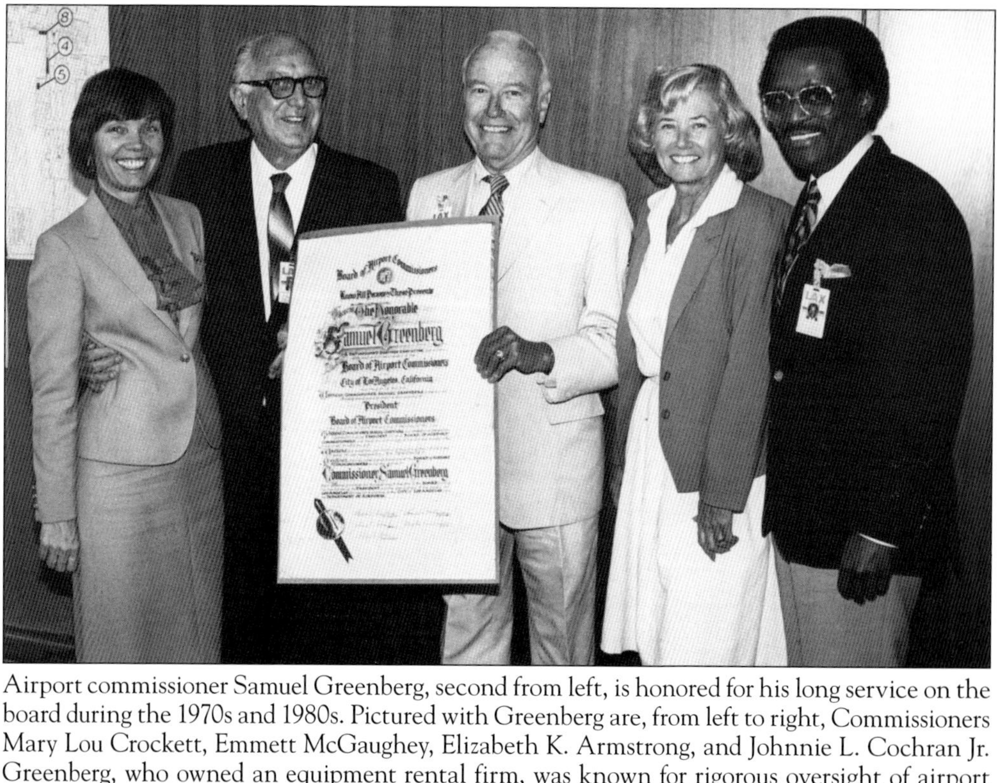

Airport commissioner Samuel Greenberg, second from left, is honored for his long service on the board during the 1970s and 1980s. Pictured with Greenberg are, from left to right, Commissioners Mary Lou Crockett, Emmett McGaughey, Elizabeth K. Armstrong, and Johnnie L. Cochran Jr. Greenberg, who owned an equipment rental firm, was known for rigorous oversight of airport administrative and operational expenses. The board's meeting room was named in his honor.

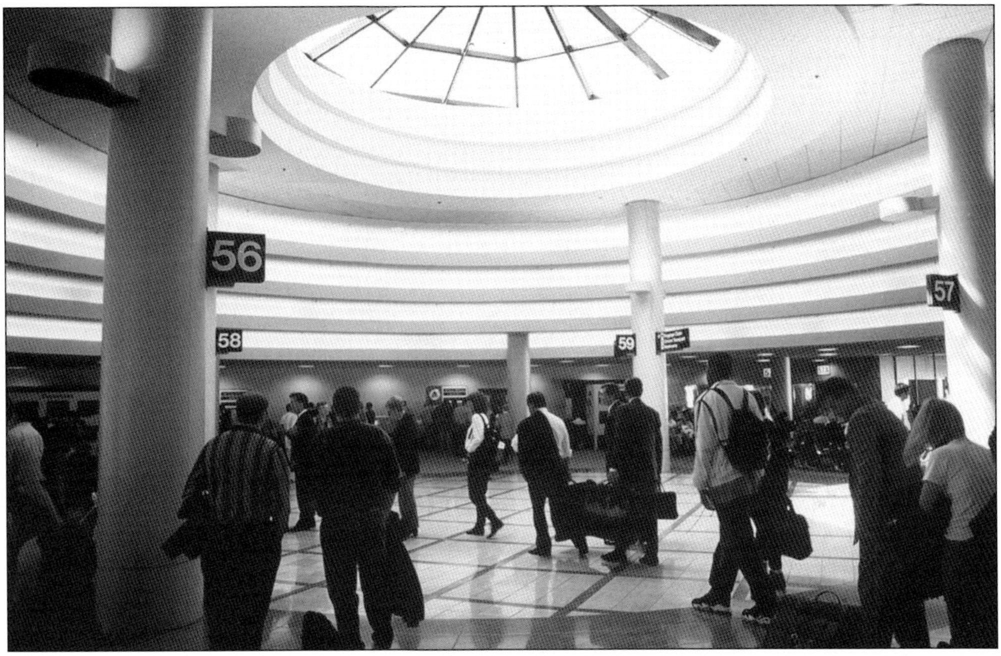

This shot shows the refurbished interior of Terminal 5, also known as the Delta Terminal. In 1987, Delta merged with Western Airlines of Los Angeles and took over the Western hubs at Los Angeles and Salt Lake City. Based in Atlanta, Delta once was known as the "Airline of the South."

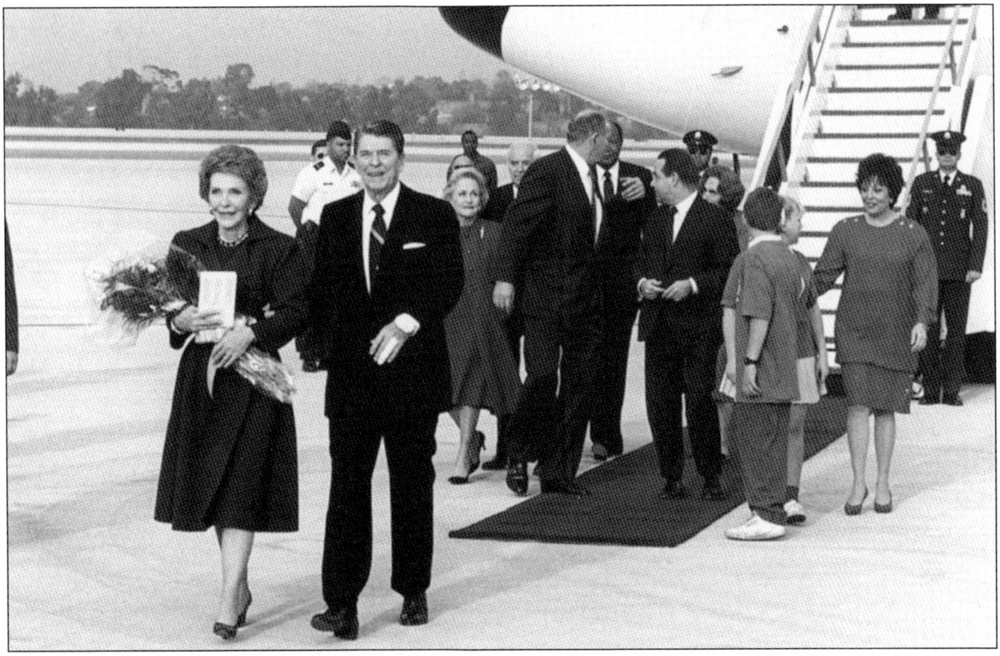
Pres. Ronald and Mrs. Nancy Reagan are welcomed at LAX in 1989 en route to their Santa Barbara County ranch. Reagan frequently used LAX as governor of California from 1967 to 1975 and as president from 1981 to 1989. Occasionally his trips from the White House to his ranch on Air Force One bypassed LAX to land at Vandenberg Air Force Base. The former Air Force One, a Boeing 707, now is on exhibit at the Reagan Presidential Library in Simi Valley, California.

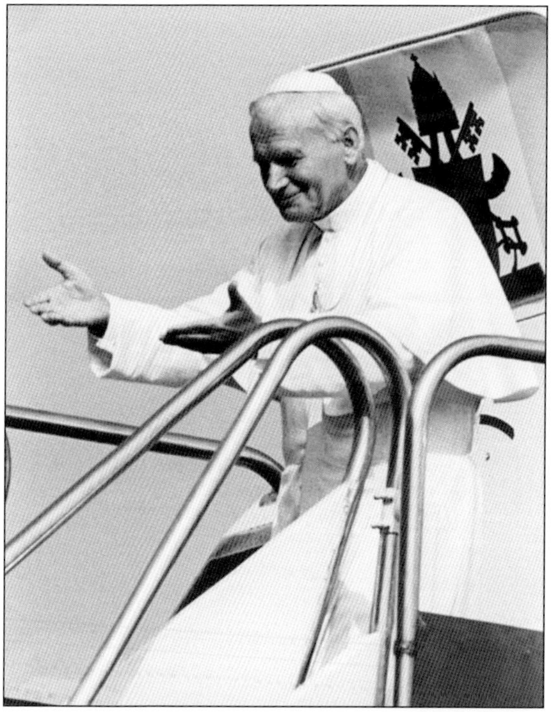

Pope John Paul II arrives at LAX in 1987, the 10th year of his reign as the worldwide leader of the Roman Catholic Church. The pontiff, who began life as the Polish-born Karol Jozef Wojtyla, served 26 years in Vatican City until his death in 2005. He used LAX more than any other pope and was known as the most traveled pontiff in history, having visited more than 100 nations during his reign.

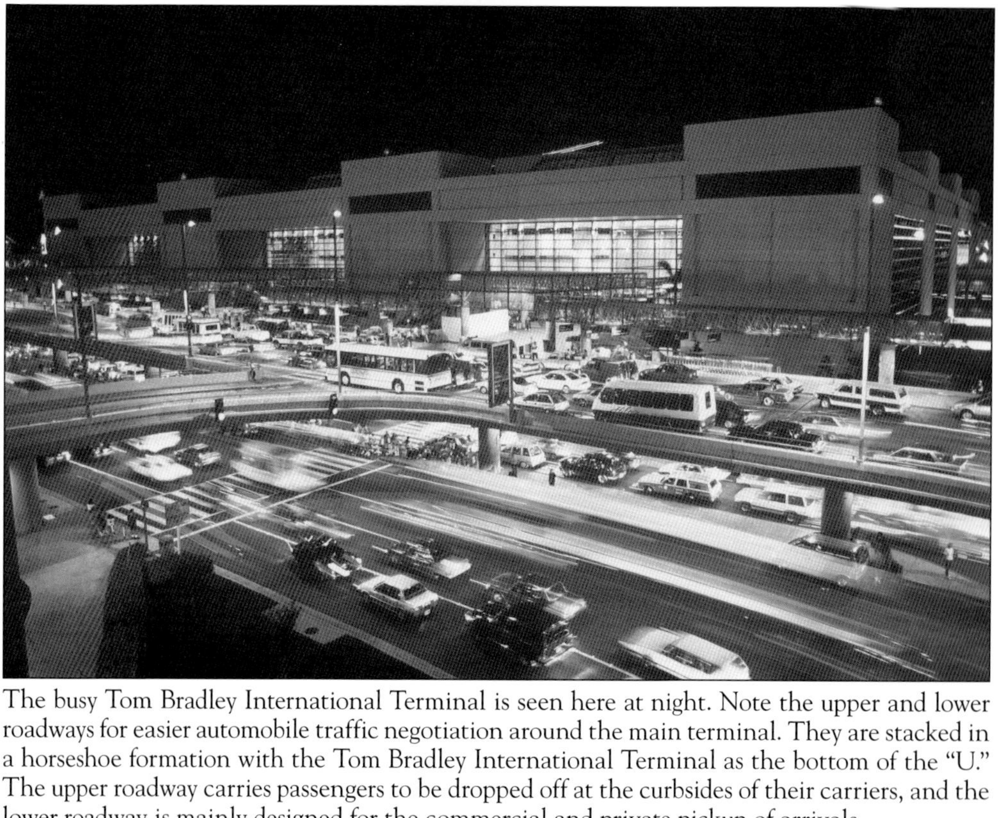

The busy Tom Bradley International Terminal is seen here at night. Note the upper and lower roadways for easier automobile traffic negotiation around the main terminal. They are stacked in a horseshoe formation with the Tom Bradley International Terminal as the bottom of the "U." The upper roadway carries passengers to be dropped off at the curbsides of their carriers, and the lower roadway is mainly designed for the commercial and private pickup of arrivals.

Six

Into the 21st Century

Major growth in air travel and air cargo marked the 1990s and made modernizing the airport for the 21st century a vital concern. Hangar No. 1 (the only building remaining from Mines Field) was designated a National Historic Landmark and the Theme Building a City of Los Angeles Cultural and Historic Landmark.

Tom Bradley International Terminal underwent a $14-million renovation in 1997, adding 35,000 square feet of eateries and shops. The LAX Gateway and its pylons, some over 100 feet tall, were lit in August 2000 to welcome the Democratic National Convention.

United Airlines completed a $300-million renovation of three terminals and built a new cargo facility in 2001. American Airlines completed a $250-million renovation of Terminal 4 in 2002.

On September 11, 2001, terrorists hijacked four flights—three of them bound for LAX—and flew them into the New York World Trade Center, the Pentagon, and a field in southern Pennsylvania. Immediately following the attacks, LAX employees worked diligently and stoically to secure the airport and transport thousands of stranded passengers. The airport was closed for the first time in its history—for two and a half days—as 178 aircraft sat grounded on the airfield. LAX was among the first U.S. airports to reopen after security recertification. Since then, LAX has led U.S. airports in implementing a myriad of new federally mandated security measures to enhance public safety.

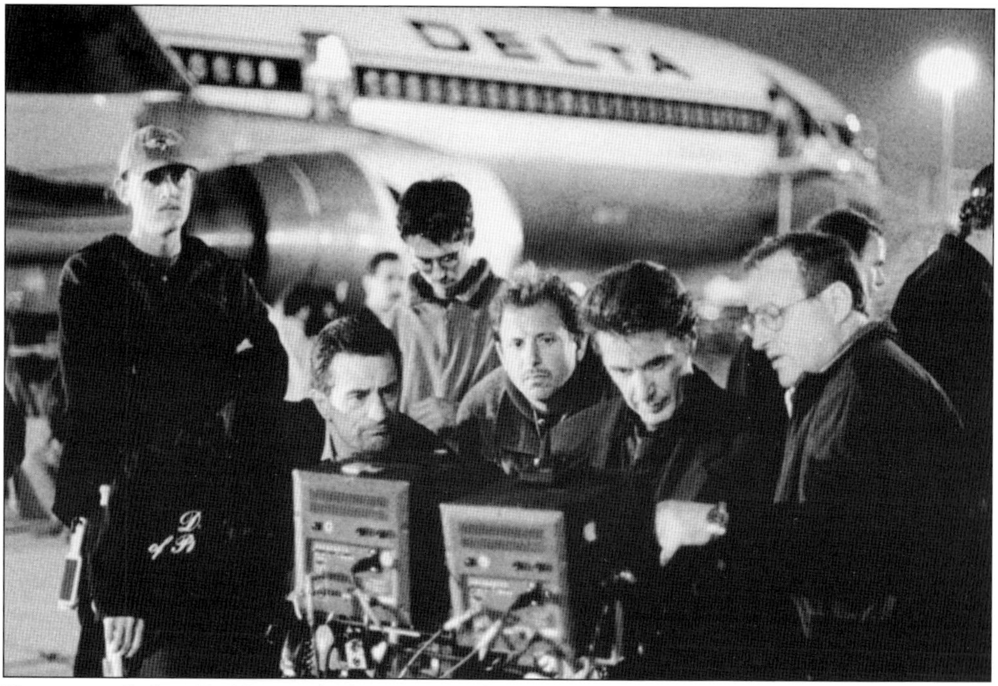

Here actors Robert De Niro and Al Pacino watch the rushes from the crime thriller *Heat*, directed by Michael Mann, at LAX facilities in 1995. Among the many movies shot at the airport were *Speed*, *Rush Hour*, *Jerry Maguire*, *Almost Famous*, *Mission: Impossible II*, *Mulholland Drive*, *Swordfish*, *Adaptation*, *Catwoman*, Steven Spielberg's *Catch Me If You Can*, and Quentin Tarantino's *Kill Bill Vol. II*.

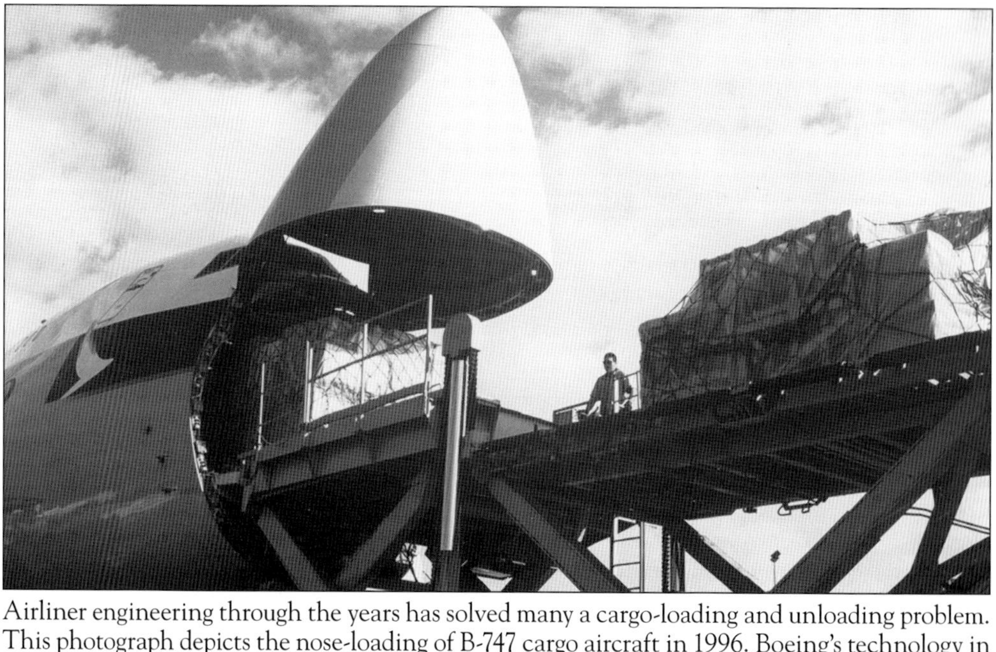

Airliner engineering through the years has solved many a cargo-loading and unloading problem. This photograph depicts the nose-loading of B-747 cargo aircraft in 1996. Boeing's technology in the giant cargo arena has led to the Boeing 747 Large Cargo Lifter, also known as the Dreamlifter, of which there are two in the world with a third on the way as of 2007.

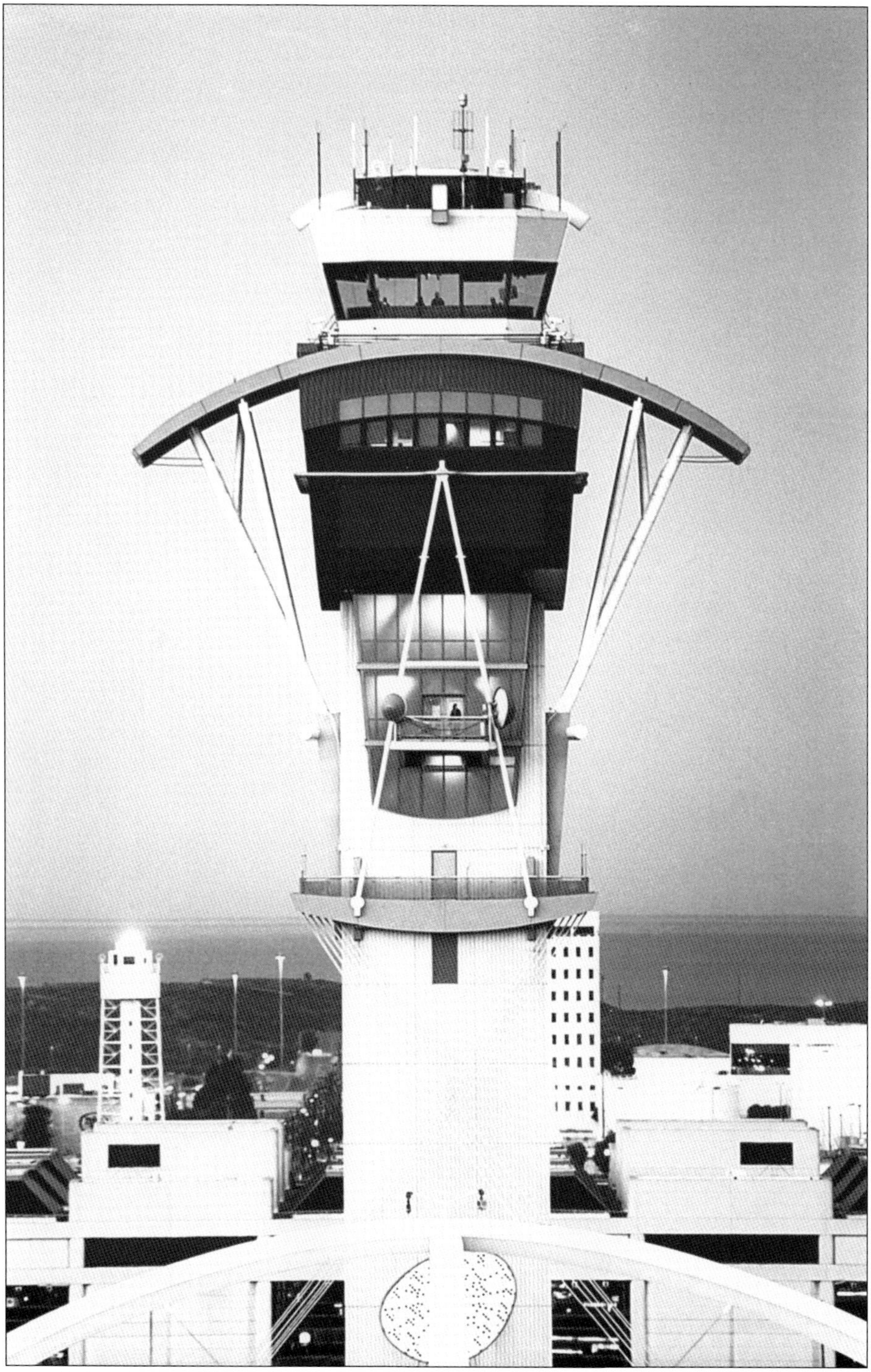

The new LAX Air Traffic Control Tower is seen in 1996. The new tower, replacing one that had served since 1959, was a cooperative effort of the Federal Aviation Administration and Los Angeles World Airports. The more centralized location and increased height of the new tower permitted an improved view of aircraft operations throughout the airport.

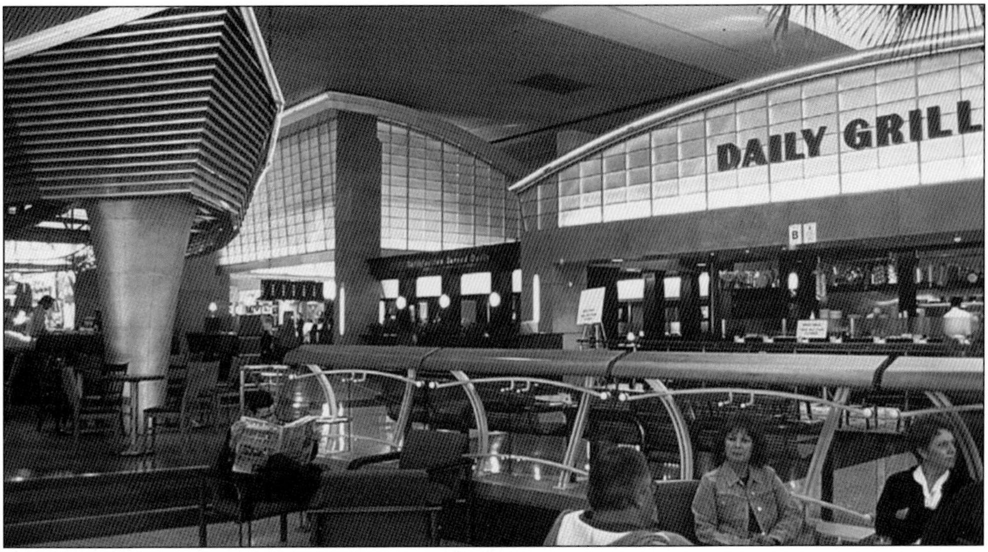

The interior of Tom Bradley International Terminal is shown in 1997. This terminal, built in preparation for the 1984 Olympic Games, occupies a site once devoted to commuter aircraft passengers. Mayor Tom Bradley served as the city's chief executive for 20 years, longer than any other mayor of Los Angeles before or since.

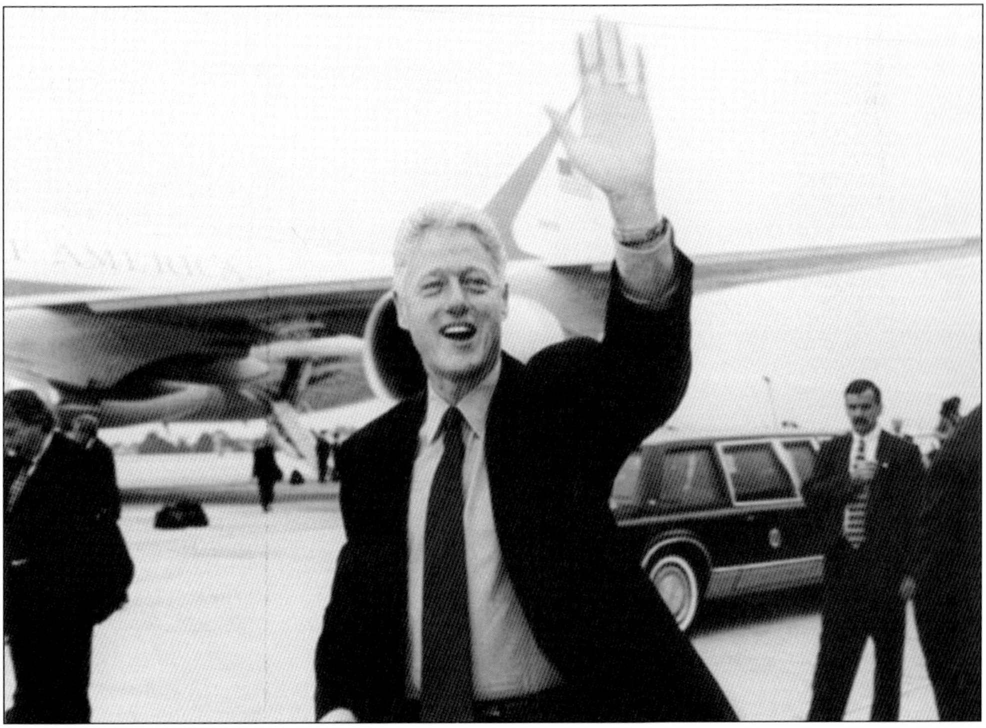

U.S. president Bill Clinton was photographed here in 1999 during one of his many swings through LAX. Democrat Clinton enjoyed a warm relationship with Hollywood's liberals and would travel through LAX often, including for the August 2000 Gala Hollywood Farewell Salute to Bill Clinton, held at a private Brentwood estate and featuring such attendees as First Lady Hillary Rodham Clinton, John Travolta, Cher, Brad Pitt, Muhammad Ali, and Diana Ross.

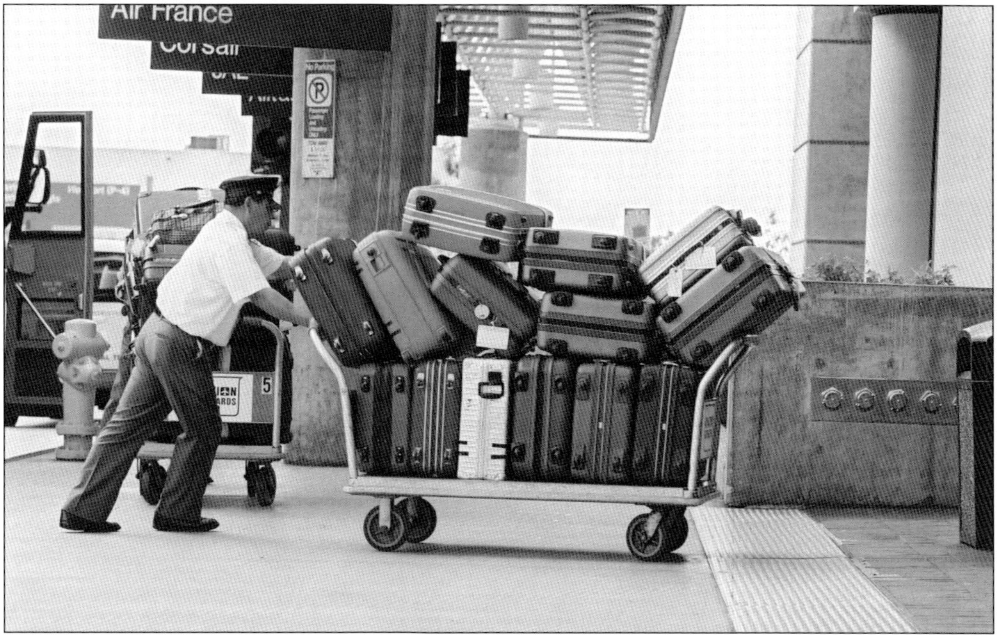

The luggage volume expanded at LAX in 1999, as depicted above. But 9/11 brought stricter luggage supervision. Standard operating procedure called for each piece of stowaway and carry-on luggage to be X-rayed before it made it into a terminal.

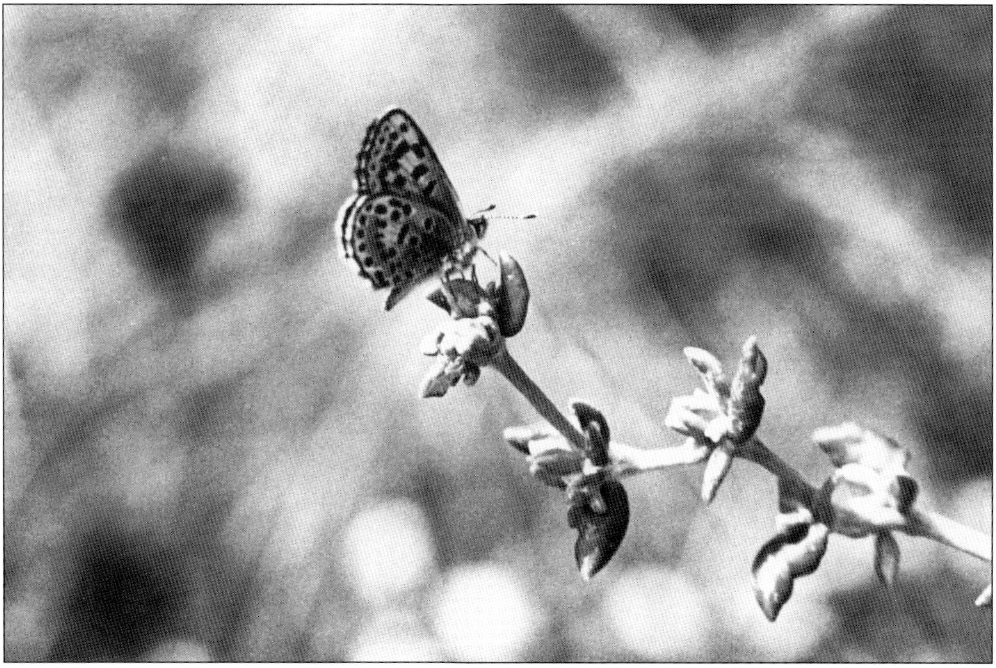

One of the most protected groups of any species at LAX is the El Segundo blue butterfly. This once dwindling species numbered in the replenished tens of thousands on the LAX dunes, according to a 2000 count. Known by the scientific name *Euphilotes bernardino allyni*, the El Segundo blue is believed to only exist on the LAX dunes, the nearby Chevron refinery site in El Segundo, and at Malaga Cove on Palos Verdes Peninsula.

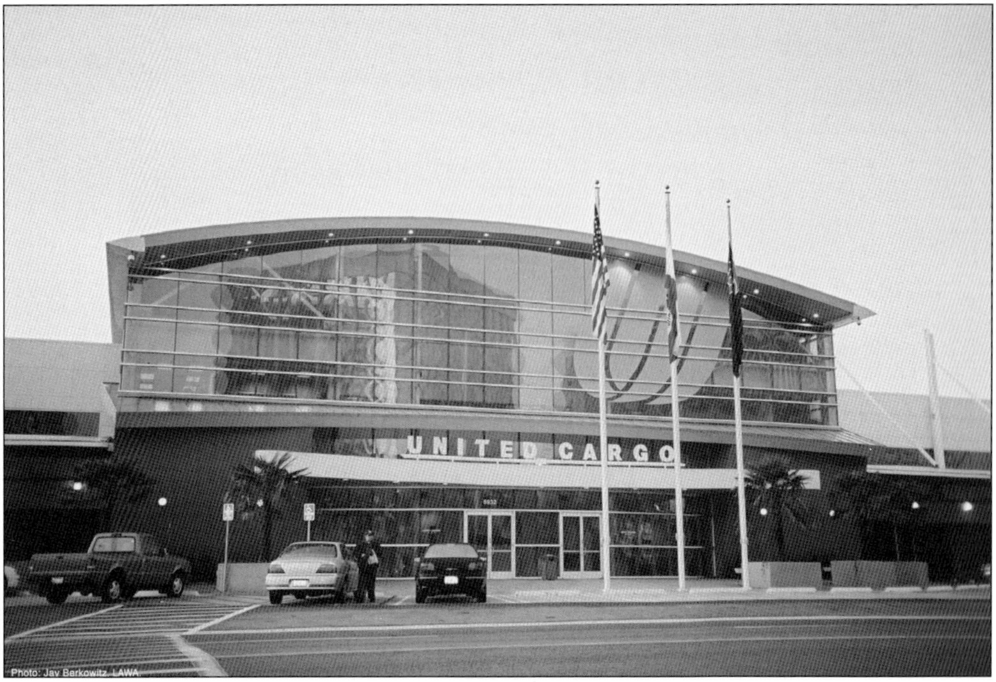

United Airlines cargo terminal is depicted in 2001. This huge cargo facility is a reminder that cargo transport remains a key component of airline operations and profitability not only for United but for many other air carriers.

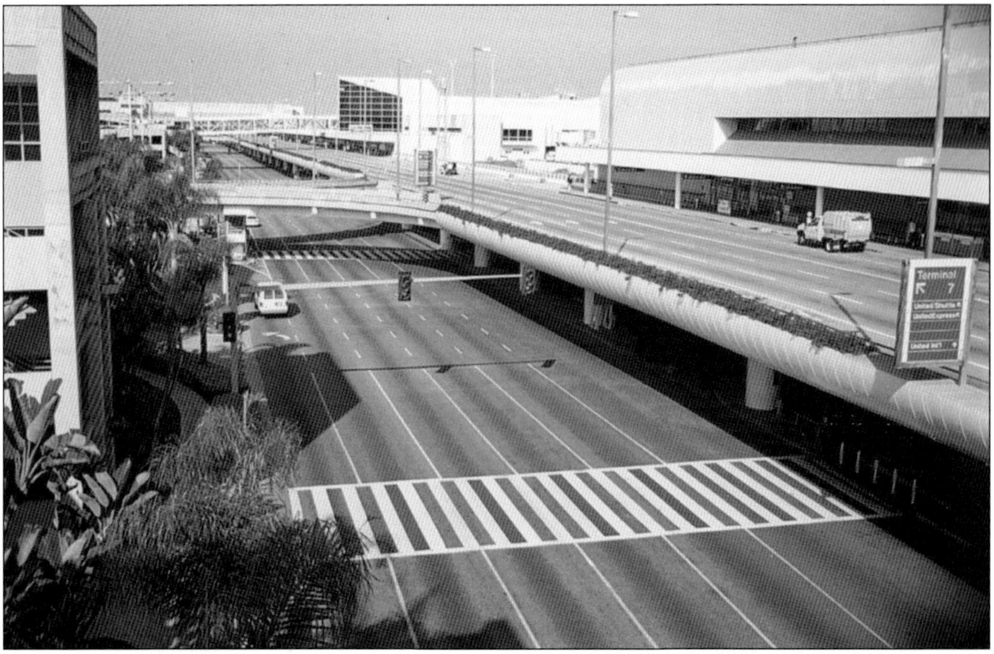

This is the eerie, quiet LAX roadway and curbside on September 11, 2001. All civil aircraft operations were halted in Los Angeles and across the United States in the aftermath of the 9/11 emergency. When air travel resumed, passengers faced tightened security procedures administered by the federal government.

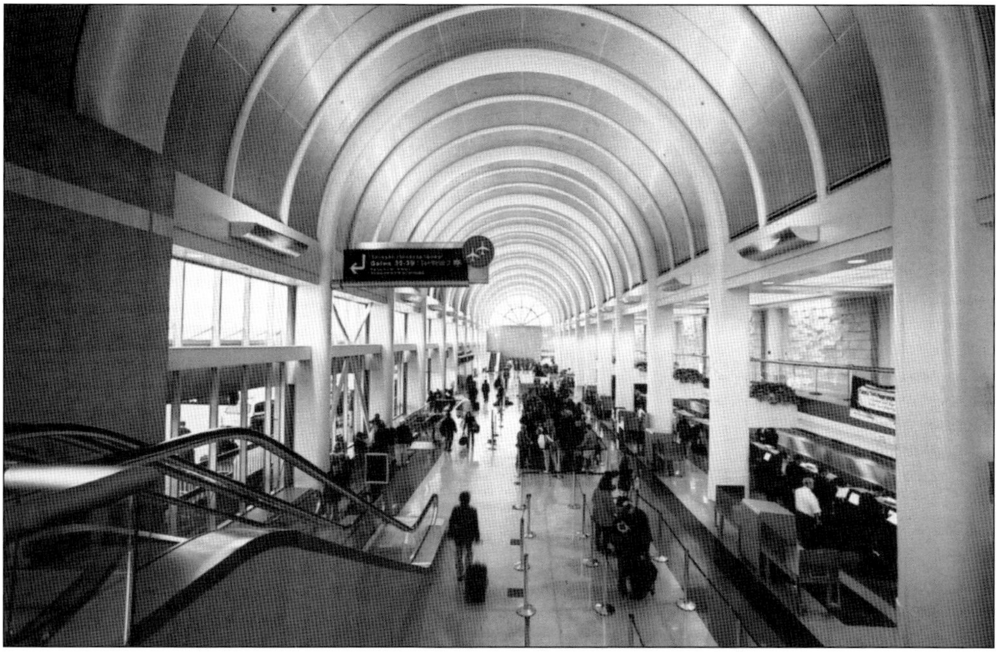

The updated American Airlines terminal is depicted in 2002.

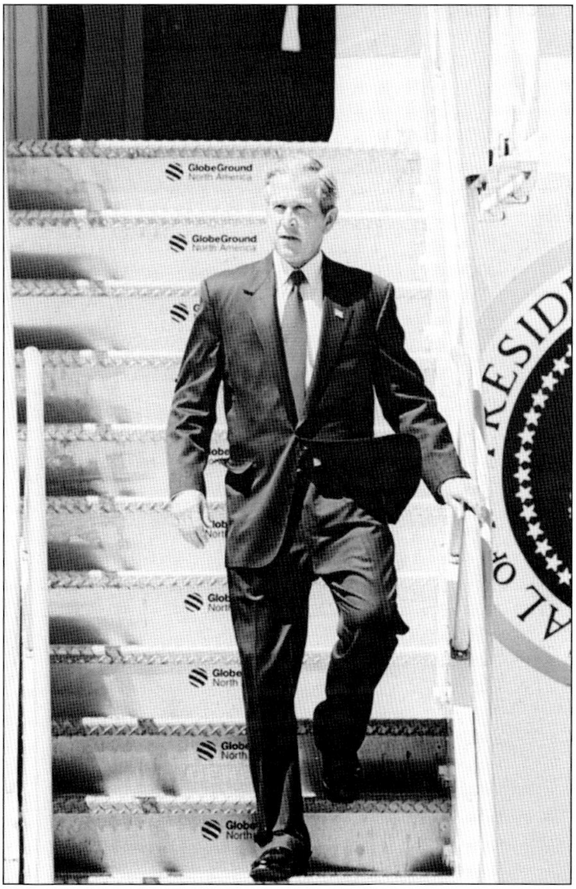

Pres. George W. Bush is seen here in LAX in 2002, the year after he was inaugurated as the 43rd president of the United States. The former managing general partner of the Texas Rangers baseball team of the American League, Bush also served a term as governor of Texas prior to his ascension to the highest post in the land.

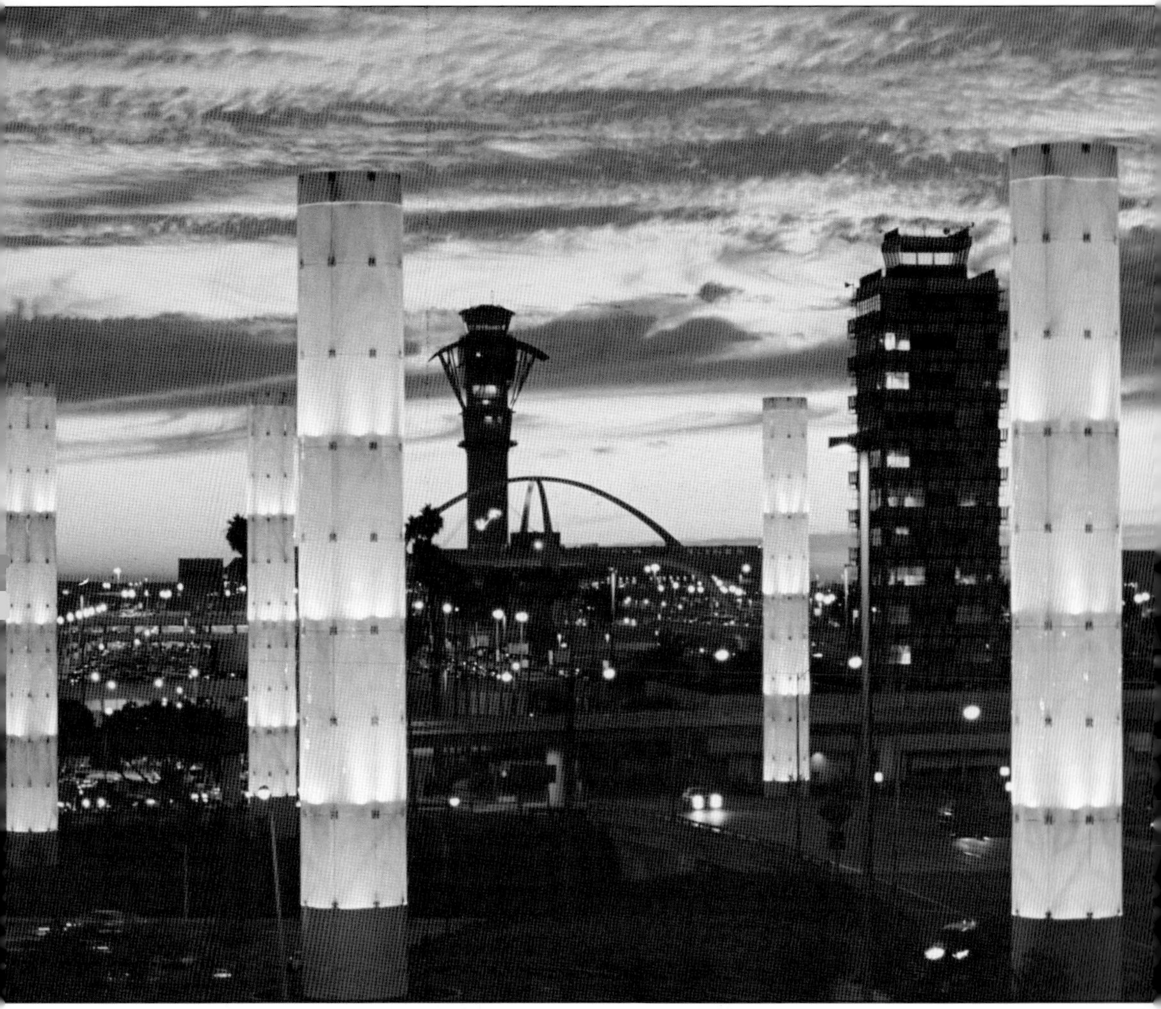

Here is the LAX Gateway at sunset, with the Theme Building and control tower at center, in 2004. As the airport entered the 21st century, its advantageous Pacific Rim location continued to enable its dominance as the nation's busiest origin-destination airport, meaning one where travelers begin and end their excursions rather than simply changing planes.

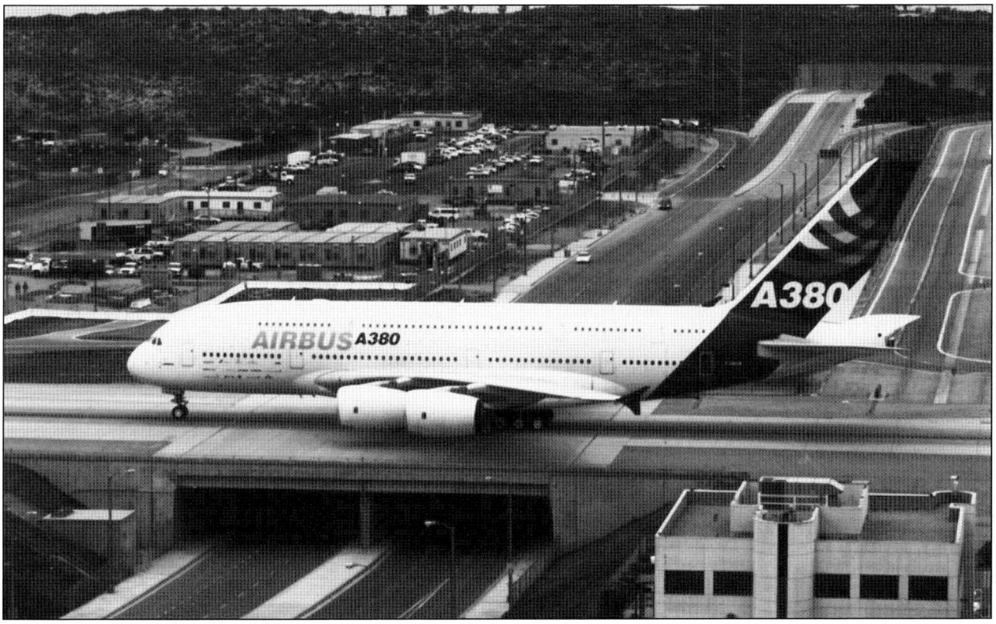

The coming of the Airbus A-380 in the first decade of the 21st century mandated major renovations at LAX. This huge aircraft required new passenger gates and other terminal modifications as well as significant redesign and modification of certain runways and taxiways.

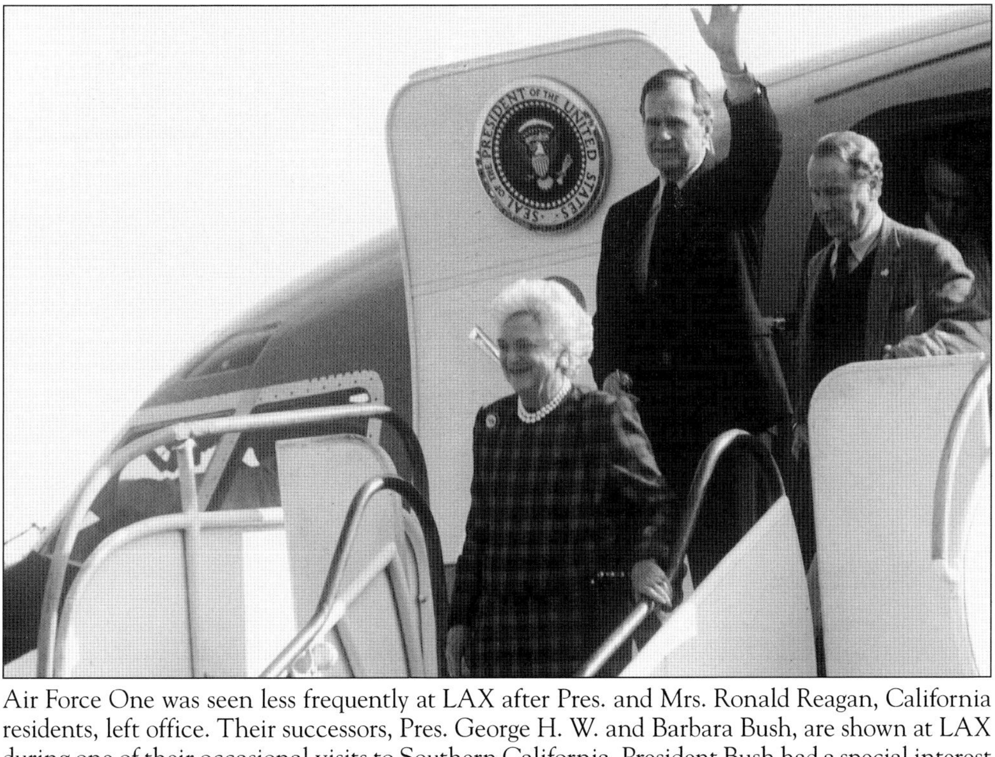

Air Force One was seen less frequently at LAX after Pres. and Mrs. Ronald Reagan, California residents, left office. Their successors, Pres. George H. W. and Barbara Bush, are shown at LAX during one of their occasional visits to Southern California. President Bush had a special interest in aviation, having earned the Distinguished Flying Cross as a carrier pilot in the Pacific theater during World War II. George H. W. Bush was president from 1989 to 1993.

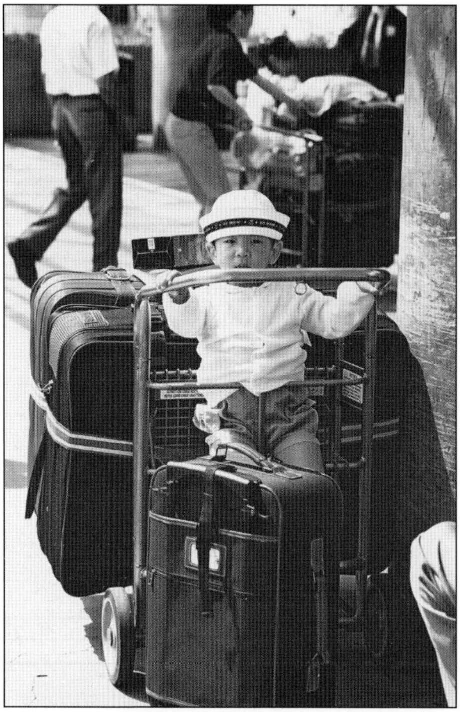

Children were seldom seen during the early years at Mines Field. Later, as air travel became safer and less expensive, parents frequently brought their children along on vacation flights. Airlines at LAX and elsewhere arranged special procedures for the comfort and safety of children who needed to travel alone.

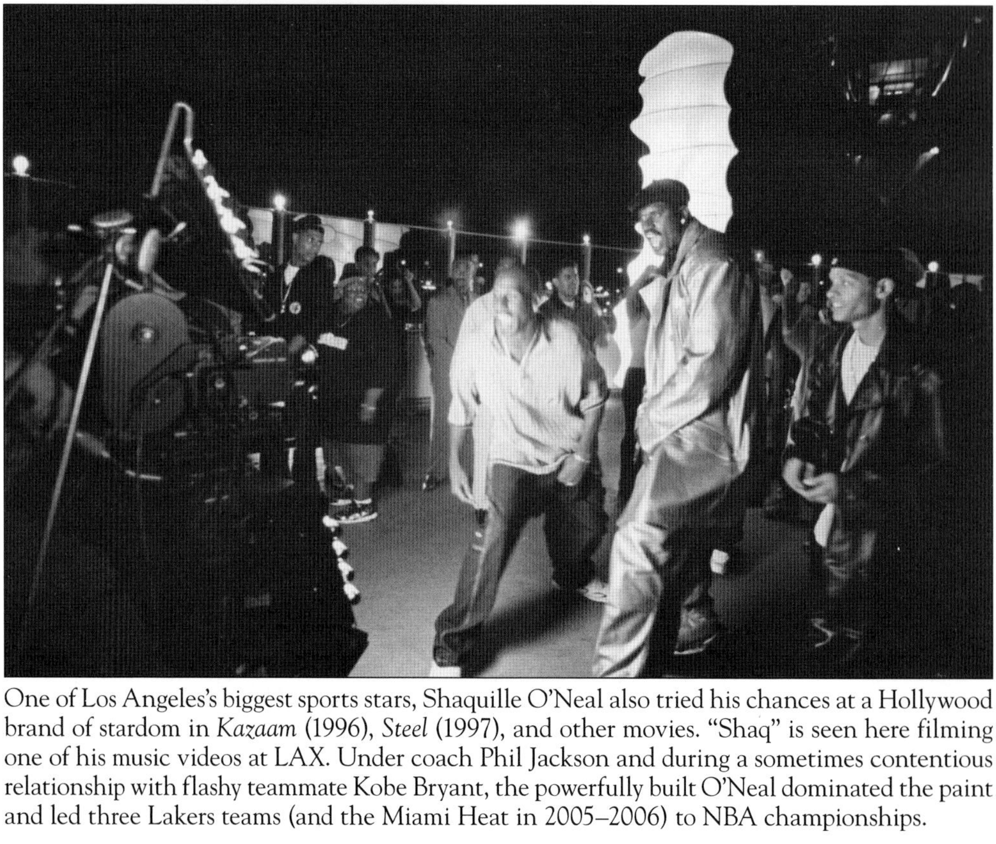

One of Los Angeles's biggest sports stars, Shaquille O'Neal also tried his chances at a Hollywood brand of stardom in *Kazaam* (1996), *Steel* (1997), and other movies. "Shaq" is seen here filming one of his music videos at LAX. Under coach Phil Jackson and during a sometimes contentious relationship with flashy teammate Kobe Bryant, the powerfully built O'Neal dominated the paint and led three Lakers teams (and the Miami Heat in 2005–2006) to NBA championships.

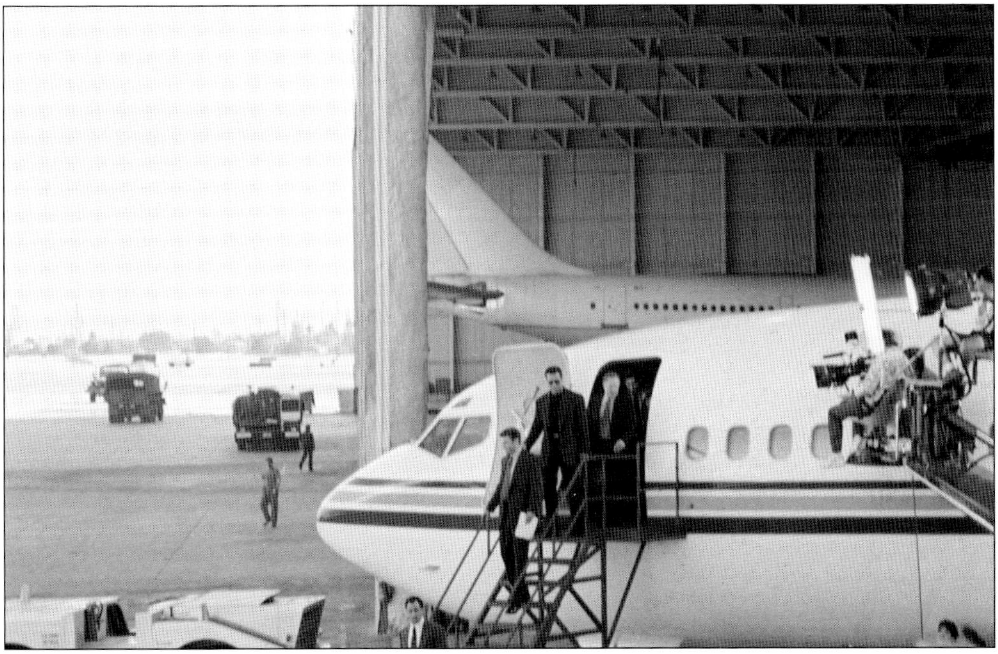

California governor Arnold Schwarzenegger and his entourage arrive at LAX. Note the remote location of the arrival at an aircraft hangar away from public passenger terminals. Security concerns require that airport arrivals and departures of political leaders and many celebrities be conducted at such remote sites. Schwarzenegger, a former multiple-time world bodybuilding champion, then a top box-office movie star in such films as *The Terminator* (1984) and its sequels, *Predator* (1987) and *True Lies* (1994), was sworn in as governor on November 17, 2003.

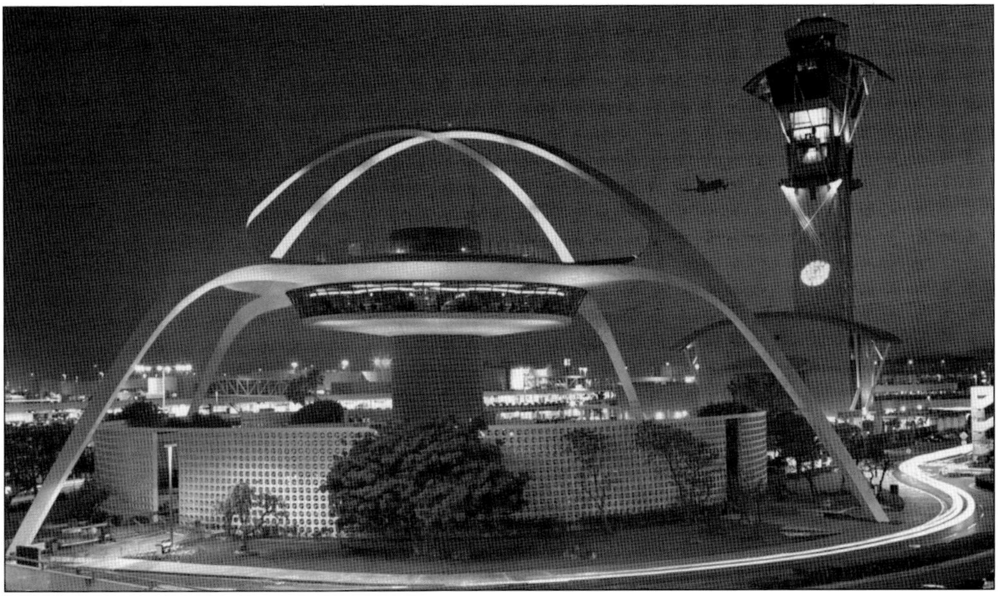

The Theme Building (left) and FAA Control Tower are the two structures most recognized at LAX by Los Angeles residents and visitors. In fact, surveys have established that the Theme Building, which houses the Encounter restaurant, is the most recognized building anywhere in Southern California.

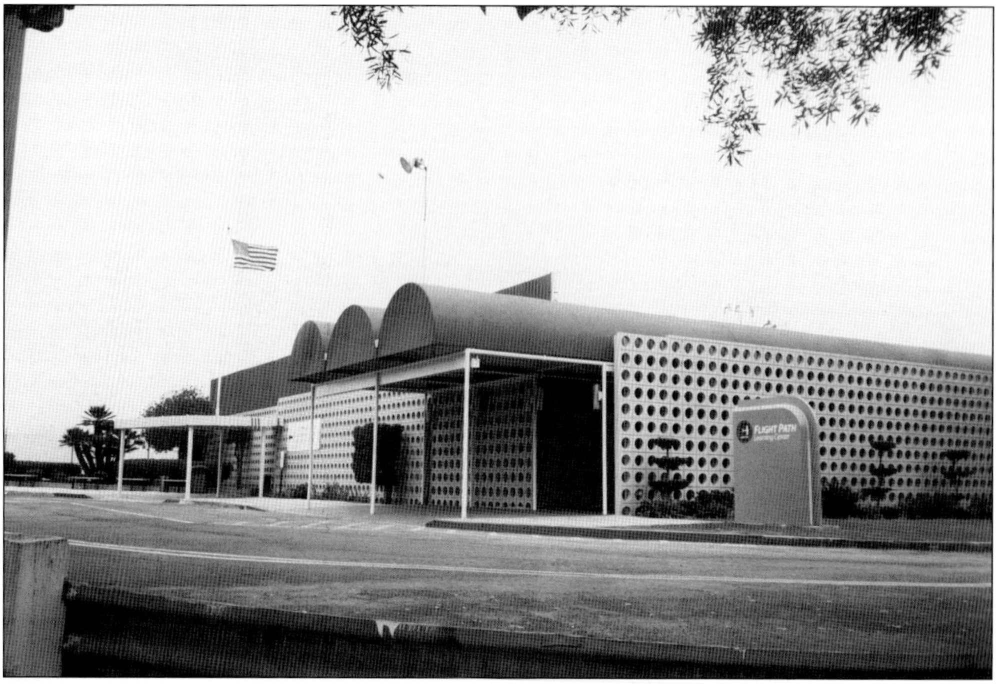

The Imperial Terminal, which once served charter flights on the south side of the LAX airfield, is now the Flight Path Learning Center and Museum. Flight Path houses airport and airline memorabilia and features student tours, flight simulator instruction, and numerous community events.

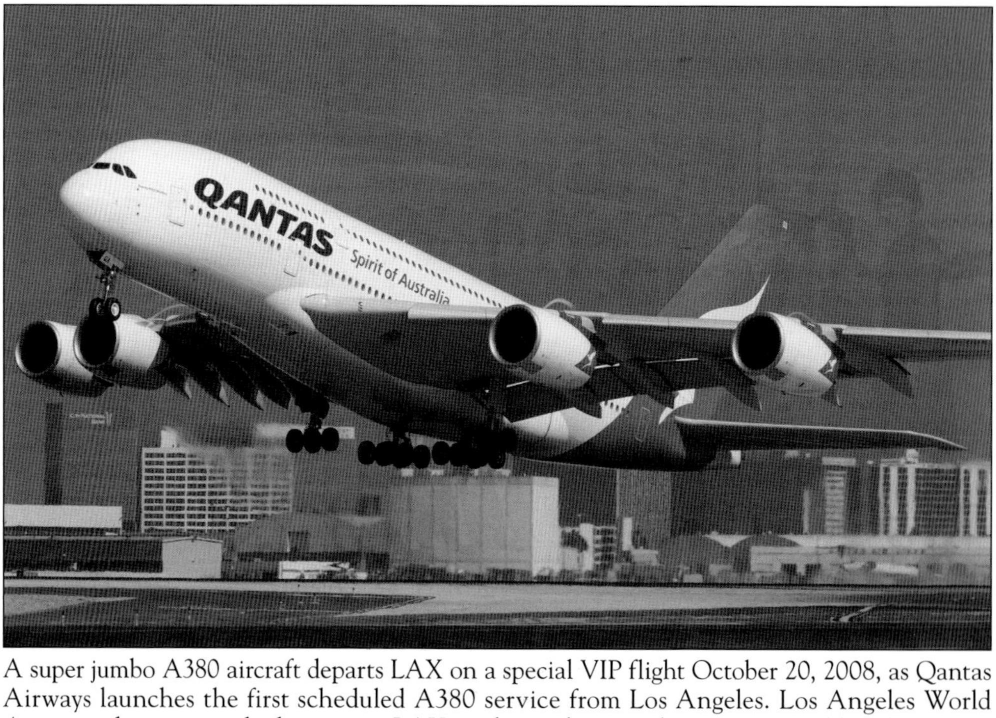

A super jumbo A380 aircraft departs LAX on a special VIP flight October 20, 2008, as Qantas Airways launches the first scheduled A380 service from Los Angeles. Los Angeles World Airports, the agency which operates LAX, authorized major changes in airfield and terminal gate configurations to accommodate the new aircraft.

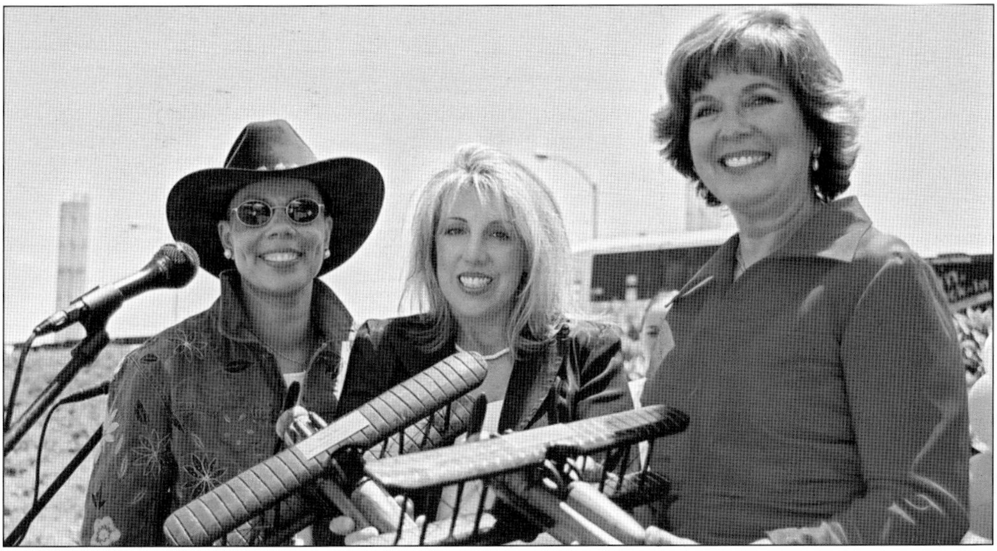

Celebration of LAX's 75th anniversary in 2003 included a community concert in the airport's flag courtyard at Century and Sepulveda Boulevards. Pictured from left to right are Los Angeles World Airports executive director Lydia H. Kennard and country music stars Shirley Myers and Susan Raye. Myers and Raye performed the hit song, "L. A. International Airport." Raye's original 1971 version of the tune had reached the Top 10 on country music charts. The song was rerecorded by Myers with updated lyrics for the 75th anniversary. Kennard officiated at numerous anniversary events, including opening of the airport's new Flight Path Learning Center and Museum in the Imperial Terminal.

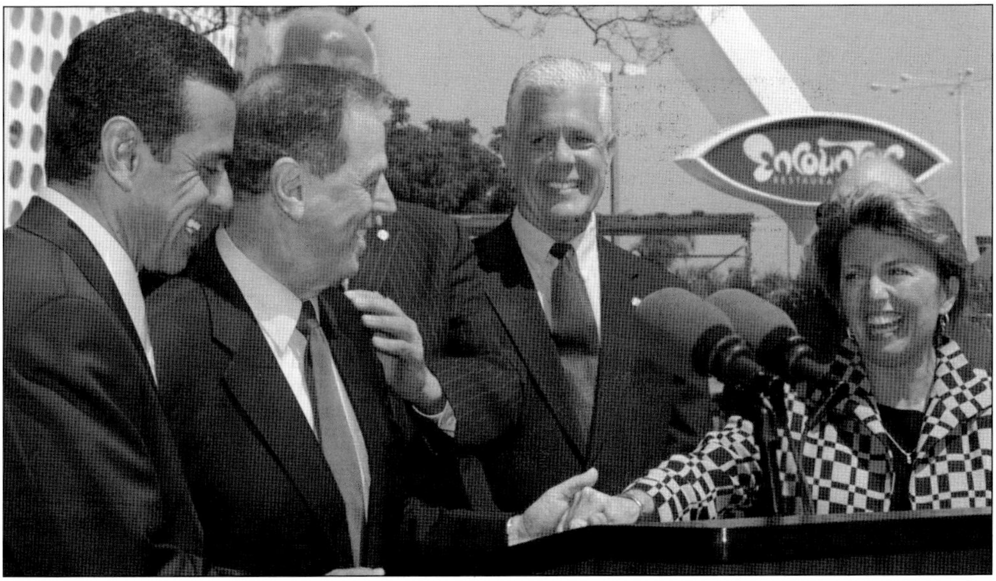

A partner in the operation of the LAX Flight Path Learning Center and Museum is Los Angeles World Airports, the city agency which operates LAX. Gina Marie Lindsey, the agency's current executive director, is a leading supporter of Flight Path's educational mission. Pictured with Lindsey are, from left to right, Los Angeles mayor Antonio Villaraigosa, Airport Commission president Alan Rothenberg, and El Segundo mayor Kelly McDowell. In background, partially shown, is Los Angeles City councilman Bill Rosendahl.

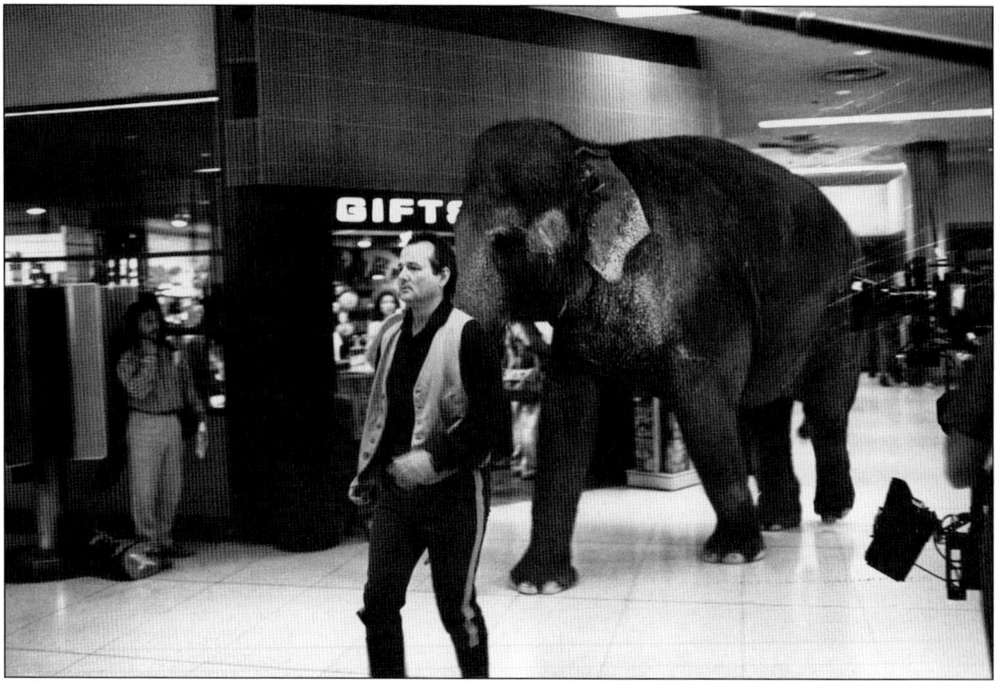

Travelers encountering movie or television filming at LAX are likely to see a favorite entertainer, such as Bill Murray here, or, also in this case, even an elephant. Murray starred with the pachyderm in the comedy *Larger Than Life* (1996). Passengers do not seem to mind stepping around cables or shielding their eyes from bright lights if there is an opportunity to view production on a television show or catch a glimpse of a film-land celebrity.

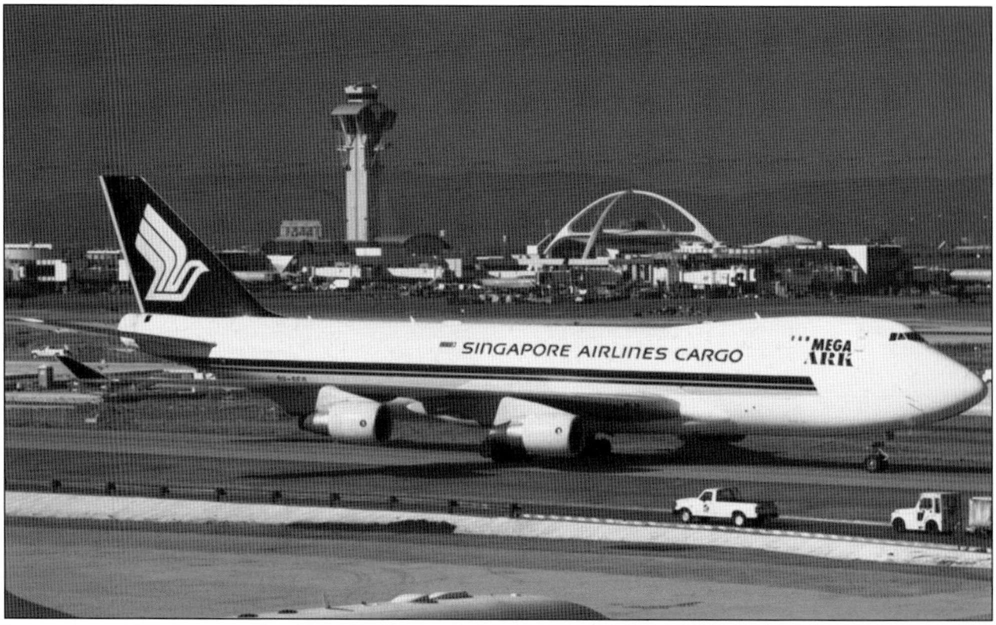

International passengers and cargo captured an increasing percentage of LAX air traffic as Los Angeles became one of the most important cities on the Pacific Rim. Singapore Airlines is one of numerous foreign flag carriers with regular scheduled service to LAX.

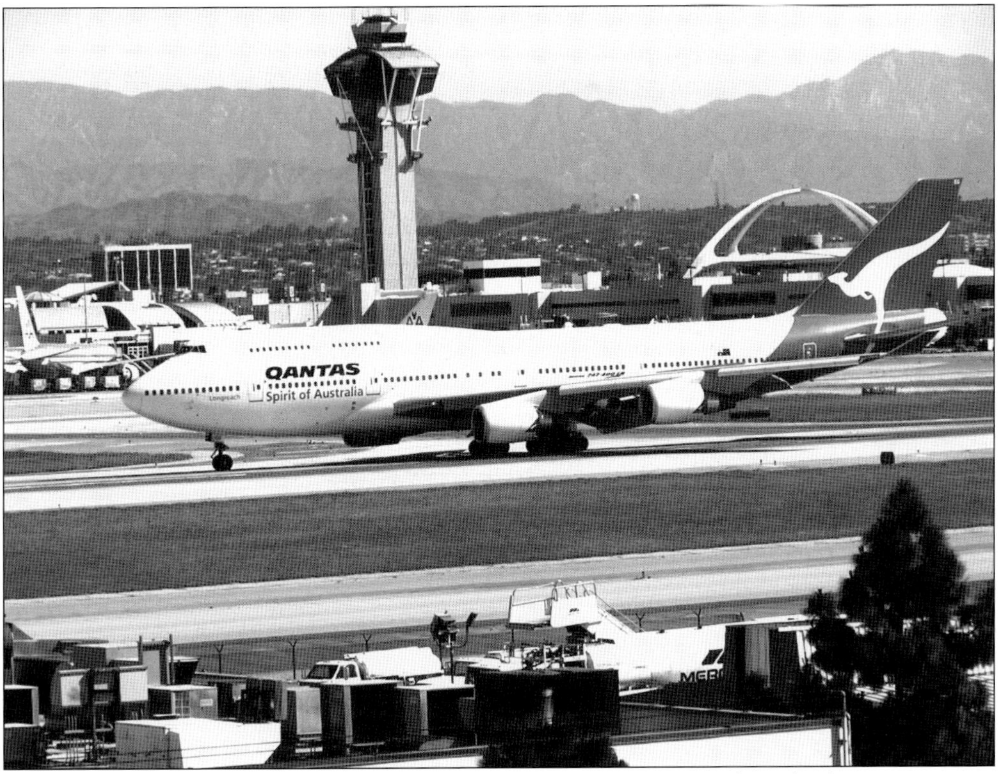

This Qantas Airlines 747 from Australia is a daily visitor at LAX. Plans for future passenger facilities at the airport will necessarily include greatly expanded areas for international passenger processing, including additional customs and immigration checkpoints.

This 21st-century aerial view of LAX clearly indicates that the airport has almost completely utilized its 3,500-acre site. Although LAX is one of the world's busiest passenger and air cargo fields, it is relatively small in physical size compared to other major airports.

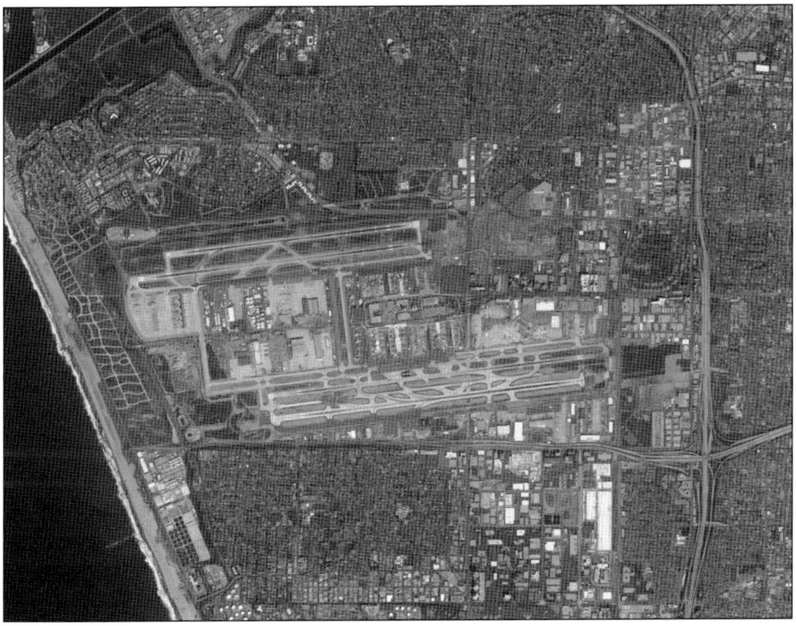

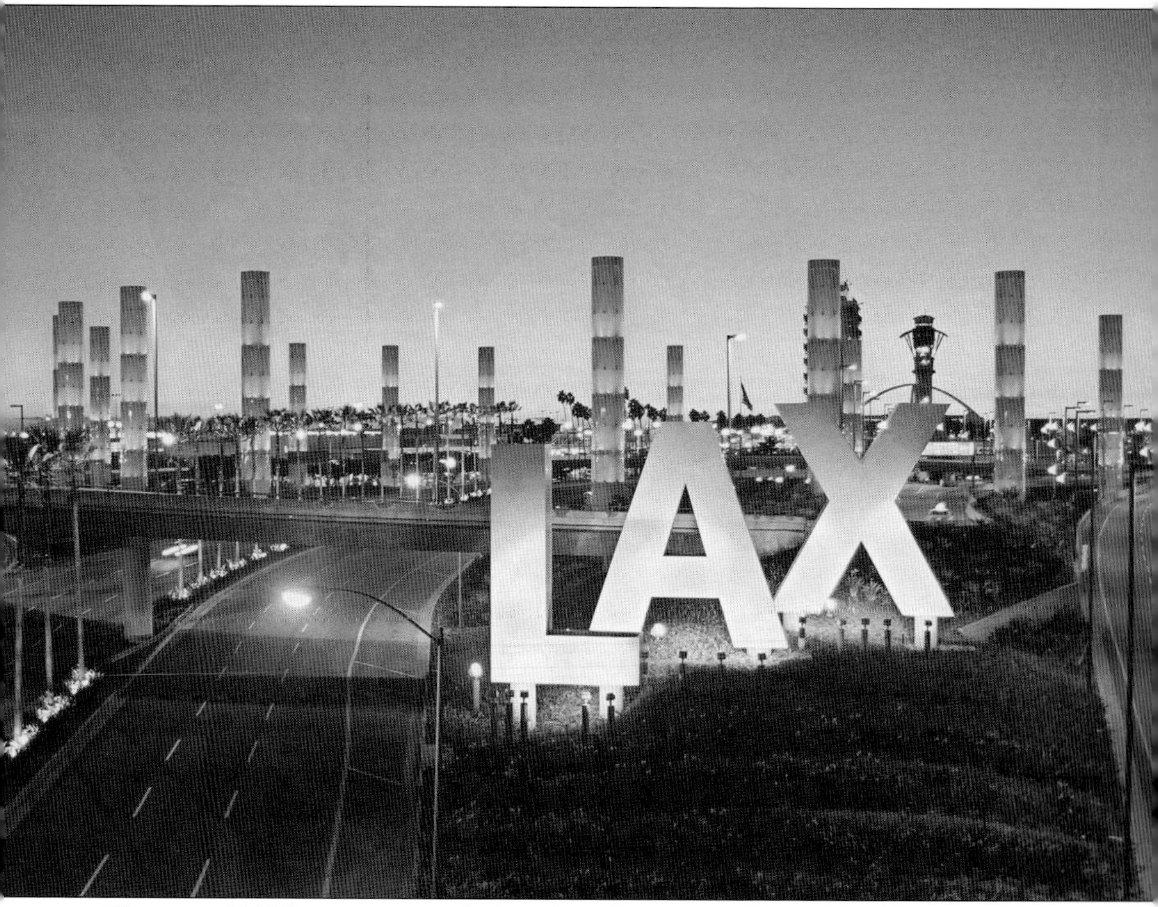

The iconic "LAX" sign is seen with the pylons that greet arrivals to the airport entrance from the east on Century Boulevard.

BIBLIOGRAPHY

Archer, Robert D. *Airliners of LAX: Los Angeles International Airport 1956–1976*. Miami, FL: World Transport Press, 1997.

Bullock, Freddy. *LAX: Los Angeles International Airport*. Osceola, WI: MBI Publishing Company, 1998.

Carpenter, Dr. Ford A. *Preliminary Report on the Airports or Landing Fields of Los Angeles*. Los Angeles: Department of Meteorology and Aeronautics, Los Angeles Chamber of Commerce, 1926.

Cusack, Victor A., Harrison Lewis Whitney, and William A. Schoneberger (ed.). *A Symbol of Los Angeles: The History of the Theme Building at Los Angeles International Airport, 1952–1961*. Virginia Beach, VA: Donning Company, 2005.

Friedman, Paul David. "Fear of Flying: The Development of Los Angeles International Airport and the Rise of Public Protest over Jet Aircraft Noise." Santa Barbara, CA: University of California, Santa Barbara, master's thesis, October 1978.

Lloyd, Earl A., Kenneth Sampson, Tom D. Cooke, and Bryant Hall. *Master Plan of Airports*. Los Angeles: County of Los Angeles Regional Planning District, 1940.

Los Angeles Department of Airports Historical Review. Los Angeles: Los Angeles Department of Airports, 1995.

Moore, Clifton A., et al. *Los Angeles Department of Airports 50th Anniversary Annual Report 1977*. Los Angeles: Los Angeles Department of Airports, 1977.

Moran, Tom, and John K. Waters. *LAX: Los Angeles International Airport—from Lindbergh's Landing Strip to World Air Center*. Canoga Park, CA: CCA Publications, 1993.

Pereira and Luckman, Architects. *Master Plan for Los Angeles International Airport*. Los Angeles: Pereira and Luckman, 1953.

Schoneberger, William A., et al. *75: The Heritage of Los Angeles World Airports: 1928–2003—Celebrating 75 Years of Connecting Southern California to the World*. Los Angeles: Los Angeles World Airports, 2003.

Scott, Denham S. *A History of Early Aviation and Its Pioneers in Southern California, as Written by Denham Scott and Published in Southern California Industrial News 1966–1969*. Hawthorne, CA: Western Museum of Flight, 1969.

Story, Harold H. *Summary of Factors Pertaining to the Los Angeles Municipal Airport*. Los Angeles: Los Angeles Department of Airports (DOA), 1933.

www.lawa.org/lax/laxHistoryMain.cfm

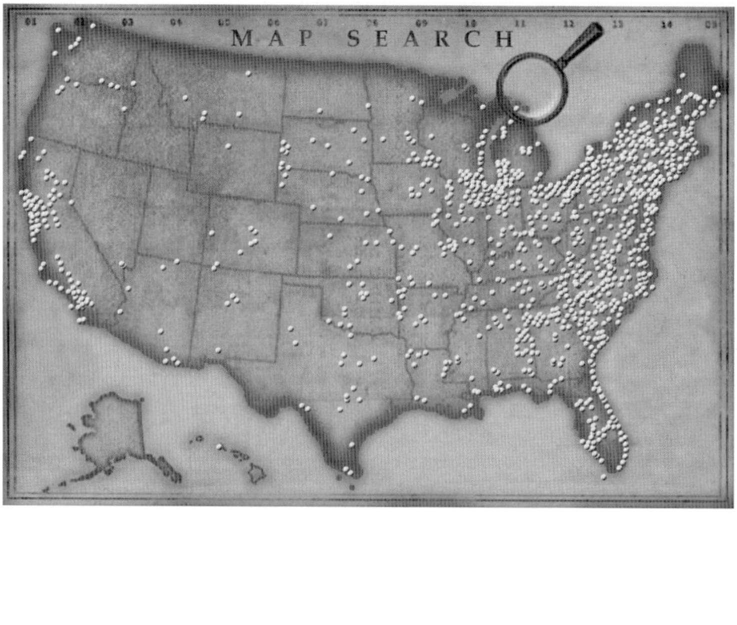

MAP SEARCH